The United States
& The Soviet Union

JOHN RICHMAN

The United States
& The Soviet Union

The Decision
To Recognize

Camberleigh & Hall, Publishers
Raleigh, North Carolina

© 1980 by John Richman
L.C.C. No.: 79-92564
ISBN: 0-935880-00-3

Camberleigh & Hall, Publishers
P.O. Box 18914, North Hills Station
Raleigh, North Carolina
27619
Printed in the United States of America

Contents

Introduction

These are not the best of times for the United States of
America. Events in countries around the world seem to be
crowding each other for headline space to announce new
problems for this nation. Iran, Pakistan, Cambodia, Cuba,
Nicaragua, Portugal, Somalia, Ethiopia, Lebanon, Angola,
Yemen, Turkey, Greece, Chile, Bangladesh, Viet Nam, Viet
Nam, Viet Nam, Viet Nam: it seems one can spin a globe and
randomly select any area of the world and find a problem for
the United States.

The adjustment to this state of affairs has been difficult
because it hasn't always been this way. There was a period
following the end of the Second World War when the United
States had the respect of all and the admiration of most. For
those who remember that shining moment in the life of this
nation, the burning question remains, what has gone wrong?
Some, particularly alumni of our government and its security
establishment, look back and conclude that the United States
just didn't meet the challenge. The country was not sufficiently
dedicated, not sufficiently disciplined. For most the answers
seem more complex, in fact, too complex. This country had a
governmental apparatus for identifying international problems,
clear and forceful policies for meeting the difficulties, and a
national consensus in support of those policies. But it all just

never quite seemed to work the way it was supposed to. Now, as the memory of that golden moment in America's history begins to fade, the question is being asked less often. In today's world it seems to be more and more only a mildly interesting historical irrelvevancy.

Every generation believes that it is taking a modern approach to the problems it encounters. Governmental decisions are made by people who believe that they are realistically responding to today's authentic challenges, but foreign policy makers, like everyone else, are products of their times. Their decisions are not poured from the decanter of pure reason but are made within the context of a dominant world view. In any age the available range of policy conclusions is severely circumscribed by historical assumptions, and interpreting the lessons of history is unfortunately always a subjective and problematic endeavor. The knowledge of the past from which a synthesis for understanding the present is drawn can never be complete, and current policies are in many ways influenced by the unnoticed intellectual baggage of prior generations. Many important assumptions that underlie our current world view are routinely accepted without fully understanding or even remembering the context in which they were first given form. The American interpretation of the role of the Soviet Union in world affairs and its significance to American well being is richly marbled with these quiet assumptions.

The fundamental concern of U.S. policy makers is the Soviet Union's desire to expand its influence and control around the world. Since the end of World War II the U.S. has regarded this as its principal foreign policy challenge. One does not have to read Secretary of State Henry Kissinger's memoirs to understand the overwhelming importance of this idea within the councils of government or indeed throughout our culture. So dominant has this concern with Soviet expansion been that it has not only shaped America's relationship with that country but it has also profoundly affected America's relationship with every other country in the world. It has influenced the way the United States has responded to political, economic, and military events everywhere in the world, and how this country perceives and responds to change itself. Further, so powerful an idea has not been contained within the realm of diplomacy, and it has also had a significant impact upon internal developments in this country's domestic institutions and mores.

If we are in any way to improve our ability to understand ourselves and the world in which we live it is necessary to better understand the origins and development of our attitude towards the Soviet Union. What American foreign policy has been creating in the rest of the world since the end of World War II and what the American government and public thinks it has been doing are wildly divergent. The occurrences in Iran at the end of 1979 were not an aberration, the peculiar consequence of a religious fanatic who accidentally found himself in power, but were, rather, a direct consequence of this country's ordered and consistent post war foreign policy, a policy at whose core resides the American preoccupation with the Soviet Union. This obsession with the Soviet Union is an idea with a long, if not clearly remembered, history.

The Russian revolution of 1917 presented the American government with its first decision regarding diplomatic policy towards the Soviet Union. After a short period of flux, the policy settled upon was a fixed and determined hostility. During the 1920's this remained the consistent philosophy of the American government, and long after France, Germany, and England had recognized the new Russian regime, the United States still refused to contemplate such a move. The United States government considered the existence of the communist government as an implicit threat to itself and steadfastly refused to recognize such a government's existence. Although hostility towards the Soviet Union was widely spread throughout the culture, it was centered during this era in the American State Department. When FDR took office in early 1933 he inherited the foreign policy bureaucracy of his predecessors, but he brought to the Presidency strong and different views regarding Russia.

This is the story of how FDR and his State Department worked together and against each other to create a new policy towards the Soviet Union. In a broad sense the interactions between FDR and his State Department in the making of Russian policy were a reflection of how different ideas and ways of thinking in the culture encountered each other within the government and the results that obtained. The results of that intragovernmental clash of ideas in the early 1930's had a significant effect upon the events of succeeding eras and is still having a significant, if less clearly recognizable, effect upon the way our lives are being led today. In a narrower sense it is the story of the functioning of bureaucracies and, in particular, the functioning of the State Department bureaucracy under FDR. In less than two years the world view of the State Department bureaucracy shaped the options available to a thoroughly independent President. The working relationships that evolved during FDR's first year in office tell much about FDR's attitudes towards his State Department and how these attitudes were translated into behavior that affected policy. The ultimate failure of the American recognition of the Soviet Union to evolve beyond being a discreet diplomatic act, or to significantly affect international political relationships, was in large part due to the way in which FDR comprehended and related to his State Department. Many of the rather unusual aspects of that relationship, which were later to become so pronounced during World War II, were already present during the first few years of the Roosevelt Presidency.

How FDR moved the country towards diplomatic recognition, why he did so, and why he conducted the negotiations in the manner in which he did are questions that have not been fully answered. There was also much symbolic meaning in the method FDR used to deal with the Russians that has not been appreciated by later generations. The reaction of the State Department to FDR's new approach to Russia has remained even more obscure, as has how the State Department's opposition led to a breakdown in the negotiations. What actually occurred during these negotiations was radically different from the American memory of it. This memory failure was of some consequence because the Soviet refusal to pay its debt, as agreed upon during recognition, became an object lesson in the risks of dealing with the Russians for a whole generation of American policy leaders.

The recognition of Russia, rather than resolving the differences between FDR and his State Department, served to accentuate and solidify the separation between them. Emerging from the recognition proceedings were two American governmental policies towards the Soviet Union, one centered in the White House, the other in the State Department. This duality would remain until the creation of a new consensus and the return to dominance of the State Department view shortly after the end of World War II. It was the updated version of that view that caused the country to turn from the strength that comes from tolerance and confidence to the obsession with power that comes from fear.

The United States
& The Soviet Union

I

Finding the Way

FROM THE TIME OF HIS INAUGURATION, PRESIDENT ROOSEVELT WAS
considering a change in America's relation to the Soviet Union.
His first words in opening official contact with the Soviet Union
in October 1933 referred back to this initial intention. "Since
the beginning of my administration, I have contemplated the
desirability of an effort to end the present abnormal relations
between the hundred and twenty five million people of the
United States and the hundred and sixty million people of
Russia."[1] Some advisors such as James Farley and Sumner
Welles have written of being told by Roosevelt of his intention
to recognize even before he took office.[2] Among those who
knew the President-Elect well there was little doubt as to how
he felt, and even when this intention was not specifically artic-
ulated his advisors understood that America's relationship to
Russia would change after the inauguration. Unlike the preceding Republican administrations when Secretary of State
Frank Kellogg could not discuss the Soviet Union without
"hysteria" and some State Department officials could not bring
themselves to mention the Soviet Union by name, Russia was
discussed openly in practical terms by FDR's advisors without
accompanying emotional harmonics.[3]

Rexford Tugwell, a close advisor who was soon to be appointed Assistant Secretary of Agriculture, in a January memo to Roosevelt casually referred to Russia as "our greatest free market."[4] Tugwell's principal interest in Russia, however, was not trade but wheat. Russia as a large wheat exporter was necessary to the creation of an international wheat cartel to drive up prices by controlling exports. To acquire an understanding as to how Russia felt about this, Tugwell spent the evening of January 23, 1933, at the apartment of Peter Bogdanov, the head of Amtorg, the Russian trading company in the United States. In the course of the conversation Tugwell told Bogdanov that he "believed recognition would come faster in an atmosphere of calm and quiet than in one in which agitation was being carried on." Tugwell recorded in his diary that he "repeated the request to Bogdanov, which FDR had agreed was important, that all pressure and agitation be avoided." The Russian "promised to assist in every way."[5]

The assumption upon which Tugwell and the other advisors were working was not whether the Soviet Union should be recognized, but how it should be done. Public opinion was the difficulty. There had been a broad anti-recognition consensus in the twenties, and although public opinion in America had noticeably shifted during the previous years, it was difficult to determine the strength of the remaining feeling. There were certainly individuals and organizations still adamantly opposed to the idea, and Roosevelt was receiving, both before and after he took office, strong representations from various labor, business, religious, political, and ethnic groups against the move.

The new President's advisors had differing opinions as to the remaining strength of these forces. Farm Credit Association chairman Henry Morganthau was one of those who felt the force of public opinion still to be politically dangerous. Soon after taking office Roosevelt charged Morganthau with developing trade with Russia. Morganthau thought this a risky venture and he dealt cautiously with Amtorg through two intermediaries, but the uncertainty of the public mind gave Morganthau the occasion for some overdramatic self-promotion with his boss. He told the President that he had been praised by Ray Moley for "doing one of the most courageous things that anybody had done so far in Washington." Morganthau said that if the negotiations with Russia turned out well he would be a hero but if they turned out badly he would have to leave Washington.[6] Others felt the public resistance to recognition of the Soviet Union was no longer an important factor. Felix Frankfurter, an advisor who had much influence on FDR, was one of those that felt this way. On March 20, 1933, Frankfurter was visited by Boris Skvirsky, chief of the Soviet Information Bureau in Washington, who "mentioned the great shift in American opinion in regard to Russia as evidenced by the countless calls that come to him to speak on Russia." Frankfurter recorded in his diary that he "had no doubt of this change in attitude. . . . We talked of recognition procedure, stressing the importance of the broad gesture: recognition first and then talk about the special items of complication between the two countries. There would be little dissent on this because of the awareness of trade possibilities between the two countries and the growing ridiculousness of trying to work on any world problems, especially disarmament and the Far East, with complete disregard of Russia. . . ."[7]

For those who thought the United States should recognize the Soviet Union there seemed to be a great many practical reasons to support their thinking; the simple foolishness of the two vast countries not having any official contact, the supposed Russian market for American goods, Russia's effect upon the world military equation, and Russia's necessary place within any successful wheat cartel. Speculation has concerned which of these factors was the most influential in FDR's decision to establish relations, but in spite of 15 years of non-recognition, the fundamental question still remained for FDR as it had remained for his predecessors, why withhold recognition? Preceding administrations did not recognize because their repugnance for communist values was combined with a real fear of communism's potential strength. It was this fear that FDR, with a far truer sense of the real America than his predecessors, totally lacked and without this fear non-recognition had no basis. There is a nice story told by Tugwell of how FDR interpreted events in which others could so clearly see dangerous radicalism. On the morning of July 29, 1932, FDR sat in his bed reading *The New York Times*' description of the eviction of the Bonus Army from Washington and the razing of their village. FDR referred to a page of pictures in the newspaper as "scenes from a nightmare" and said he "ought to apologize for having suggested him [President Hoover] as candidate in 1920." He then went on to recall why he had held a high opinion of Hoover. He said, "What hadn't been realized was that the man was actually a sort of timid boy scout leader. . . . Now look where he was. He had surrounded himself with guards to keep away the revolutionaries." FDR said that there was nothing left inside Hoover but jelly and maybe there never had been anything else. Hoover should have talked with the leader of the Bonus Army when he asked for an interview, and when the two hundred veterans marched up to the gate, he should have asked a delegation in and sent out for coffee and sandwiches for all. Instead Hoover had called in the army. As for the revolutionary danger that Hoover thought he could so clearly perceive, FDR "pointed at the pictures in the *Times,* reminding me [Tugwell], as he had done before—pridefully— that during his four years as Governor in a state troubled by depression, he had never called out the National Guard." He had been subjected to the same scared cries for action as Hoover had been. "The fat cats had wanted him to, several times, when they were scared; but he never had. His answer

6

had always been that suppression would not be effective when there were real grievances. It would only make matters worse. They went on suggesting that the country was in danger of revolution and that discipline was needed, but he had refused." Tugwell asked FDR what he actually said when he was counseled to take some action and FDR "grinned for the first time in that talk. He usually let them go on, he said; if he argued too much with them, they would go away and say he was a softie, a coddler of radicals." The implications of Hoover's treatment of the Bonus Army was such that he was tempted to feel sorry for him except that he felt sorrier for those people. He felt that "they must be camping right now alongside the roads out of Washington. They must be sleeping cold. And at least some of them had families. It was really a wonder that there had not been more resentment, more radicalism, when people were treated that way."[8] Unlike the leaders of the previous administrations, FDR simply lacked the gut fear of domestic communism.

From the beginning of his term FDR determined to use trade as a means of acclimating the American public to official contact with the Soviet Union. On April 13 FDR had Colonel Hugh Cooper, President of the American-Russian Chamber of Commerce, visit the White House. Afterwards FDR talked off the record with reporters about their discussion concerning "the possibility of selling things to Russia. . . . We talked about the need in Russia for all kinds of machinery and materials of various kinds."[9]

This signal to those who were interested in and who closely followed the government's attitudes towards trade with the Soviet Union was a deliberate gesture by the President. Trade with the Soviet Union was a policy that already had a constituency. Commercial relations between the two countries during the 1920's had not been stopped by political hostility towards the new Russian government and the general trend of American exports to Russia during the decade had been steadily upwards, topping the $100,000,000 mark in both 1930 and 1931. During some of these years the U.S. was the Soviet Union's largest source of foreign goods, and many important American firms such as Ford and General Electric joined in this growing commerce.

This growth in trade between the two countries was the result of the initiative of individual American businesses and was in no way the planned or encouraged policy of the American government. Although trade was not officially forbidden, the government kept as many obstacles to the generation of commercial relations with the Soviet Union as possible. When the American government removed the ban on trade in mid 1920, the State Department instructed its offices around the world as to the limited nature of the step. "You will, therefore, take no action which, officially or unofficially, directly or indirectly, assists or facilitates commercial or other dealings between American citizens . . . and any persons, interests, or institutions . . . now under the control of the so-called Bolshevist authorities."[10] Throughout the 1920's the U.S. refused to consider government credits to the Soviet Union, and unlike most of the other industrialized countries, refused to provide any payment guarantees to American businesses for their exports to the Soviet Union. Further, the Republican administrations did everything possible to prevent the Soviet Union from securing the dollars necessary to pay for purchases in America. They discouraged long-term credits by private business, refused to allow the sale of Soviet securities within the U.S. and banned all Soviet gold shipments on the theory that it had been expropriated from its rightful owners.

During this period the Soviet Union encouraged the belief in a great untapped Russian market for the absorption of American products. It seemed to the Bolshevik leaders, that America, the most successful of the capitalistic states, would have to respond to such enticing opportunities for commerce

8

and profit. Although this approach by the Soviet Union had conspicuously failed to secure the desired results from the business oriented Republican administrations of the 1920's, it nevertheless remained a regular element in the Russian attempt to secure recognition. When Soviet imports from the U.S. dramatically fell off to about the $10,000,000 level in 1932, these arguments seemed more relevant to many Americans, and not only those in the business community, who saw a need for doing everything possible to promote trade with Russia in order to help fill the unused capacity of the factories idled by the depression. FDR was not one of the people who felt this way, but he began his move towards political recognition by exploiting this already well-established issue. In early 1933 there was as yet still no clear consensus in the American business community for recognition, as there was not in most other elements of American society, but there was clearly a large body of business opinion which supported the idea and would respond to encouragement.

FDR assigned the task of developing commercial relations to Treasury Secretary William Woodin, and Woodin worked through an intermediary in contacting Amtorg regarding the sale of American cotton. Amtorg's immediate response was that the U.S. had "a lot of excess merchandise which they were willing to take but did not actually need at once and could not absorb in their current budgets. They thought it would be helpful for us to take this merchandise off our hands and give us this long term [ten year] obligation for it."[11] In typical fashion, FDR also assigned this task to Morganthau, and before Woodin responded to Amtorg's reply Morganthau's intermediary had made another proposal to Amtorg. Meanwhile Amtorg, receiving official instructions from Moscow, called in Woodin's intermediary, and gave him a list of 6 major items they would be willing to purchase on 5 to 6 year terms. Morganthau thought the Russians were considering his proposition as a counter offer to Woodin's and that they were "doing some oriental bargaining by reducing the length of the credit from ten to six years."[12] The Russians were actually setting before the Americans the official Soviet position regarding potential purchases. Amtorg's first response was probably made locally and their second response became Moscow's official position regarding potential purchases, and remained basically the same when presented to Smith Brookhart of the AAA in July, and Jesse Jones of the RFC in September.[13] Morganthau reported to FDR that difficulties were arising because of the two separate sets of negotiators and that Amtorg was becoming confused. FDR responded as he characteristically did when his multiple delegations of authority first brought two subordinates into conflict; he told Morganthau that he was removing Woodin's intermediary from the case.[14] Six days later Morganthau was back with the same complaint, and this time FDR, again typically, told him to get in touch with Woodin and work out the problem together.[15]

FDR also found an occasion during the first few months of his administration to initiate a political gesture towards the Soviet Union. On Saturday afternoon, May 13, FDR turned to the State Department to help him draft an appeal for disarmament to the heads of nation. FDR had come into his Presidency with a stereotype of the personnel in the State Department as supercilious sons of the well born who had no real understanding of the events in America and who, clinging to form, were timid of operating except by the book—cookie pushers, as many reporters called them. During the interregnum FDR was kidding Moley about being properly attired for their upcoming meeting with Hoover and asked if he had striped pants and top hat. Moley was looking none too happy and FDR went on, "but what worries me is the spats. The State Department boys will be wearing theirs."[16] Then FDR roared with laughter. On a more serious note, FDR alarmed Secretary of State Henry Stimson when on their first meeting on January 9, 1933, he asked if "the members of the Foreign Service were wealthy young men who got entirely out of touch with American affairs."[17]

Upon assuming office FDR added weak leadership to the burden of the stereotype already borne by the State Department. Having decided to be his own Secretary of State, FDR did not appoint men of strength to either of the two top positions in the Department. Neither Secretary of State Cordell Hull or Under Secretary William Phillips were forceful men and this fact was amply recognized by their contemporaries. Among the many such references to this aspect of Hull's character were those made by Secretary of State Henry Stimson in his diary. After his first meeting with Hull during the interregnum Stimson wrote, "he gave me the impression of being much older than I am, although he is four years younger, and he seemed rather a little bit senectified. . . . On the whole I got a rather discouraging impression of his vitality and vigor."[18] After his second meeting with Hull on the following day, Stimson's reservations regarding Hull were more specific . "He [Hull] spoke in a way that intimated that Roosevelt had told him that he intended to be his own Secretary of State, and Hull had apparently knuckled under to it."[19]

In choosing William Phillips as Under Secretary, FDR was appointing another man of limited personal strength. When Secretary of State Stimson heard of Phillips' appointment, he characterized Phillips as "a fine fellow, but without the necessary force to push things at such a time as this."[20]

The State Department's work on the appeal to the heads of nations two months after taking office quickly reinforced FDR's preexisting biases regarding the State Department. Secretary Hull and Under Secretary Phillips spent Saturday afternoon with FDR turning out a rough draft, which the State Department was to refine by Monday. On Sunday Hull, Phillips, and key subordinates Jay Moffat, and William Bullitt spent most of the day turning out a finished draft, but when it was shown to FDR in the evening he "reintroduced into the draft many of the features that we [the State Department] had been objecting to and had completely rewritten one page." As a result Moley was called in on Monday to rewrite the speech.

After accepting Moley's draft FDR wanted to include Soviet President Kalinin among the heads of state to whom the message would be addressed, but Phillips objected, insisting that in the opinion of the Solicitor General it would constitute recognition.[21] FDR said it wouldn't, included Kalinin, and when later asked by reporters if it meant recognition, said no. Although FDR officially denied its importance, the press, of course, picked up on the inclusion of Russia as he had intended. Moffat disparaged the inclusion because it deflected attention from the main issue and Phillips was unhappy because it meant soothing the Japanese. "Bill Phillips," Moffat felt, "as usual, showed timidity wherever the Orient is involved."[22]

Two weeks after his appeal FDR met with reporters and was plainly upset. Arthur Krock of *The New York Times* had somehow learned of the appeal for disarmament before it was made and had written a story saying that the United States was going to guarantee the security of France. Consequently when FDR's actual message arrived, instead of being heartened by the expression of moral support, the French were let down by the omission of the guarantee.[23] FDR blamed Phillips for the leak. He later told Morganthau that "Phillips had telephoned to New York and asked Frank Pope's opinion of the message, Pope being the lawyer for Morgan." The President said, "'What could be more stupid?' He said, 'Monday afternoon it was around Washington that I was going to send an important message to Europe, and Arthur Krock that evening wrote an article saying I was doing something which would guarantee security in France.'"[24]

On the day following the appeal to the heads of nations FDR met with Chairman of the Reconstruction Finance Corporation Jesse Jones, Morganthau, and representatives of the government of China for the purpose of arranging a loan to that country for the purchase of American wheat and cotton. FDR wanted to show support for China in its struggle with Japan and he was using the loan to accomplish a political end. He would soon use a loan to Russia in the same manner. Thinking of this first loan in moral and not economic terms, FDR told Jones, "'Do not make the Chinese pay too quickly for this transaction and do not make the interest rates too high.'"[25] When Secretary of Agriculture Henry Wallace learned of the loan he felt that it was a threat to his agricultural policy and was concerned that it portended a basic shift in government policy. Although Morganthau was involved, the loan was totally irrelevant to agricultural policy, but only FDR knew it and Wallace wrote to the President to protest that "it is dangerous to loan money to other nations to buy your surplus unless you are definitely prepared sooner or later to receive goods in equal value from them. . . . It is an aspect which the Republicans overlooked during the period 1921 to 1929 which had a lot to do with bringing on the depression and the Republican defeat."[26] Wallace was articulating a feeling that many Democrats including Hull had regarding the dangers of foreign loans, and this concern would later affect Hull's response to financial agreements with Russia.

Jones worked out the terms of the loan to China over the next few weeks and on June 5 he publicly announced that a credit of $50,000,000 would be extended to the Chinese government at 5% interest. On the day of the public announcement of the loan to China Morganthau forwarded to Jesse Jones a request from Amtorg for 35,000 bales of cotton on two and a half year terms. Four days earlier, A.J. Rosenshein, the

President of Amtorg, had written to Morganthau explaining that Amtorg Chairman Bogdanov, the man whom Morganthau's intermediaries had been dealing with, was absent from the office due to illness, and that in his place Rosenshein was suggesting a new and smaller deal for 35,000 bales "without prejudice" to the larger one.[27] Whether the Russians would have purchased this cotton under ordinary circumstances or whether they finally came to understand the reason behind all the trade feelers issuing from FDR's lieutenants is impossible to say. However, determining FDR's intentions would not have been difficult since they were already being reasonably accurately speculated about in the press. Two days prior to Amtorg's request to Morganthau the Washington *Herald* ran a story covering the appointment of Smith Brookhart as special advisor to the Agricultural Adjustment Administration captioned "US Promoting Trading Plans with Soviets."

> Resumption of trade relations with Soviet Russia under Government sanction was seen yesterday in the appointment of former Senator Smith W. Brookhart. . . . Through other sources it was learned the Government has worked out a comprehensive scheme for direct trade relations with the Soviet government, tantamount to recognition.[28]

Jones began negotiations with Amtorg directly and during these discussions the quantity of cotton under consideration was increased from 35,000 to about 70,000 bales. On June 13 Jones received an entirely favorable credit report on Amtorg from the Chase National Bank.

> this corporation has maintained an important and satisfactory account with us. . . . In the performance of its trade activities in this country, this corporation has issued its acceptances for substantial amounts in settlement of its purchases of American machinery and other

14

American products. We are informed that all of such acceptances were made payable at our office. To the best of our knowledge they have always been promptly paid at maturity. The same applies to all other obligations assumed by the corporation in the course of our business connection, and our relations with its officials have been uniformly pleasant since their inception.[29]

On the same day Jones decided to make public his negotiations with the Russians. The publicity itself was another step in the use of trade in easing towards political contact. In his public posture FDR remained aloof from these mundane arrangements. "At the White House," *The New York Times* reported, "it was said that the President had not been advised of any application by Amtorg, and therefore no comment could be made."[30] FDR's standard procedure at news conferences was to deny whatever Russian story that had just made the news had anything to do with recognition.[31]

The basic structure of the cotton sale was determined during two meetings set up by Jones on June 16, the first with FDR and the second with Morganthau and Under Secretary of the Treasury Dean Acheson. Because Amtorg "was owned by Russian interests" it was decided that unlike the loan to China it would be preferable for an American company to borrow from the RFC to finance the trade.[32] To fulfill this function Jones turned to Anderson, Clayton & Company of Houston, which had earlier in the year proposed to sell Russia ten million dollars worth of cotton on terms, if the RFC "would consider refinancing the transaction." Before receiving an answer from the RFC the company had withdrawn its request after hearing that the Russians were exporting cotton themselves.[33] Anderson, Clayton, however, did have a history of successful trade relations with the Soviet government during the 1920's, and they accepted Jones' proposal. By June 24 Jones had all the pieces in

15

place and lacked only FDR's approval. It was Saturday and because Amtorg was anxious to start their purchases Jones asked for a response by Monday from the President, who was then sailing in the Atlantic. Jones told the President that the terms of sale were good and that "Amtorg has agreed to these terms because of its great anxiety for the immediate purchase and shipment of some of the cotton."[34] The terms of 30% down with the remainder due in 1 year at 5% interest were more severe than the terms of 10% down, 15% due in 90 days, the remainder due over 3 years at 5% interest extended to China, but Secretary Wallace did not have to be concerned; like the loan to China, this was essentially a political and not an economic transaction.

When Jones did not hear from the President by Tuesday, he contacted Morganthau who was preparing to join the President at sea.[35] FDR, after talking the matter over with Morganthau on the 29th, gave Jones his approval. Jones released the story on July 3rd when the story began to break in England at the London Economic Conference after a meeting between Moley and Maxim Litvinoff, the Soviet foreign minister.[36]

II

William Christian Bullitt

THE LONDON ECONOMIC CONFERENCE PROVIDED A FORUM IN WHICH members of FDR's government could establish contact with representatives of Soviet Russia. Henry Morganthau, Sr., chairman of the American delegation to the wheat conference met with Litvinoff "to discuss the possibilities of Soviet cooperation on a wheat agreement. . . . Litvinov received Morganthau cordially and gave immediate assent to the principle of such an agreement."[1] Cordell Hull met with Litvinoff to discuss "economic principles," but Hull had too much on his mind to give much attention to such a meeting.[2] Moley, too, was preoccupied and only remained a few minutes at a meeting with Litvinoff arranged by Bullitt.[3] Bullitt, however, had two meetings with Litvinoff, during which relations between the United States and the Soviet Union were frankly discussed.

Bullitt was not a career diplomat. He was an energetic man of 42 who during a colorful and varied career had at one time worked as head of Philadelphia *Public Ledger*'s Washington bureau and as chief of the Current Intelligence Section of the U.S. delegation to the Peace Conference following World War I. During his career he had personally negotiated a peace treaty with Lenin, publicly and sensationally castigated Presi-

17

dent Wilson's peace policy before the U.S. Senate, written a pot boiler of a novel, and co-authored a psychological analysis of President Wilson with Sigmund Freud, and he was now a newly appointed Assistant to the Secretary of State and chief executive of the U.S. delegation to the London Economic Conference.

Bullitt, had been appointed to the Department of State just two months previously, but he had had to scramble for it. His personal relationship with the President had only begun during the previous fall, and a semi-official mission to Europe for FDR during the winter had ended very badly for Bullitt. As a result he was not a member of the new government on inauguration day and at that moment his prospects seemed quite limited. But the combination of enthusiastic charm and supreme self-assurance that made him one of the few people to call the President by his first name in spite of their only recent association soon worked to secure for him the position of Assistant to the Secretary of State.[4] This position allowed Bullitt the access to the President necessary for the continued building of a relationship on a personal basis and also led to an influential and important position within the American delegation to the London Economic Conference. From London Bullitt sent telegrams and long personal letters to the President outside of State Department channels regarding his interpretation of events and giving his advice for handling policies and personalities. His relationship with FDR continued to strengthen after his return from London, and by the time the year was out his association with the President would lead directly to an appointment as the United States' first ambassador to the Soviet Union. As ambassador, Bullitt became so pivotal to relations between the U.S. and the U.S.S.R. and his unusual personality so significant in affecting events that it is worth tracing his career.

William Christian Bullitt was born to all "the advantages that come with established wealth and a three-hundred-year-old American name: security, culture, social position."[5] His

18

ancestry contained many flamboyant dissenters with whom Bullitt identified including Patrick Henry's sister, Fletcher Christian of the Mutiny on the Bounty, and Captain William Christian "who was hanged, drawn, and quartered for opposition to Cromwell."[6] Bullitt "would talk of his relationship with 'Grandma' Pocahontas, Patrick Henry, Lawrence Washington, Thomas Walker (the guardian of Thomas Jefferson), and various others."[7]

Bullitt had intelligence, energy, a flair for the dramatic, an uncompromising and melodramatic vision of life, but most of all the attribute that distinguished Bullitt was personal charm. Throughout his career Bullitt showed the ability to gain the personal confidence of governmental leaders on either side of the Atlantic. As an undergraduate at Yale, Bullitt was voted "most brilliant senior" and placed second as "most versatile." He was elected president of the Debating Society. He was an editor of the Yale News, a member of Phi Beta Kappa, and was the first man selected for the senior society of Scroll and Key.[8] His father wanted him to study law but it did not suit him and after one year he dropped out of Harvard Law School to take a job as a ten-dollar-a-week beat reporter for the Philadelphia *Public Ledger*. With the total self-assurance that was so much a part of his personality he soon began submitting editorial page analyses and within six months was made a member of the editorial staff.[9] He went to Europe on his own expense as war correspondent to the Central Powers and when he returned his articles "had made him something of an authority on foreign affairs."[10] In September 1917 Bullitt was made head of the *Public Ledger*'s newly opened Washington bureau. He was now 26. In this new job, Bullitt developed social contacts with many government officials, including Colonel House, and in December of 1917 Bullitt secured an appointment as a special assistant in the European Division of the State Department.[11] Here Bullitt worked during the last year of the war.

19

After the fighting ended Colonel House acceded to Bullitt's request to be a member of the American delegation to the peace conference and appointed him as one of his secretaries for the conference. A few days later Bullitt was assigned further duties as chief of the Current Intelligence Section.[12] The intelligence mystique soon captured him, and during the conference he became obsessed with there being a dictograph in his heater.[13] When Colonel House mentioned the idea of sending a secret investigating commission to Russia to look for a way to disentangle the allies from their military expeditions to that country, Bullitt responded enthusiastically.[14]

Bullitt disparaged the conventions of the society he was born into as inappropriate to the modern age. His brother described him as having "an intense dislike for the rigidity of the ruling classes and of the status quo."[15] The Russian revolution had immediately caught his imagination as the shape of the future and on his own initiative he had begun to send "unsolicited memoranda to Colonel House, to William Phillips, even to President Wilson, suggesting a means by which Russia . . . might be swung back to fighting with the Allies."[16] "Every principle of liberalism," he had written, "impels toward the recognition of the Sovjet [sic.]."[17]

Now on February 17th Bullitt was asked by House to go to Russia, but his instructions beyond gathering information were vague. Bullitt went to Russia and when he returned he brought back a peace proposal from Lenin, but the peace conference had become strained while he was away and Wilson never acknowledged Bullitt's mission and Lloyd George publicly denied it and all knowledge of the emissary. Bullitt called it "a most egregious case of misleading the public, perhaps the boldest that I have ever known . . . so flagrant was this that various members of the British mission called on me . . . and apologized for the Prime Minister's actions."[18] To Bullitt's disappointment regarding the Russian treaty was added disillusionment when he read the full peace treaty. Bullitt addressed his letter of resignation to Wilson telling him that "Russia, 'the acid test of good will,' for me as for you . . . has not even been understood. Unjust decisions of the conference . . . make new international conflicts certain."[19] He had previously invested Wilson with an unblemished nobility, but he now turned on him with the same intensity with which he had adulated him. When he was summoned to appear before the Senate Committee on Foreign Relations, chaired by anti-League of Nations spokesman Senator Henry Cabot Lodge, Bullitt broke all the unspoken rules by his sensational testimony. After both President Wilson and Secretary of State Lansing failed to provide information about the original American peace plan, Bullitt provided the committee with the President's original proposal from the President's typewriter. Bullitt provided the committee with peace conference minutes refused by the President and the Secretary of State as well as notes to private conversations in which the Secretary of State had disapproved of the treaty.[20] After Bullitt testified Senator Lodge said, "I have no defense to make of Mr. Bullitt's breach of confidence. That is his affair."[21] Under Secretary of State Phillips wrote, "'The tragedy of the week . . . has been the Bullitt affair' . . . After that William Phillips had hoped he would never have to see Bullitt again."[22] Bullitt's testimony made his name for the moment synonymous with treachery. In 1919 FDR himself wrote to Herbert Swope, "'I really want to look you over and see for myself whether you are still the good old Swope or have taken on the manners and customs of a Billy Bullitt.'"[23]

Bullitt's government career was over. But for one of his position money was never a problem, and he spent much of the new decade in Europe researching the origins and conduct of the World War and writing two unusual books. In his research he interviewed most of the important men of the war period and maintained contact with many who were still politically powerful, such as Colonel House back in America. His first book was a novel entitled "It's Not Done," meaning that in proper society one must behave in the appropriate fashion. The thrust of the novel was that the behavior and attitude of American "society" was obsolete in the modern world. The novel's protagonist was doomed to personal unhappiness because of his belief in the old values that no longer worked. The plot boiled with recurring coincidences, secret dealings, blackmail, and an endless series of melodramatic crises. More than literary license, these were to Bullitt the ingredients of life. If his novel reveals an active imagination, international politics held no less a claim upon his fancy. Bullitt saw intrigue in everything. To the men who worked with him in the Roosevelt administration, Bullitt's view of politics resembled an unpublished chapter from his novel.

Raymond Moley wrote of Bullitt, "I had by this time clearly made out the values and limitations of Bullitt. He was pleasant, keen-minded, idealistic, and widely informed. On the other hand, he had a deep and somewhat disturbing strain of romanticism in him. Foreign affairs were, to his imaginative mind, full of lights and shadows, plots and counter-plots, villians and a few heros—a state of mind that seemed to me dangerous, if not constantly subjected to the quieting influence of some controlling authority."[24] Herbert Feis wrote of Bullit, "One other newcomer in the Roosevelt entourage puzzled me, even while he attracted me. . . . He was a fluorescent sort of fellow to whom diplomacy was an incessant drama. Its lurid scenes, strange characters and bold possibilities incited his imaginative interest."[25] James Warburg wrote of Bullitt, "He had a brilliant and often original mind, an irrepressible sense of humor, and an inclination toward dramatic, preferably clandestine adventure."[26]

Another aspect of Bullitt's novel is of interest. The villain of the piece succeeds because he is unencumbered by scruples and is willing to do whatever is necessary to gain his own selfish ends. The protagonist, whose motives are finer, fails because he is bound to a code which proscribes his ability to retaliate. That much is fiction. The fact is that Bullitt, a man who viewed himself as an idealist, never failed when representing the American government in any negotiation to do whatever was necessary to secure complete compliance with his own position. Bullitt may well have seen himself, unlike the protagonist of his novel, as an aristocratic idealist who knew how to fight for his finer ends.

Bullitt's second book was a psychological analysis of Woodrow Wilson in collaboration with Sigmund Freud. The book's thesis, introduced by Bullitt, was that "the President's breakdown resulted largely from the strain of convincing himself that the Versailles Treaty accorded with his avowed principles."[27] By early 1932 this second book was complete, and Bullitt, looking to Roosevelt and a reentry into American government, began pressing House for an introduction. Against House's advice Bullitt took a tour of the capitals of Europe to enhance his authority as an expert on foreign affairs.[28] After returning to America Bullitt gave up on House's influence and looked up Louis Wehle, an old friend of FDR's, "to open up the way for him to Roosevelt."[29] Wehle was much taken with Bullitt's travels and concluded that he was "probably the best informed American on foreign affairs."[30] Wehle wrote FDR recommending Bullitt highly and in response Louis Howe offered Bullitt a job in the New York City campaign headquarters in the section handling the preparation of material for speeches.[31] In early October Wehle secured for Bullitt a personal meeting with FDR but still nothing happened.[32] Finally, Bullitt decided it was time to do the European tour ploy again and sent Wehle to suggest to FDR "a voluntary service that Bullitt might render." Wehle told FDR that he "thought it would be helpful if Bullitt on his own initiative and resources were to make a special tour of England and the Continent; he could get up-to-date

23

information. . . . I [Wehle] said such a tour should be Bullitt's private venture; and I felt he would be discreet in keeping it so." Hoover had by now begun involving FDR in the war debt problems, and FDR responded to Wehle that "he could see no harm in Bullitt's going over 'purely on his own for a look-see.'" Devising a secret code with Wehle, "Bullitt quickly sailed for England."[33] On his trip across Europe Bullitt met with Mac-Donald, Chamberlain, Lothian, Lansbury, and Cripps in London; Herriot, Berneger and Leger in Paris; and Buelow and Von Neurath in Berlin, and as Bullitt cabled home reports of these meetings, Wehle decoded them and passed them on to FDR.[34] These meetings established Buliltt's credentials with FDR and upon his return he reported to FDR on European conditions on the day following Norman Davis' report on the same subject. In his letters home Bullitt had laid down the sort of broad self-promoting hint that he worked so well, telling Wehle that "all the men in the [French] Foreign Office feel deeply the inadequacy of our representation here. Berenger said to me: 'Is it not possible to impress on the incoming American Government the necessity of sending us an Ambassador who speaks French fluently.'"[35] Wehle swallowed the bait whole and when Bullitt was out of the room for a few minutes he told Roosevelt, "'There is your man for Paris.'"[36] Paris was too much of a jump but the meeting did finally permit Bullitt personal access to the President, and when Stimson impressed FDR in January with the importance of the war debt problem and currency stabilization, FDR allowed Bullitt to visit Europe again, this time as his personal representative.[37] While Bullitt was in England, however, his mission leaked to the press and the papers said that he was in Europe to forgive most of the debts.[38] Actually Bullitt was a complete hard liner on the debts, but the damage had been done. The great publicity destroyed his usefulness and he returned to America incognito and moved in with Wehle under the name of Mr. Williams.[39] The mission itself was misconceived and contributed directly to Chamberlain's uncompromising speech at Leed's, but FDR didn't recognize this. Bullitt's problem as far as FDR was concerned was the publicity, because it brought back memories of Bullitt's sensational breach of confidence during his testimony before the Senate many years before.

Shortly, Bullitt came out of seclusion, but his attempts to secure an appointment through FDR came to naught and as inauguration day passed and the new administration came into office it became evident that he was not going to become part of the new goverment on the strength of his own relationship with FDR. He began to cultivate Moley as his patron and "not long after the administration got under way, Bullitt appeared in Washington and established himself near my [Moley's] rooms in the Carlton Hotel. Bill managed to see me often there and in my office. And he was always welcome, for I found him interesting, informed, and helpful. He spoke again and again, during these visits, of his desire to fit in somewhere, and it seemed to me that he would be eminently suitable for either of two places open in the Department—the Assistant Secretary-ship and the position of Special Assistant to the Secretary." Moley became Bullitt's champion in the new government. "For what seemed like a long time," Moley wrote, "I reminded the President almost daily that there was an obligation of sorts to Bullitt—with no noteworty results, I admit. At last I prepared a little memorandum about Bill's appointment and several others, which the President initialed. Armed with this, I went to Phillips, who thereupon showed more emotion than I knew he was capable of. He bitterly reminded me that Bill had been 'disloyal' to the Wilson administration."[40] Moley prevailed, however, and Bullitt was given the position as Special Assistant because it did not require Senatorial confirmation.

Bullitt immediately became involved with James Warburg, Herbert Feis, and Moley in preparing for the London Economic Conference and once appointed Bullitt was not shy about using his position to reestablish a personal relationship with the President. Now, after having been intimately involved for two months in the preparation for the conference, Bullitt was in London in the capacity as Chief Executive of the American delegation.

Bullit's first meeting with Litvinoff was for the purpose of securing Russian support for James Cox, of the American delegation, as chairman of the monetary committee. Hull had hoped to chair the economic committee, but when FDR publicly announced against submitting any tariff reduction authority to Congress that position was effectively precluded. The American delegation decided to support Cox against Bonnet of France as chairman of the other major committee and Bullitt set about earnestly lobbying the other delegations. His competitive spirit aroused, he "contended that Washington would be offended if he [Bonnet] were chosen and that the prestige of the United States was involved."[41] Litvinoff was glad to pledge his vote to Cox but others were more reluctant.[42] In lobbying for Cox and for other American positions Bullitt demonstrated no understanding of proportion. His brother wrote that "to Bill most decisions were either black or white; he had very little use for compromise in his character. Something was right or wrong, and he seldom chose the middle ground."[43] This tendency was strengthened whenever Bullitt dealt with the English because he was frankly an anglophobe. Bullitt, according to his brother, "had a distinct bias against the British that went back to his childhood when England was engaged in the Boer war in South Africa. His sympathies were all with the Boers. His sense of identification with his ancestors imbued him with the spirit of resistance to Great Britain and his heroes were the leaders of the revolution."[44] Bullitt's attitude towards the British was further enforced when Lloyd George publicly denied all knowledge of Bullitt's mission to Russia during the peace conference. "This

26

whole sordid and shabby exposition of the dealings of Prime Minister Lloyd George and of the statements made by him and the members of his government in the House of Commons left a mark on Bullitt which," in his brother's opinion, "was to take over twenty years to erase. This episode should be kept in mind when reading his letters to Roosevelt wherein he sometimes violently expresses his distrust of British diplomacy and the dependability of their statements."[45] After working with Bullitt, the British Ambassador to the U.S. would later say of him, "In general I should say that he likes Englishmen, but hates the English," and in the files of the British Foreign Office are such handwritten statements as "evidently a very dangerous intriguer."[46] James Warburg relates in his autobiography how Bullitt responded to one small difficulty at the London Economic Conference. A major concern of Congressman McReynolds' of the American delegation "was to get his daughter presented at Court. In trying to arrange this, Bullitt very nearly caused a major crisis in Anglo-American relations by telling MacDonald's private secretary that, unless Miss McReynolds received the desired invitation, the American delegation would pack up and go home."[47]

Bullitt's approach to the negotiations was no different on more serious matters. Prime Minister MacDonald told Cox that "during the contest for the presidency of the Monetary Commission between Bonnet of France and myself [Cox], Bullitt went to 10 Downing Street with the ultimatum that if the English did not join in support of the American delegation it would take the first boat home."[48] MacDonald was critical of Bullitt's behavior throughout the London Economic Conference. He later told Henry Stimson that he felt that Bullitt "had done some very dangerous and arbitrary things . . . at one stage of the negotiations when there was a difference of opinion between the British and the Americans, Bullitt went to a British delegate and threatened to tear up the Naval Treaty and build

27

the biggest Navy in the world; also to tear up the Kellogg Pact, etc."[49]

That was Bullitt's manner with the British, but what of his dealings with the French with whom he felt himself sympathetic? After FDR's bombshell renouncing even a perfunctory statement regarding currency stabilization, the French wished to adjourn the conference immediately and hold the U.S. responsible. By his own account Bullitt approached the French Premier with a threat of political blackmail. Bonnet had a few months earlier rejected a private offer of currency stabilization from FDR, and Bullitt made it plain that he would step out into the corridor and tell the entire story to the press if Bonnet persisted upon adjournment. Bonnet said he doubted that Bullitt could be as mean as that, but Bullitt left no question that he could.[50]

In one of his many private communications to FDR during the conference Bullitt gave FDR his advice for dealing with the French. "The whole French attitude towards us at the moment is one of contempt and I think it would be healthy to let them know that our personal affection for them will not prevent us from refusing to support them in any way if they continue to behave as they are now behaving." Bullitt also wrote in the same letter that "it seems to me that the time has almost come for us to make it clear to the French that we feel that they have rejected with contempt our effort to collaborate with them in foreign affairs, and that we should back such a statement by appropriate actions."[51]

Bullitt was no subtle gamesman using disproportionate force with cool calculation to effect negotiations, but rather he was a romantic man who became emotionally committed to the righteousness of whatever position he took, and who was consequently incapable of understanding anything less than total power. When he was through he came away with the feeling that not only were the positions of the opposition inferior but that the opposition was made up of inferior men. There is no temperance in Bullitt's descriptions of his opponents. Of Mac-Donald, Bullitt wrote, "He is the damnedest, squirming eel in the world." Of British Foreign Minister Simon, Bullitt wrote, "the trouble with Simon is that when they circumcized him, they threw away the wrong piece." Of French Premier Bonnet, Bullitt wrote, "Bonnet is, of course, beyond reach. He is as cooperative as a rattlesnake."[52]

Bullitt's contacts with Litvinoff of the Soviet Union were much less volatile. In their first meeting Litvinoff told him that his representative in America was Boris Skvirsky; in the second meeting Litvinoff asked Bullitt if the U.S. contemplated recognition. Bullitt replied that FDR's "general attitude was friendly, as he could see from the fact that our representatives at this Conference, even the Secretary of State, were meeting him and talking with him as if he were a human being and not a wild man, and that trade negotiations were in progress in Washington." However, Bullitt said that he did not have "the slightest idea" when the President "might consider it desirable to recognize Russia; that it might be soon; that it might be a long time; that he should not count on immediate recognition, but that he should not be surprised if you [FDR] should recognize Russia." Litvinoff was relying on the prospects of trade to stir the American appetite for recognition, and he told Bullitt "that the English argued with him continuously that it was not fair for Russia to trade with the United States since the United States had not recognized Russia." Litvinoff had made something of a stir at the Conference by holding out the possibility of a one billion dollar Russian market for foreign trade, but interest quickly subsided when it became clear that this market was contingent upon the extension of long-term credits. The newspapers had noted that the target of the speech could be ascertained by the currency (dollars) in which this potential market was calculated. Bullitt in reporting these discussions with

29

Litvinoff included the self-promoting hint that he worked so well. "Litvinov, of course, said that if Russia were recognized he hoped I would be sent as Ambassador to which I replied that I could not think of a worse one for the post and that I should repeat the same remark to you. I have no idea that you would contemplate such a thing, but I should like to argue with you against it if by any chance someone should suggest such an appointment to you."[53] By denying his interest he was nevertheless planting the idea that he was thought by people of importance to be a fine choice.

It is interesting to note that Bullitt and Hull, after being in office only a few months, had already both become sensitive to aspects of Soviet behavior traditionally made much of by the State Department in the belief that they proscribed recognition. During Bullitt's discussion with Litvinoff he told him that if the U.S. did recognize, "an absolute pledge from the Russian Government to refrain from all propaganda directed against our institutions" would be required. The Soviet style of justice when applied to foreign nationals was another problem made much of by the State Department. When the Chinese ambassador to Russia called on Hull during the conference to urge American recognition Hull said "that the matter was under careful consideration at Washington and that all phases were being kept in mind. I [Hull] did remark that the recent experiences of the British was not especially encouraging."[54] Hull was referring to the arrest of some British citizens working in Russia on charges of economic espionage. This episode had already become an important factor in the Secretary of State's attitude concerning the recognition of Russia.

30

III

The State Department's
Russian Experts

In Washington, the chief of the Eastern Europe Division, Robert F. Kelley recognized that these new contacts with the Soviet Union reflected an attitude which made recognition a possibility. Kelley was adamantly against such a change and he quickly moved to make the State Department's objections known to the new President. Since he began functioning as chief of the division in 1925, Kelley had effectively used his position as the governmental expert on the Soviet Union to influence official policy against recognition. Herbert Feis, a participant in and a historian of these events, described Kelley's outlook this way: "Since he considered the world revolutionary aims and practices of the Soviet Union precluded the maintenance of friendly association with it, he would have been content had the American government refrained from any at-

31

tempt to enter into closer relations with its government." Kelley felt communism was a threat to all non-communist governments and he produced a plethora of studies and recommendations under the guise of scholarly examinations of the problems, which were potently effective bureaucratic weapons in an active campaign against recognition. This aspect of Kelley's bureaucratic skill was never sufficiently appreciated by his peers. Kelley was routinely described by Feis as "reliable and industrious in his study of, and reports on, Soviet affairs."[1] This lack of appreciation resulted from the fact that Kelley was simply articulating the feelings of many of the regular foreign service officers who, having similar outlook and value structure, shared his antipathy towards the Soviet Union.

The concern with the dangers of communism was broadly dispersed within the State Department and during the first year of FDR's presidency Washington received such information as "a Bolshevik move planned against all national currencies" from its Paris embassy, a report that the Comintern headquarters in Europe was a steamship line in Copenhagen from its Warsaw embassy, a report of a communist bogus passport plant from its Berlin embassy, the names of three Swedish sailors believed to be communist couriers from its London embassy, and a report on the latest Comintern official line as interpreted by the local communist press from its Madrid embassy.[2] However, the focus of the communist monitoring activity was the Eastern European Division's legation at Riga, Latvia. Here the major function of the Russian section of the Legation was the study of all aspects of Russian life, and much effort was expended analyzing and interpreting events within the Soviet Union for Washington's use. From Riga, Kelley received information on Russian gold shipments, agencies of Soviet propaganda outside Russia, the names of Americans in Russia believed to be communists, policies and activities of the Communist International, Russia's international monetary condition, translations of Russian publications of all kinds, and generally all aspects of Russian life and communist behavior.[3]

The State Department's concern with communism was not a temporary aberration, but was a consistent policy that had within a few years of the Russian revolution become solidified into rigid opposition. As do all wars, World War I had altered the flow of change within society and had thrown up challenges to accepted values. The great conflict had destroyed the firm ground of rational progress upon which the confidence of the prewar era had stood and the outlook of the world that emerged from the war was very different from the one that had gallantly marched off to battle. In spite of American enthusiasm for the post–war New Era, an assured confidence in a better future could never really be secure for a generation that had first-hand knowledge of the senseless and futile carnage of trench warfare, and who had seen that carnage develop such momentum that it could not be stopped while the capacity for destruction remained.

Within the general assault on values by such a terrible war, a particular event resulting from that war, the Russian revolution, made that challenge more direct and quite specific. The new communist values challenged established economic systems by disparaging private property and challenged established religious systems by denying God. Because of this confrontation of basic values, the Russian revolution was the type of event that had major impact on its times and forced everyone who thought about human society to confront it and somehow come to grips with its meaning. The revolution was so novel an event in history that it seemed to hold a kaleidoscope of meanings. Different groups of Americans looked at the revolution and saw a totally different phenomenon. As the policy of the Russian government continued to evolve, it gave off ambiguous impulses to an American society that further defracted meanings through the lens of the change occurring within itself. To

American observers the continuing Russian revolution seemed to be many things.

There were those, however, to whom the existence of the Soviet government meant simply a continuing evil challenge. Communist proclamations of an impending proletarian world revolution under a communist dictatorship seemed to these people to be nothing else than a direct challenge to all organized government. The new communist government's "dizzy illusions of the imminence of world revolution" was met in the State Department with an instinctual antipathy.[4] "The Soviets wish us to assist them," Phillips wrote in December 1917, "to communicate with the socialistic elements in this country which are striving for our own overthrow."[5] "A declaration of war on all existing governments and law and order," was the way Secretary of State Robert Lansing responded to a Soviet note in January 1918.[6] Hostile to communist values, ignorant of the import of the peculiar state of Russia's prerevolutionary society and the impact of war upon that society, made anxious by the loss of the confident expectation of progress that had been destroyed by the machine guns, tanks, and gasses of the battlefield, the men of the State Department would soon come to see in the communist revolution the creation of a new and implacable enemy.

The confusion of the U.S. government's decision to participate in the allied military expedition into Russia in 1918 helped to firmly establish and solidify the hostility of these men towards the young Soviet government. The allied expedition was far too small to accomplish any military goal, but it did provoke Russian feelings against foreign invaders which the Bolshevik government used to solidify its control of the country. The expedition escalated the struggle and created new forces of destruction, which horrified American observers. The blind spot of 20th century U.S. foreign policy has consistently been the inability to understand how American actions affect events within other countries. As was anticipated by those who opposed the expedition, the communists in the rage of the struggle destroyed their opposition and the bloody purges that resulted accelerated the obliteration of moderate positions within Russia. In addition, the American participation needlessly created mutual antagonisms between the two governments, severing on both sides the tenuous link of feeling and diplomacy between the two countries, and with it the possibility of future American influence upon the new Russian government. American diplomats in Eastern Europe observed the destruction of the Russian people and ideas with whom they most sympathized and their intellectual dislike of the communists became hardened by personal experience. As a consequence, fear and distrust of the Soviet government made them view every future Russian action with suspicion. The kaleidoscope had collapsed for many of these men into a narrow shaft of distrust.

These men had little understanding of the mechanisms of societal change. They were unable to comprehend fully the means by which so small a group had been able to secure the control of so vast a country and they feared its unidentifiable strength. As a result, the revolution appeared to them to be larger than it was and the possibility of like occurrences seemed always ominously threatening. Many accepted the Soviet challenge totally on its own terms and viewed the United States as being involved in a monumental global struggle with communism. As Secretary of State Bainbridge Colby explained in 1920, the U.S. would not recognize the Soviet Union because it had a government which was "determined and bound to conspire against our institutions; whose diplomats will be the agitators of dangerous revolt; whose spokesmen say that they sign agreements with no intention of keeping them."[7] Nine years later Kelley explained the U.S. government's objections to the Russian government in similar terms. "The essential difficulty lying

35

in the way of the recognition of the Soviet government is not certain acts of the Bolshevik régime, such as repudiation of debts, the confiscation of property, and the carrying on of propaganda in the United States; but the Bolshevik world revolutionary purpose, of which these acts are manifestations."[8] Kelley's clear delineation of the central idea underlying all his "statements of policy towards the Bolshevik régime" meant that these specific causes for complaint were largely irrelevant to the American government's official policy, as that policy had been based instead upon what was considered to be the fundamental Russian revolutionary challenge. This fact did not, however, prevent Kelley from using these complaints effectively in arguments within the American government to maintain a policy of non-recognition.

Kelley had much influence within a State Department whose personnel largely shared his general outlook. His serious and scholarly professional demeanor contributed much to his ability to continually reinforce governmental hostility towards the Soviet Union. Kelley was a superb bureaucrat who fully comprehended the power of recognized hierarchal authority. He understood that his influence upon peers and superiors flowed upwards from his division, and he ran his division in a manner that perpetuated the fundamental orientation of his analysis and continuously produced information in support of it. "A scholar by instinct and dedication," Kelley required novice diplomats assigned to his division to obtain a solid Russian cultural background through the study of Russian history, literature, and language.[9] Kelley's serious academic approach was also manifest in his collecting "the best library on Soviet affairs in the United States. He had elaborate and voluminous files of materials collected from every possible source on every aspect of Soviet life."[10] When Litvinoff arrived in Washington to negotiate recognition he remarked that "the division of Eastern European Affairs in the State Department had better records on the history of Soviet diplomacy than did the Soviet Foreign Office itself."[11] Kelley not only had a better library than the Soviets, he also took his library more seriously. Whereas the Soviets paid homage to the writings of their founders while adopting interpretation according to the exigencies of the moment, Kelley's respect for the writings of the founders knew no bounds for he was convinced the Russian future was determined by the book-bound words of the past. Kelley interpreted all Soviet actions in terms of the theoretical communist writings. Because the theoretical writings said that communists were the vanguard of a world revolution against capitalistic states, Kelley interpreted all Russian diplomatic endeavors as actions whose goal was world revolution. As the new men were trained in the orthodoxy of the old, Kelley's bias became firmly established as the bias of the Russian Division. Referring to Kelley's influence upon him while on his first tour of duty in Russia, Charles Bohlen wrote, "Yet I could not but be fearful of accepting the Bolsheviks at face value, Kelley's skepticism was healthy. My feelings were shared by most of the Soviet specialists, including Kennan."[12]

Unable to comprehend the real nature of the enemy's seemingly great powers, Kelley engaged in a largely artificial struggle which placed enormous importance upon words, both Russian and American. He devised strategies and defenses against the challenge which were as ineffective as had been the allied military expedition, and as irrelevant as was his principal weapon of non-recognition. Unfortunately for the continuation of his policy, the legalisms that often resulted could not have been more uninfluential with the new President, who had come into office seeking a way to recognize the government of 160,000,000 Russians.

Kelley knew that the change in the government's attitude towards the Soviet Union in the early summer of 1933 did not originate within the top level of the State Department. Both

Hull and Phillips were far too cautious to attempt to alter the status quo regarding the Soviet Union in the face of the major obstacles presented by their expert, and both men had been sufficiently sensitized to at least some of the problems to have already developed reservations regarding recognition. It was apparent the impetus for the change originated at the White House, and Kelley prepared for Phillips, who was functioning as the Acting Secretary of State while Hull was in London, for forwarding to FDR, an analysis of the problems precluding immediate recognition.

Kelley titled his analysis "Problems Pertaining to Russian-American Relations Which in the Interests of Friendly Relation Between the United States and Russia, Should be Settled Prior to the Recognition of the Soviet Government."[13] As the title makes clear, Kelley's theme is that America's goal was not relations with the Soviet Union but friendly relations, a much different endeavor under his definitions. "The fundamental obstacle . . . is the world revolutionary aims and practices of the rulers of this country. It is obvious that, so long as the Communist regime continues to carry on in other countries activities designed to bring about ultimately the overthrow of the Government and institutions of these countries, the establishment of genuine friendly relations between Russia and those countries is out of the question." Even if the efforts are ineffective, they prevent friendly relations and if friendly relations are not possible, then no relations should be established. "Even when these activities do not constitute a present menace to the established order, the systematic interference of a foreign power in the domestic affairs of a country constitutes *ipso facto* a source of deep resentment and unavoidable friction." This whole issue is an item of importance to recognition only if it is vested with significance, by no means a foregone conclusion, and although the State Department leadership, including Bullitt, quickly accepted Kelley's testimony as to its significance,

38

FDR never did. Kelley in fact is dissembling a bit here. He believed that the Soviet leadership would never abandon its ideology of revolution and once the American government accept communist activities in America as obstacles to recognition, then recognition would become a dead issue. For this reason Kelley emphasized throughout his analysis that the obstacles must be cleared up before and not after recognition.

"Another serious difficulty" to friendly relations was the confiscation of American property in Russia which occurred after the revolution as well as the failure of the Soviets to honor the debts of predecessor governments. These American investments are not in Kelley's analysis mundane financial transactions determined by the relationship of risk versus return but are elevated to the level of moral principles based upon the accumulated wisdom of human history. Kelley argued that the Soviets had failed "to observe certain generally accepted principles governing the conduct of nations towards each other . . . which the experience of mankind has demonstrated are vital to the satisfactory development and maintenance of commerce and friendly intercourse between nations." The maintenance of standards in international obligations had been a fairly effective argument within the State Department, particularly among those who didn't quite have the gut animosity towards the Soviet Union shared by the members of the Eastern European Division. Secretary of State Stimson had relied upon this particular argument in denying recognition in September of 1932 and it was the principle one of the many reasons that Ambassador Joseph Grew in Japan remained against recognition in the fall of 1933.[14] But Kelley's gun fired more than one kind of shot, and Kelley's papers on the problems of recognition contained something that everyone could object to. Whereas international moral obligations appealed to the mindset of many within the State Department, the idea of affronts to private property could be counted on to appall those who made an ideology of capitalism, and in cognizance of this fact Kelley headed this section "Question of Repudiated Debts and Confiscated Property."

"A third major problem" as Kelley saw it was the Soviet government's monopoly on foreign trade which "in carrying on commerce with foreign countries, had a natural advantage over individual business concerns in such countries. In practically every country trading with Russia endeavors have been made, usually with little success, to find ways and means of putting trade relations on an equal footing and removing the disadvantages under which the individual businessman labors in dealing with the Soviet monopoly of foreign trade." Kelley is writing from the perspective of a political ideologue and not a commercial man. The businesses represented by the American-Russian Chamber of Commerce, operating with great excess capacities, were anxious to acquire Russian orders even at reduced levels of profitability. The businessmen wanted a government organization to provide long-term financing, some minimal safeguards, and a clearing home for trade information. Kelley wanted an organization strong enough to nullify the purchasing power of the Russian trade monopoly. That the Russians would under these circumstances most likely place their orders with other countries was not to Kelley's way of thinking a loss. An indication of the enthusiasm with which Kelley looked upon trade with the Soviets may be garnered from the response he prepared for Phillips to a May 13th request from Lehman Brothers for guidance in this area. Lehman Brothers wrote that "we do not wish to enter into any negotiations of the above-mentioned general character with the Soviet Government or its commercial representatives unless we obtain such assurances as you may wish to give us that efforts to facilitate Russian-American trade would not be contrary to the policy or wishes of the United States Government."[15] The official State Department response prepared by Kelley was:

> In reply to your letter of May 13, 1933, you are in-
> formed that the Department of State cannot undertake
> to express any opinion with respect to the advisability or
> propriety of any foreign loan undertaking. Individuals
> and corporations engaging therein do so upon their own
> responsibility and at their own risk.[16]

This reply was made at the time that FDR through other agencies of the government was actively seeking to arrange trade
between the countries.

The fourth major obstacle was that the communist idea of
justice was so alien to American standards that conflicts were
sure to arise. "For example, the Soviet conception of espionage,
especially economic espionage, is of such a broad nature that
almost every foreigner in Russia commits acts which may
readily be interpreted as violating the laws on this subject." In
early 1933 some English engineers had been arrested by the
Soviets for economic espionage. This was the recent English
experience that Hull alluded to when expressing his reservations with regards to recognition. Kelley recommended that an
agreement protecting the "life and property of American citizens in Russia" should be signed to remove this obstacle before
recognition.

On July 27, Phillips handed a copy of Kelley's analysis to the
President, making it in effect a State Department position. It is
worth noting here Kelley's bureaucratic experience. He did not
squander memos at government levels that did not determine
policy. This memo was not written for the Under Secretary but
for the Under Secretary to pass on with his endorsement to the
President.

IV

===

The Incomparable
Max Rabinoff

THE RFC LOAN TO ANDERSON, CLAYTON & CO. FOR THE PURPOSE OF
financing the sale of cotton to Russia successfully accomplished
FDR's purpose. It created further interest in Russian trade, it
made official contact with Russia less exotic to the general
population, and it called widespread attention to the anoma-
lous state of political relations between the two countries and
thereby made societal pressures for recognition more visible.
Many businessmen came to Washington to investigate the
Russian market and from across the country many more wrote
letters of inquiry to the State Department, the Department of
Commerce, and the RFC.

Among these interested businessmen were the representatives of Anderson, Clayton & Co., who continued to meet with
Amtorg in an attempt to build a larger deal; but is soon became

apparent to these men and the officials of the RFC with whom they were in contact that the government's usefulness in such more ambitious transactions was quite limited. FDR soon realized that the trade issue had taken the country as far as it could towards recognition, and consequently in the late summer FDR's attention began to move away from commercial and towards political contact with the Russians. When the trade issue ceased to be politically useful, FDR would drop it entirely.

As had everyone else, FDR had been forced to confront and resolve the challenge of the Russian revolution. He accepted it on its own terms but in his own restricted and limited way. He understood the revolution as a Russian attempt to improve Russian existence, and discounted the pretentious theories of worldwide applicability, particularly in relation to America. It was not the political theories of the communists that disturbed and drew a reaction from him, but their philosophical claim regarding what was important in determining how human lives should be led. He most responded to and refused the Bolshevik emphasis upon things material and their corresponding rejection of the spiritual. In his view this was the Soviet challenge. He was not going to permit relations between the two countries to be defined by the Russians on the basis of their own obsessive materiality with their talk of billion dollar markets and economic opportunities. His whole conduct of the negotiations with the Soviet Union leading to recognition was to be a deliberate avoidance of the economic issues as denial of Russian assumptions which defined the U.S. simply in terms of the quest for profits. Consequently, trade was important to FDR only for testing domestic political forces and for moving the country closer to political contact. When trade became no longer useful, FDR would systematically ignore it and other economic issues.

At this same time it was apparent to Kelley that a major shift in policy regarding Russia had occurred and that under

FDR the State Department no longer had a primary role in determining policy regarding the commercial issues. In fact Kelley found his views all but ignored as it became clearer that other branches of the new administration were actively reaching out towards economic contact with the Soviet Union. Washington buzzed with plans for capturing the Russian market that Kelley unaccustomedly found himself unable to counter. As a reult, at the very time that FDR's interest in trade and similar issues was diminishing, Kelley and his subordinates were increasingly focusing upon these subjects. Not understanding the real source of this sudden surge in business agitation towards trade with the Soviet Union, the State Department's Russian experts considered the Administration's growing interest in that country as being a political response to this growing political force. In their view the President, by naively acquiescing in such a shortsighted and politically expedient move, was not demonstrating a true understanding of the Russian threat.

Members of Anderson, Clayton & Co. and Amtorg worked together during July to consummate the RFC financed sale of cotton to Russia, and during these contacts consideration was given to the possibilities of a larger cotton deal. The RFC was proposing three-year financing, but by the end of July Amtorg had received definite word from Moscow that the terms were too short to consider as the basis for an arrangement. Moscow had told Amtorg that any additional cotton "is not a strict necessity; and that their budget for the next five years does not provide more foreign exchange than is required for the most urgent necessities. Therefore, they said they can take this additional cotton only if payment for it can be deferred to six years hence."[1] Lamar Fleming of Anderson, Clayton & Co. gave the Russians an extract of the law enabling the RFC which did not provide for any financing of any kind longer than five years.

Fleming reported the results of his discussions to Jones along with his impression that Bogdanov and Rosenshein were in most respects being frank with him.

In mid-August Fleming and Will Clayton dined with Bogdanov and Rosenshein for the purpose of continuing the discussion of the larger deal. The Russians lowered their credit requirements to five years but would go no further. Clayton, after disclaiming any authoritative knowledge, suggested that Bogdanov consider Jones' position and the care he had to display regarding "public opinion, Congressional opinion, and the press, not only out of regard for your [RFC] Board's position and that no detail in the Corporation's relations with Russia might arouse a criticism that would embarrass the evolution of our general policy towards Russia." Clayton suggested that the farsighted approach from the Russian's point of view would be to accept a credit with annual installments of two, three, four, and five years instead of one payment at the end of five years. Fleming reported to Jones that "Bogdanov seemed impressed by this reasoning, but said nothing that would indicate that he saw a possibility of winning Moscow to anything shorter than five years."[2] Constrained by limited foreign exchange, the Russians said they did not feel they needed the additional cotton enough to justify the purchase for less than five-year terms.

Although the law limited the RFC's options in the financing of agricultural sales, its provisions regarding industrial sales were far more stringent. Essentially the law provided that in this area the RFC could not bear any risk at all. The RFC could loan directly to a manufacturing company only if that company put up American securities for the full amount as collateral, or if a bank "of undoubted solvency" guaranteed the RFC loan. As another alternative the RFC could finance the sale by lending to a bank but only if the bank assumed the entire risk. Because of these limitations the RFC's lack of usefulness in

46

financing industrial sales to Russia emerged during July and August.

During the summer the RFC and The White Company had had a series of discussions regarding the financing of a $12,000,000 Russian order for heavy duty trucks.[3] Amtorg was willing to pay for these trucks with a note bearing 5% interest, due in three years. The White Company was willing to accept the risk of up to about half the value of the note, and the discussions with the RFC revolved around whether the RFC would accept the remaining risk. The company had already had to lay off thousands of employees because of decreased business, but the low profitability of the proposed sale, being at a level simply to keep about "3,000 skilled mechanics" employed during the coming winter, did not warrant the company's assuming the full risk. In early August the company informed the RFC of the terms of financing under which it would accept the order. After a conference at the RFC the company agreed to look at the situation again but on August 8 they reported back that "we carefully weighed this Russian transaction again from every angle, material costs, labor increases, the amount of investment we could afford to make in relation to profit and risk in the proposition," and that they finally decided that the deal would either have "to stand or fall" as previously presented.[4]

As a possible alternative the company's bank wrote the RFC that they would be willing to handle the three-year note for the company but only "without recourse," that is without assuming risk. Having just brushed by a collapse of the entire banking system, the risk of foreign loans held no attraction for Cleveland bankers. By August 18 the attorneys for the White Company agreed with Stanley Reed, general counsel for the RFC, that The White Company would remain liable if the bank handled the note "without recourse." This being the case, the arrangement would suit neither The White Company, who did not want the entire risk, nor the RFC, which could not make a loan under that condition. The RFC's lack of usefulness for financing industrial sales had become apparent and by the end of the month the RFC was advising American manufacturers that "we have thus far found it rather difficult to be of assistance in financing the export of commodities other than agricultural products due to the rather restricted wording of the law under which we operate."[5]

During the summer Morganthau was less directly involved in developing trade with Russia. However, the intermediaries that Morganthau had used to make contact with Amtorg had developed grandiose ideas about the possibilities of Russian trade and had formed a group to develop a plan for handling the $240,000,000 market they foresaw. During the early summer they met with members of the RFC to present their plan and one of the intermediaries went so far as to take the plan to Moscow. In late July the group informed Bogdanov of the plan and on August 1st they met Bogdanov in the offices of Dulles and Jaretzki (Sullivan and Cromwell) to present the plan's major details. The plan called for a 6% regular interest rate plus an additional 3% interest "to be used in refunding pre-Soviet obligations," a provision to which Bogdanov immediately objected. There were probably a number of difficulties with the plan, but the factor that made all the other difficulties irrelevant was that the plan depended upon RFC financing, and as the summer wore on the difficulties here were becoming too apparent.[6]

This was not the only group trying to develop a plan for financing Russian trade that summer. Attracted by the prospect of a burgeoning trade with Russia, a myriad of schemes were being developed and promoted in Washington. The plan which for a short time carried the most consequence was developed by a promoter named Max Rabinoff, or as he was dubbed in a flak newspaper story "the incomparable Max Rabinoff."[7]

Rabinoff, born in Russia, returned there in the employ of Remington-Rand in 1928 and while in that country met E.C. Ropes, who in the summer of 1933 was chief of the Russian Division of the Department of Commerce. Rabinoff's ideas for financing the coming Russian export trade impressed his friend who began giving personal references for him. Ropes told businessmen "that he knows of his own personal knowledge that Mr. Rabinoff is the only man who has ever been able to get business from the Russians for Americans, all others having failed."[8] Ropes sent inquiries from businessmen regarding the exporting of their products to Russia to Rabinoff and not to Amtorg. Through Ropes, Rabinoff was able to contact almost everyone in the government concerned with doing business with Russia and by early August Rabinoff had convinced the enthusiastic Smith Brookhart of the worthiness of his plan. Consequently, on August 8 Brookhart chaired a conference at the Department of Agriculture whose principal purpose was to present Rabinoff's views and to form a committee to implement them. The conference, actively promoted by Rabinoff, was attended by about 40 people, including representatives of almost every government agency anxious to keep abreast with what seemed to be the latest important development.

Brookhart began by giving "a general summary of existing business conditions in Soviet Russia, together with a survey of trade and credit relations as now existing with European countries which have recognized the Soviet Union." Brookhart then introduced Rabinoff as a man who had much experience as a counselor to American firms "which have established trade relations with Soviet Russia."[9] A few months later when some of the businessmen at the meeting tried to determine from Ropes which companies it was that Rabinoff had represented, only three names could be secured from him. When questioned, two of the three denied any relationship with Rabinoff and the third reported that the "connection with Rabinoff had been satisfactory, but that for some time past they had been dealing directly with Amtorg."[10] After Rabinoff's presentation the government officials were dismissed from the meeting and a committee of businessmen was set up to work on the development of the export bank that Rabinoff proposed. Two members of this committee met with the just returned Secretary of State the following day, and according to a Treasury Department official who was following these events "Secretary Hull evidenced considerable interest and approved of the suggestion made by his callers that they seek an interview with President Roosevelt and present the matter in detail to him."[11]

It was a strong performance by Rabinoff but his plans began to run into difficulty in mid-August when Bogdanov complained to Morganthau that the Department of Commerce was sending inquiries concerning Russian trade to Rabinoff instead of to Amtorg.[12] Morganthau immediately followed up Bogdanov's complaint, and within a week the Department of Commerce and the Department of State were writing explanations of why they made such referrals. The particular request for information had been originally sent to the State Department where Earl Packer, the Assistant Chief of the Eastern European Division, after agreeing with Ropes by telephone as to the form of the reply, forwarded the request to Ropes for an answer.[13] While disclaiming responsibility for Rabinoff's plans, Ropes suggested that Rabinoff be contacted to provide the trade information desired.[14]

In promoting the legitimacy of himself and his plans, Rabinoff was receiving help from the State Department as well as the Commerce Department. Whatever the personal reasons of Ropes for providing the assistance, the State Department reasons were political. Earl Packer felt that the centralized export bank proposed by Rabinoff would provide an effective counterweight to Amtorg's monopoly purchasing position, and he was not pleased with Amtorg's complaint. "The question could be raised" Packer replied, "whether a corporation (the Amtorg) owned by foreign interests has any right to complain of an action taken by a Department of this Government in the matter of informing an American firm to get in touch with an American citizen with respect to questions concerning trade with the country owning such corporation. What Amtorg desires is, of course, to have the Government recognize its monopoly position here." Both Packer and Kelley had been in touch with Rabinoff "on several occasions" even prior to the meeting arranged by Brookhart and they liked his idea for a centralized bank. In forwarding the request for information to Rabinoff they were doing what they could to organize American business to combat Amtorg. Packer explained that "initial hostility of the Amtorg Trading Corporation to this scheme was to be expected, since the Corporation would upon its execution be faced by a central organization of exporters, a position which obviously might operate somewhat to cramp Amtorg's style, since the latter would be less able to play off the price quoted by one exporter against that quoted by another."[16]

Rabinoff's plan depended upon RFC financing, and by late August Packer recognized that this would be a problem, but he didn't have the expertise to evaluate the merits of the plan. He and Kelley accepted the plan because they so much desired the function it would serve. A few days prior to Packer's explanation of his actions, J.A. Marcus, a Foreign Trade Marketing Specialist for the AAA wrote a scathing report on the workability of Rabinoff's plan. The executive vice president of the American Foreign Credit Underwriters of New York had been given a copy of the plan by Rabinoff and after reading it and finding the plan "vague and hardly operative," gave a copy of the plan to Marcus for his opinion. Marcus reported that "without claiming to have consulted Messers. Stalin, Kalinin, Molotov, Rosenholtz, not even Bogdanov, I can state definitely that THE RUSSIANS WOULD NEVER, NEVER CONSIDER

SUCH A PLAN, THAT THEY WOULD CONSIDER IT AN INSULT TO THEIR INTELLIGENCE, AND THE MERE FACT THEY CHOSE TO DISCUSS WITH ANYONE SUCH A PLAN WOULD BE A REFLECTION UPON THEIR CREDIT STANDING THROUGHOUT THE WORLD. . . . The whole affair seems to be so ridiculous that it is a wonder to me that anyone in the Government Departments has seen fit to give it any attention." Marcus also reported that "from the standpoint of the American manufacturer, the absurdity of this ill-conceived plan is so obvious that I shall not dwell at length on this subject. . . . How they could have considered such make-shift of a plan to be acceptable to either the American indus-trialists or the Russians is a mystery to me."[17]

V

———————

The Cuban Revolution

WHEN HULL RETURNED FROM LONDON FDR SENT HIM A TRANSLATION
of a Russian article entitled, "Soviet-American Relations" with a
short cover note, "I think you may care to see this from a
Russian semi official paper."[1] Hull's first five months in office
had been dominated by the London Economic Conference, and
with the conference behind him the issue that filled the void
was not Russia, but Cuba. On August 11 Hull wrote Norman
Davis that "I have been overwhelmed with the Cuban and other
emergency problems since my arrival."[2]

Many within the State Department saw in the radicalism of
the Cuban revolution a consummation of Russia's global rev-
olutionary intentions. These men understood too little of
Cuban nationalism and too much of the theoretical claims of
Russian communism. The American ambassador to Cuba,
Sumner Welles, had a better understanding of the social prob-

lems which prompted Cuban instability, but he was not prepared to see the Cuban government in the hands of students and enlisted soliders and he was professionally committed to the succession of a reorganized democratic government under the leadership of Carlos Manuel de Céspedes. As a result of his endeavors in favor of Céspedes and against the young revolutionary government, Welles directly fed the anxieties of the diplomats in Washington. These men misunderstood the instability in Cuba, and Welles's biased reporting further increased their apprehensions, particularly with regards to the role played by Russia in these events. The result was that in the late summer the State Department became much concerned with communism in Cuba. The Cuban revolution put fear into the State Department, and it succeeded in turning Cordell Hull into an opponent of recognition. By successfully linking the issues of subversion and recognition in the minds of the newly appointed State Department leadership, resistance within the Department against the idea of recognition was much strengthened.

Welles, the new American ambassador selected by FDR, had been deeply involved in easing the exit of the Cuban dictator, Machado. In early August events in Cuba approached the crisis, and on the night of August 12 Machado abandoned the struggle and fled Cuba. A new government favored by the American ambassador was created under Céspedes, but the sudden removal of established authority unleashed uncontrollable forces harshly suppressed by the old regime. In the societal turmoil the Cuban students were to Welles an unexpectedly powerful force. In mid-July Welles had dismissed the student groups as unimportant but by August 15 he was calling them "the most pernicious element in Cuban public life."[3]

As the normal social restraints disappeared and the strident oratory for rights and demands spilled over the society, it was not long before many Americans began to see communist manipulations behind these events. Welles was visited "by a delegation of 30 of the most prominent American businessmen in Cuba. They expressed themselves as exceedingly disturbed by the social and labor unrest which is current in Cuba and certain of them appear to be firmly of the opinion that Communist agitators 'under the pay of Russia' are seizing their opportunity through the formation of unions and the promotion of syndicalism to plan the overthrow of the Cuban Government and the installation of a Communist regime." In transmitting the businessmen's message back to Hull in Washington, Welles took pains to point out that labor and social unrest were not necessarily a Russian import. "I do not believe," Welles wrote "that Communist theories as such have as yet any support among the laboring classes. The present situation, disturbing as it is and increasingly serious as it may become, is primarily due to the fact that the laboring classes have suffered under an absolute dictatorship for the last three years; that their leaders have been arrested and frequently assassinated; and that any organization of labor has been made absolutely impossible." Even more important in contributing to the unrest in Welles' opinion were Cuban living conditions. "The average laborer on the plantations has been paid less than the minimum amount required to feed himself and his family and the conditions of distress and actual destitution which exist cannot be exaggerated." Welles summed up that while he recognized that some foreign agitators were stirring up trouble he could not "see any indications of the 'red menace' which certain Americans doing business here are fearful of."[4]

The communist danger, however, was on the minds of some people in Washington as well. On August 9, even before Machado's fall, Earl Packer sent a copy of some New York *Daily Worker* articles denouncing the American role in Cuba to the Latin American Division of the State Department because of their "possible interest in connection with the situation in Cuba." The articles, with such titles as "Machado Brutal Watch-

Dog for U.S. Imperialism" and "Cuban Communist Party Most Advanced of All in the Caribbean Area," claimed the communists to be "in the lead of the fight against Roosevelt-Welles intervention."[5] These articles were not passed on as a curiosity item, but as illustrations of the significance of the communist involvement and of the seriousness of purpose with which they undertook that involvement, and under Kelley the Eastern European Division took everything the communists wrote very seriously. To Kelley communist words had special qualities that projected them in the marketplace of ideas with more animation than their competition. The key to understanding Kelley's position is fear, fear of communist words and actions and fear of the potency given them by foreign support. He wrote that it was "entirely erroneous" to assume that communist propaganda was merely descriptive of a communist utopia and how to reach it. Rather it consisted "of forming, subsidizing and actively directing and controlling from Moscow a small strongly disciplined group of communists in each country whose purpose is to 'win over the majority of the working class' and bring about the development of conditions within each country which will be favorable to a revolutionary, armed *coup d'etat* under communist leadership and the resultant establishment of a communist government." Thus Kelley felt communist propaganda "resolves itself into active interference in the domestic affairs of each state concerned,—directed and controlled by an alien power and inimical to the continuance of the existing order in, and the existing government of, each such state."[6]

The communists, Kelley felt, had developed a "doctrine of world revolution" and Kelley had no doubt about the basic communist aim either in the U.S. or in Cuba. He wrote that the purposes motivating the communist movement in both the United States and in Latin America should be considered together, because the Communist International had from the first laid down one basic aim for these communist parties: "'. . . the

56

destruction of the last stronghold of capitalist imperialism, the overthrow of the North American bourgeoisie, is the task of the workers and peasants of all the American countries.'" Kelley explained that "the quotation is from a letter written by the Communist International to the Mexican Communist Party in 1923. It was published by the American Communist Party, and the directions contained in it were formally accepted as binding the latter."[7] Because the United States Communist Party was the largest and strongest "it is believed that the American Communist Party has assumed a position of leadership with respect to many phases of the communist movement in Latin America, and that this has been done pursuant to an order given by the Communist International in 1926."[8]

Kelley followed the changing organizational tables and institutional relationships of the various communist organizations with an eye for detail, which information he used to produce a legalistic synthesis of the motley communist pronouncements and communications. Kelley knew communist policy better than the communists. The impression the reader is left with after reading a number of his documents is that Kelley interpreted communist words as if they were written on stone tablets. If on occasion the masses failed to respond to the eloquence of communist argument or the proletariat uncomprehendingly ignored the historical imperatives of their teachings, it may be certain that Kelley never did. Unknown and forgotten communist hacks could always be assured that their work was being read, studied, and excerpted for Secretaries of State and even Presidents.

With all the emphasis of communism, Hull himself was quickly becoming sensitive to the issue. When told during a telephone conversation with Welles on August 15 that the port workers were remaining on strike, Hull's response was, "What is the matter with them? Are they in the hands of the communists?"[9]

Welles received much approbation for the creation of the Céspedes government, but his aspirations for the new government were short-lived because on the night of September 4 Fulgencio Batista led a mutiny of the enlisted ranks against the army's officer corps. In his study of these events, *The Making of The Good Neighbor Policy,* Bryce Wood concluded that "this sudden end of the Céspedes regime was a surprise, and must have been a great shock to Welles, for in a real sense the Céspedes government was his government, and the mutiny was a blow to his newly gained prestige no less than an attack on the position of the traditional ruling groups in Cuba."[10]

At one o'clock in the morning of September 5, Welles telegraphed the first news of the mutiny back to Washington. Welles' immediate assessment of the political character of the mutiny was that it had been "fomented by the extreme radical elements. The subversive movement has been announced by radio from the various barracks and in all probability violent disorder will break out before morning."[11] The situation was extremely fluid but by 10:00 A.M. Welles had garnered and wired to Washington a copy of the new government's proclamation signed by Batista "and is likewise signed by a group of the most extreme radicals of the student organization and three university professors whose theories are frankly communistic. Five of the signatories of this proclamation have constituted themselves an executive committee to govern the Republic." Welles' opinion of the capacity of this government was not high. "It appears hardly likely that a so-called revolutionary government composed of enlisted men of the army and radical students who have occupied themselves almost exclusively during the last ten days with the assassination of members of the Machado government can form a government 'adequate for the protection of life, property and individual liberty.'"[12]

58

In interpreting the rapidly developing events for Washington, Welles was seeking to gain the commitment of his superiors for the intervention of American troops, and the distinction between the radical students and communists was much blurred. If a reader of these early telegrams from Welles was actively seeking to differentiate between the two groups his task would have been difficult, and most of the readers of Welles's cables had no interest in any such distinction.

By 5:00 P.M. of the first day of the coup Welles was able to cable to Washington the names of the five-man ruling committee. His assessment of their politics was that one was a "communist," one "a radical of the extreme type," two were professors who "are extreme radicals" and one "a supposedly conservative businessman of good reputation who is being used as window dressing."[13]

Immediately after sending this assessment he transmitted a position statement that had just been handed him by the American Chamber of Commerce of Cuba, requesting immediate and decisive steps "to protect American lives and property and maintain order." The Chamber of Commerce felt "that the Communist element is the best organized element in Cuba today."[14] Welles also transmitted information received from the American consuls around the island which contained other references to communist activities.[15] Welles's cables to Washington contained many such references to communists and although these references did not dominate his reporting, they did serve as a constant reminder of the communist presence to those who considered this presence important. In the State Department most who read his cables did consider this presence important, and for this reason the following narrative will focus on this aspect of the American reporting of the Cuban revolution.

Immediately after sending the above information to Washington, Welles went into a meeting with the leaders of the

Cuban political parties in which alternatives to the new government were discussed. The meeting took place at the American embassy and the principal accomplishment was the conveyance by Welles of the United States government's tacit approval for the organization of political opposition to the new Cuban government. Welles reported that the political leaders "were emphatic in their declaration that the present revolutionary group could not remain in control for more than a few days and would be then in turn forced to give way to an out and out Communist organization."[16] If the State Department in Washington thought of the 1917 revolution after reading this message, the reports that followed offered no comfort. Later that evening the Chief of Naval Operations received a cable from the Commandant of Guantanamo Naval Station stating: "Situation in Guantanamo City and vicinity in grave danger. Lawless red element has control."[17] Early the following afternoon the State Department received a telegram from the Corn Exchange Bank and Trust Company stating their interest in the Hormiguero Central Sugar Company and their dismay at having received a cable stating that the "Communists have taken mill and staff held as prisoners."[18] And an hour later the State Department received a similar message from the New York Trust Company.[19]

Assistant Secretary of State Caffery was Hull's principal advisor on the Cuban crisis and on the afternoon of the 6th, in accordance with FDR's decision to consult with the Latin American nations regarding Cuba as a manifestation of his Good Neighbor Policy, Caffery met with the Mexican embassy's chargé d'affaires.[20] Assuring the Mexicans that sending ships into Cuban waters did not mean intervention was Caffery's official message (a message that he was not very successful in transmitting), but he sent an unofficial message as well. Welles's hostility to the new Cuban government as well as the State Department's concern with communist influence must have been clearly transmitted to the Mexican representative because shortly before nine that evening in Mexico City, the Mexican foreign minister contacted Josephus Daniels, the American ambassador, and expressed himself "seriously disturbed over fear of intervention in Cuba. [Foreign Minister] Puig says he knows the four men composing Junta are educated men with good backgrounds and no taint of communism. He believes that they will organize good government."[21]

The concern of the Mexican foreign office over the American government's understanding of the Cuban situation and the role of communism there was such that at 8:26 the following morning Puig wired to Hull biographical descriptions of four of the five members of the ruling commission. "I take the liberty of advising Your Excellency that we have accurate data concerning personality at least four persons who are serving as members of the Executive Commission of the new Government of Cuba, data indicating that they are not Communists, but persons of undoubted preparation, intellectual capacity and social responsibility." Included among the four was the man characterized by Welles as a communist, which characterization seems to have been passed on by Caffery. "Mr. Carbo Commissioner of Gobernación, Commerce and War, was some years ago Consul of his country; he has been and is manager of the periodical 'La Semana.' There could be no basis for the supposition of his communist affiliations due solely to the fact of (his) having visited in Moscow and then written a book on Russia that is strictly literary."[22]

Daniels was himself concerned with the State Department's interpretation of events and he "telephoned me [Hull] to give me Mexico's attitude and to urge us not to budge from nonintervention. A day or two later I received a letter from him dated September 9, saying: 'It was good to hear your voice over the telephone today. Sometimes I get lonesome for the voice of a friend in our country. It cheered me greatly when you said,

"I would rather walk from here to the South Pole than to have to intervene.'"[23] This is a quote from a letter that Hull thought enough of to include in his memoirs. However, he is quoting from the first paragraph of Daniels' letter and the first paragraph is misleading. After talking to Hull, Daniels had become so concerned that he wrote Hull a letter almost entirely devoted to denigrating the importance of communism in Cuba. Hull had told Daniels, "'We have very persistent reports that there are more or less communistic influences in there that are trying to keep anything from being done to restore order and that may be the chief trouble we have down there.'" Daniels advised Hull "that my information here is that the report of communistic influence in Cuba is very much exaggerated. In our own country and elsewhere people attribute to Communists all the agencies that work evil. I think it is so in Cuba, and if I were you I would accept with many grains of allowance the attempt to . . . [blame] on the comparatively few Communists all that goes awry . . . I am inclined to think that it is not Communists who are making the most trouble in Cuba, only they are made to bear sins of other groups."[24]

Meanwhile reports of communist influence continued to flow into the State Department from various sources. On the night of the sixth a telegram from the embassy in Guatemala arrived with the news that "President Ubico feels the Cuban situation is exceedingly grave principally because of communistic tendencies."[25] On the eighth Bethlehem Steel Company reported that "Camaguey mines forced to stop by Communists'" and the President of Munson Steamship Lines wrote that "our terminal and lighterage properties in Cuba; valued at three million dollars, are in danger under communist seizure."[26]

All these reports of communist activity did nothing to assuage the fears of Caffery who was already much concerned about communist influence. During the afternoon of the eighth

Chargé Sterling of the Cuban Embassy contacted Caffery to discuss American intervention in Cuba. Caffery made a memorandum of the conversation. "As Dr. Marquez Sterling has asked me [Caffery] if he might speak frankly to me on the question of landing marines, I said, 'I would like now to ask you frankly a question.' I said, 'We hear that Communist elements are having an unfortunate influence and are causing disturbances in many parts of Cuba; what do you say to that?' He said that he could assure me that there were no Communist elements in the Revolutionary Government; that on the other hand, it was quite possible that the Communists were causing disturbances in various parts of the Island but he believed that with the formation of a concentration government it would be easy to put down the Communists. I said 'What is this I hear about anti-United States propaganda in various cities?'"[27]

Caffery's role as interpreter of the Cuban revolution for the State Department was central to the conclusions that were being drawn in Washington concerning these events. Caffery was highly regarded by the State Department leadership, and his analyses of the situation were given much credence. Phillips considered Caffery "one of the best men in the Service in the ministerial rank" and Hull considered him one of his "real advisors."[28]

With so much concern about communism it wasn't long before the State Department began seeking the Russian hand above the Cuban stage, pulling strings and controlling events. During a conversation with Hull on the eighth, Welles, who was still seeking intervention, requested that the USS Richmond be moved into the harbor because much time would be saved in landing troops in an emergency if they were inside. Hull was concerned about the danger to the vessel but Welles replied that there was absolutely none. "The only danger," he said, "is mob excitement amongst the agitators and communists and when they have been drinking, against Americans." The mention of communists triggered a new thought in Hull's mind, causing the conversation to veer.

"Secretary: Have you access to cables coming in down there? I mean cables giving instructions from the outside to any group, communist or otherwise?"

Russian control was not an idea that sprang naturally from evidence manifest to Welles at his post in the midst of the revolution, but from an idea conceived in Washington and forwarded to Cuba. The idea was new to Welles, who had not previously given it any thought and he reacted to it slowly.

"Ambassador: I suppose that I could. I have not tried to get that. I see what you mean. I will undertake that at once."[29]

As the situation moved past Céspedes loss of power and FDR and Hull eliminated the possibility of intervention, Welles's reporting better distinguished between communists and others. Still there was communist activity to report and there were enough references during the following weeks to keep the State Department stirred up. Communist subversion in Cuba had become a significant concern of the State Department and that concern had a direct impact upon attitudes regarding the Soviet Union. Emphasis upon the importance of Russia to the continuing internal disorder within Cuba created a general apprehension within the State Department regarding any dealings with the Soviet Union and strengthened the feeling within the Department that recognition was a bad idea.

VI

═══════════

First Steps Towards
Recognition

IN MID-SEPTEMBER THE VARIOUS AMERICAN DEVELOPMENTS
regarding Russia began to come together and influence each
other. FDR decided to move from commercial to political contact with the Soviet Union, and ignoring the State Department,
he left the trade issue behind in one culminating burst of public activity. The State Department did not understand that this
was the swan song for trade in FDR's maneuvering and became
agitated at their obvious omission from any voice in the matter.
This was particularly upsetting to Kelley and his assistants
because they had recently been receiving reports from American diplomats in Eastern Europe which interpreted late economic developments there as indicating a significant weakening
in the Soviet Union's financial structure. Kelley especially did
not want to assist the Soviet Union economically just when it

seemed that they were running into real difficulty. He had some hope that the Russian financial troubles might even affect the survival of its communist regime.

Kelley's discomfort regarding trade was heightened when a parallel occurrence regarding Russian-American discussions on wheat quotas also unexpectedly came to his attention in mid-September. Again Kelley was not only omitted from policy making but had not even been kept informed of events. These omissions from any voice in determining policy regarding Russia were occurring at the time when apprehensions regarding communist subversion were being stirred by the Cuban revolution. Welles' discovery of a short telegram from Cuba to Moscow pretentiously promising 250,000 workers "mobilized for action" seemed to confirm the State Department's fears in this regard. The result was a burst of activity by Kelley to influence American policy. He worked hard towards postponing any financial assistance to the Soviet Union until after recognition, and he successfully won the State Department leadership over to his view that American moves towards recognition were a mistake. Kelley was also successful in that he was able to define which issues in contention between the two countries would have to be resolved before according recognition. Within the State Department only Bullitt remained a strong proponent of recognition, although he too accepted Kelley's conceptual structure for judging the Russians. Kelley's only failure was in not convincing the President that recognition was an error, and FDR, who was not confiding in the State Department, continued blithely moving towards recognition using his own style of personal diplomacy.

In late August Russia signed the Final Act of the wheat conference in London, and now in mid-September the U.S. Agricultural Department was looking forward to the first meeting of the Wheat Advisory Committee scheduled for September 18 to resolve the problems still remaining. One major problem was

Russia's insistence on a quota about twice what the other exporters were offering. On September 14, seeking a means to induce Russia to accept a lower quota, Secretary of Agriculture Wallace cabled Ambassador Bingham in London, the United States representative on the Wheat Advisory Committee, that a "plan now being discussed here for extention of credit to Russia through export corporation with some government assistance . . . [might] prove satisfactory alternative to induce Russian participation in wheat agreement on basis of export quota around million metric tons."[1] Herbert Feis, who received this message for transmission through State Department communications, objected to the content. It was apparent that the RFC trade financing negotiations were having some difficulties and he was concerned that credits not be held out to Russia as a bargaining chip if there were little actuality of their occurrence. Feis called Mordecai Ezekiel of Agriculture and secured his agreement to change the wording of the cable to "the whole question of financing exports to Russia is before the R.F.C. in many forms at the present time, but the outcome cannot be predicted."[2] The episode focused attention on the fact that the State Department really had no authoritative information and consequently no influence upon what the RFC was planning. To correct this Secretary Hull sent a letter to Jones on the same day requesting that if any trade proposals "approach the stage of actuality, that the Department be given a chance to discuss them with you before they are effected."[3]

FDR's purpose in seeking to finance trade with the Soviet Union had been to acclimate the American public to governmental commercial relations with the Soviet Union as a precursor to political relations, but it is now becoming clear that under the present law there was little hope for further trade contracts. This course having brought the country as far as it could, FDR was in the process of shifting directly to political relations.

On September 14 Felix Frankfurter before leaving for England was FDR's overnight guest at the White House. Frankfurter's general advice to FDR on foreign policy was to be independent and not to rely on the State Department diplomats who were too bound up in trivialities to capture his grand objectives. From Oxford, England in October Frankfurter wrote back to FDR that "the impact of events on this side makes one thing more clear than ever to me—that the guidance of foreign relations must substantially be in your own hands." There were in Frankfurter's view two reasons for this. "In the first place, there is such interaction among various issues that do not seem immediately related that vital decisions must be made by one who sees these interconnections and is not too immersed in the specific problems as they arise from day to day. Secondly, these are not days for cautious and conventional conceptions of foreign relations and hampering preoccupations with formalities and precedents quite inapplicable to present-day exigencies and complexities."[4] This sort of advice from Frankfurter had certainly been effective with FDR in the past.

During the week following Frankfurter's September 14 visit at the White House, FDR began the actions that would lead to political contact with the Soviet Union. When these actions resulted in an exchange of letters with the Soviet President, Frankfurter wrote FDR that "strange as it may seem to some of the politically myopic opponents of your Russian policy, your note to Kalinin is calculated to mark the beginning of a most important chapter in the pursuit of world peace."[5]

Although trade negotiations were at an impasse in mid-September, they still were an example of official governmental contact between the two countries. On September 15, the day that Frankfurter left the White House, Jesse Jones, who was in New York meeting Bogdanov and Rosenshein, announced to the press the current status of his negotiations with Amtorg.

Actually it was a non-story. There was no deal to report and no immediate prospects for one.

> But a deadlock seems to have been reached, it was said, and although the conferences have proceeded, the deal is now no nearer completion than it was thirty or forty days ago. . . . The RFC is willing to make the loan for a sum between $50,000,000 and $75,000,000, but cannot, within the restrictions under which it operates, make the concessions, the Amtorg officials were told.[6]

Although the follow-up story in the next day's Sunday *New York Times* remained essentially the same, it did slightly alter the prospects for success of future negotiations. Whereas the original story had indicated that an impasse had been reached, the Sunday story began with the announcement, "Additional conferences of officials of the R.F.C. and representatives of the Amtorg Trading Corporation were scheduled in a week or two." Jones was quoted as saying, "'We have gone as far as we could in offering terms to the Soviet representatives and will probably hear from them later.'"[7] "'It is all a matter of obtaining the necessary credits,' was the comment of one Amtorg official. 'If the credits can be arranged and the negotiations successfully carried through, an announcement to that effect will be then made. At present we are not in position to add much beyond that.'"[8]

As a result of these new stories there was a flurry of activity towards the RFC both from outside and from within the government. Mordecai Ezekiel of Agriculture wanted to make the loan contingent upon Russia's acceptance of a wheat quota, and the AAA sent over a list of surplus American farm products that they hoped Russia could be induced to take as part of a loan agreement. But within the government the real consequences from these stories were occurring within the State Department, which "was very much disturbed by Jesse Jones' statement in New York . . . that he was ready to loan fifty to seventy-five million dollars to Russia."[9] The State Department was particularly disturbed because they had seen a Russian telegram to Moscow reporting that Amtorg had refused Jones' loan offer.[10] They did not know how to interpret the significance of the stories, but they did know that it meant that the State Department was being bypassed in the decision making concerning Russia. Jones had made these announcements despite Hull's letter asking to be kept informed, and in fact Jones would not get around to answering Hull until September 26.[11] The whole matter of American relations with Russia was a particularly hot subject in the State Department because of a cable that had just been received on September 15 from Welles in Cuba.

> Two days ago a cable signed "Mesaejectuiva Prado 123" which is the headquarters of the Conferacion Nacional de Obreros was dispatched to the following address.
> "Profintern Solianaka 12 Moscow."
> I have not been furnished an exact copy of the cable but the text which I am told was brief contained the statement that 250,000 workers, agricultural laborers, and soldiers were now mobilized for action. I will be advised if any further cables are sent from this source.[12]

This seemed to justify all the concern about Russia's role in Cuba's revolution. Caffery was extremely concerned that the Comintern "in Moscow is directing communist leaders engaged in fomenting labor disorders in Cuba."[13]

As a result of these developments a meeting of the Division Chiefs was immediately arranged in Hull's office on Monday to discuss "the Cuban and Russian situation."[14] The problem of communist subversion in Cuba had already become linked to

70

the recognition of Russia within the State Department. The discussion in Hull's office "centered on the necessity of concentrating in this Department all activities in relation to Soviet Russia. There is great danger that with the independent offices assuming independent policies toward Russia, the confusion will be too much magnified."[15] The official concern of the State Department was its proprietary interest in any significant foreign policy matter, but at the heart of that concern was the desire of Kelley and his allies to control the issue. By concentrating control of all discourse with Russia within the State Department they would be in a position to deflect any moves towards granting recognition as well as forestalling any additional loans. The problem of loans to Russia was becoming a continuing source of aggravation. The State Department had been aware that the group which included Morganthau's intermediaries had sent a representative to Moscow and the Department had become upset when this representative had refused to keep them informed by sending back progress reports.[16]

In fact, the prevention of new loans rather than recognition had become Kelley's immediate concern and with the help of Bullitt, who had staked out Russia as one of his issues, he drew up a document for the Secretary of State arguing against such loans. This partnership of Bullitt and Kelley was mutually beneficial. Bullitt gained from the arrangement because it helped establish his credentials as a Russian expert, and Kelley gained because Bullitt became an active exponent of his ideas. Bullitt had a personal relationship with the President, which was important because the document was written not to Hull, but for Hull as a statement of his views to be signed and then given to the President. By sharing the authorship of the letter Kelley was insuring that it would be brought to the President from more than one source and given a wide hearing and strong support. Bullitt may have influenced the style of the letter, but the content was pure Kelley. In a similar situation in

71

late August, Packer had given Bullitt a copy of the July letter that Kelley had passed to the President through Phillips, with the understanding that Bullitt would present it to Hull.[17]

Kelley's and Bullitt's new letter for Hull repeated the earlier letter for Phillips in establishing the obstacles to recognition. The obstacles remained interference in the internal affairs of the United States, repudiation of debts and the confiscation of property, and differences between U.S. and Soviet economic and social structures, principally the Russian state monopoly on foreign trade. And again Kelley established that the true goal in Soviet-American relations was "friendly cooperation," and that without the removal of these important obstacles "friendly cooperation" was impossible, and of course without "friendly cooperation" recognition was impossible. But this letter, unlike the letter for Phillips, recommends a bargaining procedure to overcome these obstacles. "Thus at the moment, the Government of the United States has two powerful weapons which can be used to bring about a favorable settlement of some, if not all, of our outstanding problems with the Soviet government."[18] These are "credits or loans, and recognition." It is worth noting that the word "weapon" was chosen for this context.

As the first sentence of the letter makes clear, the essence of Kelley's immediate anxiety and the reason for the letter was the possibility of new loans "by agencies of the United States Government to facilitate Russian purchases in the United States." There is much discussion of the efficacy of withholding loans as a weapon to force the removal of the obstacles to friendly relations. Reports of Russia being in precarious financial condition had been arriving in Washington all year. In January the Estonian Minister to the U.S.S.R., Julius Seljamaa, told an American diplomat that "'under the existing conditions the Soviet authorities were without means to enter into extensive engagements abroad; they had of late even reduced very heavily their imports from Great Britain and from Germany.'"

To this report Kelley appended the note "Worth noting—Mr. Seljamaa is one of the best informed diplomats in Russia. RFK."[19] Also in January the Consul General in Prague reported that the British Consul had been told by "L. Hubbard, who is in charge of the Russian section of the Bank of England, and a well-known British financial expert . . . that he is entirely convinced that within the year the Soviet Government will default in its international debts." The British Consul also stated his own opinion after discussing "the Russian situation with various British travelers, who had just returned from Russia . . . that for the most part these travelers are of the opinion that the present Russian Government will last for two or three more years, and that they are endeavoring to obtain all of the cash business possible in that time and while it does last."[20]

Immediately following the RFC loan to Russia in July, Felix Cole, chargé in Riga, sent Washington a strongly worded analysis of Russia's financial condition. This document more than any other became the basis of Kelley's aversion to granting the Soviet Union any financial assistance.

> In its financial dealings with the rest of the world, the Soviet Government is, and has been for several months, on the verge of extreme financial difficulties. In the beginning of the current year, the German banks came to the rescue with financial credits on the security of Russia's future exports. Since that time there has been a revolution in Germany and the attitude of Germany's new rulers is undoubtedly different from that of the previous governments. Russian-German relations are becoming daily worse. It is doubtful whether Berlin would be inclined to come to Moscow's rescue again in the same way.
>
> Thus Russia is compelled to look elsewhere for extensive credits and there is no better prospect in Moscow's eyes

than the United States. The extension of cheap credits to Russia by American industry may or may not be advantageous to the enterprises concerned; to Russia it is a matter of the most urgent necessity. With payments to the extent of several millions of dollars to be met in the current year, with a curtailed export trade which is not yielding enough to meet these payments, with a vast undiminished industrial construction program in dire need of foreign assistance and foreign equipment, with former friends and supporters turning their backs—it is not surprising that Russian officials are willing to go to any lengths of propaganda and misrepresentation in order to secure financial help from America.

The Russian appeal stresses recognition; actually what is wanted are credits. And in view of this fact, I cannot refrain from pointing out once more to the Department that in the estimation of this Legation, based on years of intensive study of Russian economic conditions, there has never been a time since the commencement of commercial relations between Soviet Russia and the rest of the world, when conditions were worse for the granting of credits to Russia and when the risk involved was greater.[21]

This last paragraph has two lines drawn beside it for emphasis.

In late August Cole followed this up with the report of a discussion with "Dr. Richard Anspach, Director of the Eastern Division of the Dresdener Bank, Berlin. . . . Having been personally in charge of the arrangement of the 140,000,000 mark interim credits granted to Soviet Russia by the German banks last winter, he is exceptionally well-informed with regard to the question of German credits to Russia and the ability of the Soviet Government to meet its obligations at the present time." The report of the discussion concludes with Dr. Anspach's statement "that unless the Russian trade negotiations with England, France, and the United States should be reasonably successful, that is, unless the Russians, through these negotiations, should be able to assure themselves increased export markets or further long-term credits, Russia might indeed find itself in a bad financial position."[22]

If Kelley could help it, Russia would find neither an increased export market nor long-term credits in the U.S. Kelley and Bullitt argued in their letter to Hull that because the Russians were in such precarious financial condition the withholding of loans would be an effective weapon to force the removal of the obstacles to "friendly cooperation," and consequently no loans should be granted before the obstacles were removed. "It may be pointed out that the foreign debt situation of the Soviet government presents at the present time great difficulties. The Soviet government, for instance, was unable to meet its obligation which fell due in Germany in February of this year, and the German Government was obliged to come to its financial assistance and arrange a bank credit of approximately $50,000,000. It is generally believed in German Government circles that the Soviet Government will be unable to meet its obligations falling due in Germany next year, and that a similar arrangement will have to be made." The Soviet government was on the verge of financial ruin dependent upon the German government's future largesse, and "at the present moment the German Government, it is understood, is unwilling to increase the amount of Government-guaranteed credits now available to Russia in Germany."

Although the Soviets "it is believed, prefer at the moment credits to recognition," the value of recognition as a weapon was also enhanced by similar financial considerations because "recognition by the United States would open the private banking resources of the United States to the Soviet government and facilitate the obtaining of credits in other countries." Kelley seems to have considered these issues to be of some real import to the internal structure of Soviet society. Loans were of more importance to the Russians than recognition, but Kelley felt that even recognition "would strengthen the prestige of the Soviet government not only abroad, but also at home, where it is faced with tremendous difficulties in carrying out its industrial and agricultural programs."[23]

After Kelley and Bullitt composed this letter "they besought the Secretary of State to send" it to the President. "The Secretary fingered this letter hesitantly. He signed it and took it over to the White House but brought it back again. Being still of two minds, he had not given it to the President. But within the next day or two he succumbed to persuasion and did so."[24]

While Bullitt and Kelley argued their case with Hull the Cuban revolution continued to churn, focusing attention on communist subversion. On Tuesday, September 19, Phillips cabled Welles about a report that some Americans had been killed, but when Welles talked to Hull the following day he labeled the report as "ridiculous." "Undoubtedly," Welles told Hull, "the representatives of the owners of American interests have been down here for the last few days and have gotten a rather exaggerated idea of conditions. . . . If anything, the situation seems to be more satisfactory," although he said, earlier in the afternoon there had been a clash between government troops and communists. The behavior of communists was a theme that over the past ten days Hull's advisors in Washington had been dwelling upon.

"Secretary: Communist sentiment has increased considerably on the Island during the last two or three months?

Ambassador: Yes, and I think the people now in the Government are beginning to realize the seriousness of that condition.

Secretary: Don't you think that in recent months those communist organizers have been sent in there just for that purpose—and especially since present conditions began?

Ambassador: That is one of the things I wanted to have an opportunity to talk to you about tomorrow morning."[25]

As this debate to fully persuade Hull waxed, Judge Walton Moore was appointed Assistant Secretary of State by FDR, filling the vacancy left by Moley. More than any other of FDR's appointees Moore was Hull's man. Friends and colleagues in the Congress, Judge Moore and Judge Hull had shared regional and political values. Some Department regulars interpreted this to be a move against Bullitt, who was perceived by many to be FDR's man in the State Department as Moley had been. Hull himself regarded Bullitt with some suspicion, although Bullitt was far more sensitive to the Secretary's feelings than Moley had been. After the London Economic Conference Hull was quoted by James Cox as referring to Bullitt as "'another source of annoyance and humiliation to Cox and me. He was constantly searching for dictaphones and spies and generally made himself offensive and ridiculous.'"[26] Hull told Moffat that he did "not feel that he [Bullitt] played the game at London and would like to fill the Department with men of his own choosing."[27]

But rather than being a direct blow to Bullitt's influence, Moore's appointment effectively brought Bullitt closer to Hull. "Moore's and Bullitt's fathers had been roommates at the University of Virginia Law School and were lifelong friends. Bullitt had the affectionate regard of the Moore household, of Moore—a bachelor—and his two spinster sisters. This regard Bullitt sprightly returned."[28] Moore was a solid bridge between Hull and Bullitt and on the matter of Russia his appointment helped to bring the entire policy-making level of the State Department together in their common acceptance of Kelley's framework for dealing with the Russians. Strong differences remained, but these were differences as to the best method of proceeding from a commonly understood set of fundamental assumptions. Bullitt had been for recognition for 16 years, and no amount of persuasion could convince him otherwise, but this difference seemed greater to Bullitt than in reality it was. He thought of himself as being in opposition to the State Department regulars and he presented himself this way to FDR and his intimates, and as a result FDR accepted Bullitt's assertions regarding his independence. As Bullitt told Morganthau on September 27, "the staff of the State Department were anti-Russian and anti-recognition but that he personally had been for the recognition of Russia for a long time."[29] Bullitt sought information regarding Russia from sources other than Kelley, and when Russian "authority" Samuel Harper visited the Department in October, Bullitt questioned him at length regarding the Soviet Union. Bullitt also asked Harper "to prepare memorandum for him on six points, this to be absolutely confidential between us."[30]

This perceived difference in Bullitt's positions from Kelley's was one of appearance with little depth, and it is one of the keys to understanding later events. When during the negotiations in November Moffat ran into Bullitt and jokingly said that if Bullitt, Kelley, and Moore "could agree on anything I thought Litvinoff should undoubtedly accept it at once. He [Bullitt] said that the joke of the situation was that in spite of their different approaches to the problem, there had not been one single item on which the three were not in full accord."[31]

Although Hull remembers three meetings with FDR "after my memorandum [Kelley's and Bullitt's actually] to him," the White House logs and internal evidence indicates that the September 21 meeting established the basis for much of what occurred over the next 2 months.[32] Hull had been hesitant but now he was convinced. Years later Hull's conviction remained as an oral tradition within the State Department that the Secretary did not favor recognition.[33] Hull remembered the meeting this way.

We then ran over again the various points at issue between the United States and Russia, and talked about the steps to be taken toward recognition. I earnestly argued that three questions—no Soviet interference in our internal affairs; freedom of religion for Americans in Russia; and debt settlement—should be thoroughly taken up and satisfactory understandings reached and put in writing, by informal conferences between the two Governments, before we should invite the Russian Government to send a representative here with a view to recognition. Meantime not a single word should be uttered publicly about recognition.

The President, however, decided otherwise. His view was that we would invite Russia to send a representative here and could then discuss the questions at issue and thereafter agree upon recognition. The President decided he would send a letter direct to President Kalinin.[34]

FDR decided to initiate contact with the Soviet Union at the top level and rejected Hull's advice to negotiate Kelley's points of contention secretly and through traditional means before proceeding further towards recognition. FDR was clear on this and Hull felt FDR had rejected the well thought out and experienced approach of his State Department. Yet because FDR was still working out the mechanics of recognition, Hull supported by political realities did have much influence; more than he realized. FDR did accept Kelley's list of obstacles as problems that required solutions. Furthermore, although Hull had urged negotiations before recognition, there were many including Frankfurter who thought the U.S. should recognize Russia first and then negotiate afterwards. The approach that FDR settled on was a compromise between both positions; negotiations and recognition discussions to take place simultaneously.

To implement this policy FDR asked Hull to prepare a draft of a letter for President Kalinin of Russia. The idea of direct negotiations with heads of governments always had much appeal for FDR, and on the Russian matter he had liked the idea as early as May 9, when he had told Morganthau, "'Gosh, if I could only, myself, talk to some one man representing the Russians, I could straighten out this whole question.'"[35]

Immediately following this meeting with Hull, FDR met with Bullitt.[36] Although there is no record of their discussion, Bullitt surely reinforced Hull's message that Kelley's list of obstacles, co-authored by himself, was important and that the obstacles should be removed prior to either loans or recognition, but that unlike Hull and the State Department, he was for recognition.

While Hull and Bullitt were meeting with FDR at the White House, Feis received another Department of Agriculture telegram for transmission to the Wheat Advisory Committee in London which held out to Russia favorable consideration in the extension of credits in exchange for a lower wheat quota. Feis again objected.

> It contained a paragraph regarding Russian loan prospects which seemed to me to run counter to the substance of our [Feis and Hull] talk earlier in the day. I immediately telephoned Ezekiel over at Agriculture, and told him that this Department felt that the whole question of Russian financing was an important element in the whole Russian problem, for which the State Department had primary responsibility, and I told him confidentially that the Department was asking the President to arrange that responsibility be placed in this Department.
>
> I [Feis] therefore suggested omitting the paragraph. . . . Ezekiel said that this had been drafted by the Acting Secretary and had been discussed with Morganthau, who he understood was in charge of Russian matters and it would be very difficult to omit it or even to change it. . . . I adhered to the opinion that if the Department was

going to take the view that loans should not be made to Russia except as part of all outstanding issues, (which I have gathered was the substance of your position and of Bullitt's position), an outcome that might be long deferred, then it was too crafty diplomacy to hold out any promise of a loan, no matter how vague, in connection with this wheat negotiation.[37]

The previous day the White House had announced that Morganthau was in charge of all Russian trade negotiations. This was only a public relations move, probably made to placate the State Department while preventing it from gaining control of the issue. Recall that FDR had started on the path to recognition by delegating Russian trade to everyone while specifically avoiding the State Department. In Feis' estimation of the time that would be required to find solutions to the issues which Kelley had now convinced all were of preeminent importance, can be judged the prospects for recognition if negotiations were left in the hands of the Eastern European Division. When Bullitt returned to the Department, Feis turned to him for support, but Bullitt saw nothing wrong with falsely implying that loans or credits were dependent on the size of the wheat quota, and Feis made do with drafting a sentence "of a far vaguer character," and then convinced Agriculture to "grumblingly" accept it. Two days later news of the flap reached the Eastern Europe Division and Kelley learned of another area of intercourse with Russia of which he was not being kept informed. He immediately sent a snappy memo off to Feis, the heart of which was that the Eastern European Division "would greatly appreciate it if you would route through EE outgoing telegrams referring to conditions in or questions relating to Russia."[38] Feis, of course, agreed that he would.

Not only did Hull fail to bring back to the State Department FDR's delegation of responsibility for all Russian loans, but he

81

also brought back the possibility of a significant political move towards Russia in FDR's request for a draft letter to Kalinin. Bullitt, reflecting FDR's desire to deal with a Russian with the authority to negotiate for his government, had the conviction "that the success of the recognition negotiations depended upon the Kremlin's choice of a Soviet statesman of first-rate importance for the American mission, preferably Litvinov himself. The text was worded and reworded with the object of insuring the appointment of Litvinov."[39] This move towards Russia did not concern Kelley as much as the idea of providing Russia financial assistance, which remained for Kelley the most pressing issue. Having failed to control the issue through Hull, Kelley turned to Phillips whose long-standing relationship with the President might afford a different kind of influence on the President than Hull's titular position had been able to provide. Phillips, although currently not deeply involved in the Russian question, could still be relied upon to support any status quo if an objection to change was made. Years later Phillips recalled in both his book and oral interviews that he objected to FDR's letter to Kalinin because he felt the Soviets should have been required to make the first gesture and to have approached the U.S. before any American moves were made.[40] Phillips was in many ways the stereotype diplomat that FDR derided.

So on the following Monday, September 25, Kelley wrote a memo to Phillips. "Mr. Phillips: In connection with the President's proposed message to the head of the Soviet State," Kelley's letter began, "I recommended that the Secretary bring to the President's attention . . . the desirability of retaining in our hands one of the most effective weapons we have to obtain from the Soviet Government some measure of conciliation in reaching a solution of outstanding problems,—namely Government financial assistance, in the form of loans or credits, to facilitate American exports to Russia." Although Kelley disliked the gesture towards Russia, he could coolly use it to his best advantage. He argued that it would be "particularly unfortunate were any arrangement or agreement to be arrived at by our financial agencies which would take from our hands this weapon at the very time when consideration is being given to the question of entering into negotiations with the Soviet authorities for the purpose of reaching a settlement of existing difficulties." In the political area Kelley was the government's source of information regarding Russia, and this coupled with the weight of his official position and his personal expertise afforded him a real measure of control. In the area of loans the State Department under FDR, unlike the Department under preceding administrations, was being excluded from any participation, let alone control. If he could not control this extremely important issue, his solution was to place it behind the political problems which remained within the purview of his division. "It therefore seems essential" Kelley wrote "(1) that any pending discussions looking to our granting financial advances to Russia be held in abeyance until we have ascertained the willingness of the Soviet Government to reach a solution of outstanding problems, or (2) that, it be deemed desirable to continue such discussions, it be immediately made clear to the Soviet authorities that the conclusion of any definite agreement is conditional upon the reaching of a general settlement of existing difficulties."[41]

Hull was also becoming personally apprehensive about loans to Russia. Hull shared with Wallace and many other Democrats a strong distaste for foreign loans, associating them with the disastrous economic policies of their Republican predecessors. Hull was now developing the perception that any loan to Russia would be a continuation of this failed policy and what was worse, such a loan would act in contravention to sound tariff procedures.

83

> There is going to be a strong effort put forth by the various interests which believe that they can get a large market for American products in Russia, financed by government money, to push the matter of government recognition and a large loan. This whole move appeals to me [Hull] as exactly the kind of thing which the Harding, Coolidge, and Hoover administrations engaged in to our ultimate undoing when we stopped loaning money abroad in 1929.

> The Republican administrations loaned money abroad without any thought as to the volume of material which we would eventually have to receive from abroad in order to pay for these loans. They had no suitable tariff plan. There is grave danger that this administration is now preparing to make exactly the same kind of mistake concerning Russia.

To Hull's usual way of thinking there was nothing more upsetting to the world's economic or political systems than unsound tariff policies, but surprisingly Hull's real fear of a Russian loan comes not from the force of these powerful economic mechanisms but from the intent of the Soviet state.

> I fear that a highly centralized administration in the form of the Russians could easily cause us the most serious kind of trouble when the time for repayment comes six years hence. They could dump large quantities of goods here in our country or in other countries where such dumping would cause the maximum of proletarian discontent.[42]

Proletarian discontent! It is not hard to see who was encouraging Hull in his associating Russian trade financing with Republican economics and unsound tariff policies.

Actually Kelley, Phillips, and Hull had little to worry about on this issue from the President who, having used trade and loans to bring him to the point of political contact, was about to drop it for a new conveyance. On this same Monday, September 25, Morganthau lunched with the President, and having just been named as head of Russian loan negotiations by the newspapers asked FDR "whether in view of all the publicity he wished me to go ahead and make any loans to Russia?" FDR in turn asked Morganthau, "'What would you think of bringing this whole Russian question into our front parlor instead of back in the kitchen?' I [Morganthau] said, 'That is fine if you want to do it, but that is up to you.' He said, 'Well, I have got a plan in mind,' and I said, 'What is it?' He replied, 'Well, it will take me at least ten minutes to explain and we haven't the time now.' He said, 'However, send for Skvirsky and tell him that we have the whole Russian question under consideration and that the delay in no way is prejudicial.' We had a lot of fun laughing over his mispronouncing of the name Skvirsky, and he insisted on inserting the letter 'm,' and we both had a good laugh over it."[43] The next day shortly after noon, and less than five days after he met with Hull and Bullitt, FDR left for his home in Hyde Park to begin a ten-day sojourn away from Washington. He left without confiding to anyone in the State Department what could be next expected. Although many people had a piece of his plan no one really knew what FDR was planning, and he left behind him various degrees of confusion regarding his policy towards Russia. Having only recently learned how the forces within his government were reacting to recognition and about the issues in contention, FDR was still working out in his mind how it would all fit together. The list of problems needing resolution which he had received from Phillips in the summer was now being supported by both Hull, who was against recognition, and Bullitt, who was for it. In some form these difficulties had to be incorporated into his plans. It was also clear that the State Department except for Bullitt was against recognition.

85

Bullitt had found his opportunity and was not about to idly let events overtake him. On the day after FDR's departure Bullitt lunched with Morganthau, telling him that he was "handling the Russian matter for the State Department." Following this Bullitt began walking Morganthau to work in the morning.[44] He was cultivating Morganthau, just as earlier he had cultivated Moley and before that Colonel House. Morganthau was unsure how to respond to Bullitt's talk of Russia, but Bullitt's self-assured brashness succeeded and Morganthau confided in him. Bullitt had hoped to learn from Morganthau, but all Morganthau knew was FDR's instructions to Skvirsky. Morganthau was really peripheral to the trades by this time. He kept a foot in the door by bringing up the subject with FDR from time to time but now it was only a desire to make himself useful. To all those who were informed it had become clear that trade was dependent upon credits and the source of credits, the RFC, was closely restricted by its statute. Consequently, Morganthau was a little bewildered by suddenly being named chief of Russian trade. The day before meeting Bullitt he had received a possible explanation from Forbes Morgan who had told him that "he understood that it was the White House that had the statement given out that I was in charge of Russia in order to sit on the lid." Bullitt gave Morganthau a similar but more specific interpretation for his sudden elevation. Bullitt "intimated that it was the White House which gave out this statement that I was in charge of Russian matters in order to offset Jesse Jones' statement and to let the world know I was in charge and not J[esse] J[ones]."[45]

Actually, although neither Morganthau or Bullitt knew it, Morganthau was no longer in charge of the loan negotiations, his promotion with the press having already been withdrawn. On September 22 at an afternoon press conference FDR told the reporters, off the record, that "there was really, nothing in" the story of Morganthau's new status as head of Russian trade.

When a reporter responded, "The general impression got around that Morganthau had been designated by you," FDR passed it off as an old expedient invented to take the heat off of the State and Agricultural Departments, and he said, "That was three months ago."[46] Although the reporters knew of Morganthau's true status, FDR's government did not. It was curious but typical that the reporters now knew more about the organization of FDR's government than did the people involved.

When Bullitt asked Morganthau, "Do you know whether the President gave out this morning his statement in regard to Russia?" Morganthau at first didn't even know what he was talking about. It was Morganthau who was the net receiver of information, and he was sufficiently impressed with what he heard that afterwards he told his people "to go very cautiously in regard to Russia" because he was afraid that he would "wake up some morning to find that the President had recognized Russia."

Bullitt gave Morganthau quite a story. Much of the information was Kelley's opinion enhanced through Bullitt's always active imagination. Bullitt told Morganthau that "negotiations with Russia are far more important than just lending them some money with which they can buy goods." The Russians, he said, "are absolutely broke and that they cannot meet their payments this year, although their total payments which they owe the world do not exceed four hundred fifty million dollars. . . . In negotiating previous loans with Germany, Russia practically pledged their eye teeth." Bullitt told Morganthau, "that it means everything to Russia to negotiate this loan with the U.S.A. as their only source of credit at present is Germany and on account of Hitler's stand towards the Russians, they are naturally anxious to break off relations with Germany." Even worse for the Russians, Bullitt said, was "that there is a 50% chance that Japan will attack Russia in the Russian Maritime Provinces." However, he continued in the same melodramatic key in which he heard the world's events, "if they could negotiate a loan from us the

Japanese would naturally draw the inference that we would loan Russia money with which to buy airplanes and other war materials." Regarding all of this, Bullitt's conclusion was that Russia "would have to conclude trade agreements with us because if they were unsuccessful in the eyes of the world all doors would be closed to them for credit."[47]

Reflecting Kelley, Bullitt believed the Russians were desperate for an American loan, and this is the key to understanding Bullitt's later behavior as American ambassador. Bullitt was absolutely unrelenting in negotiations, particularly when he felt he held the strong hand, and henceforward, because of his belief in the Soviet's desperate need for an American loan, Bullitt would feel he held that unbeatable hand. Even at this early point Bullitt's competitive instincts towards Russia had already become aroused. He felt, with justification, that judging from the experience of other countries "unless we utilize every available means of exerting pressure on the Soviet government in order to obtain a settlement of outstanding problems, there is little likelihood that such problems can be satisfactorily solved."[48]

In addition to accepting Kelley's interpretation of Russia's financial difficulties, Bullitt also accepted Kelley's view of the quality of the personnel of the Eastern European Division. Bullitt told Morganthau "that the Hoover Administration had put in the Legations adjoining Russia some of our very strongest men and they have been collecting for years material in case we should recognize Russia."[49]

As had many others before him, Bullitt accepted Kelley's interpretations because of the professional and scholarly manner in which Kelley presented himself and with which he ran his division. The one issue on which Kelley failed to convince Bullitt was that Russia was an implacable enemy that must not be granted succor in any guise. But Kelley was so successful in establishing the framework with which to judge Soviet behavior and in convincing Bullitt of the financial desperation of the

Soviet government, that when the time came Bullitt's unique personality and unusual approach to negotiations would do the rest. Kelley was quite simply a bureaucratic genius. There is really no other word for it; the world we live in today is to large extent shaped by this talent he had, and Bullitt was his greatest creation. Bullitt came into government with strong and sentimental ties to Russia and with a desire for recognition. By the time he left the Soviet Union three years later, his views were indistinguishable from Kelley's. In the meantime FDR's diplomatic initiative towards Russia had been totally blunted, accomplishing recognition but nothing more, and leaving mutually acrimonious feelings of broken pledges on both sides.

VII

The Development of the
Recognition Issues

IN OCTOBER FDR SIFTED THROUGH THE ISSUES AND MADE THE
decisions that began the process of recognition. He and members of his administration consulted representatives of many
groups, and during these discussions FDR concluded that the
issues of freedom of religion and communist propaganda
would be the most influential in winning public acceptance to
the idea of recognition. Many Catholics and labor union people
were particularly interested in these issues, and they were successful in making their reservations sufficiently apparent to
cause the President to take their concerns into his considerations. Businessmen interested in commitments for governmental
support of trade with Russia fared much less well in gaining
FDR's attention to their concerns. FDR was interested in
making a statement to the Russians about the nature of the

United States as well as about the spirituality of human beings and had already deliberately turned away from the economic issues. The businessmen, however, unknowingly were quite successful in impressing Kelley, who was profoundly disturbed by their presentation. In response to their proposals, Kelley developed and sold to Bullitt and the State Department the ideas which would develop into the major focus of the Eastern European Division's attention in the few months immediately after recognition.

FDR was running Russian policy out of his vest pocket and Hull was aware of it. The Secretary of State, having remained only partially informed as to what the administration's policy to Russia was to be while FDR was out of town, requested on the day before FDR's return Bullitt's and Moore's suggestions as to how best to proceed. When he sent these opinions over to the White House upon FDR's return, his cover letter hesitatingly offered the two memoranda "attached hereto for whatever the information may be worth."[1]

FDR returned to Washington on Thursday, October 5. On Friday, Saturday, and Sunday Bullitt was a visitor at the White House. During this period while awaiting the return of the draft letter for Kalinin previously forwarded to Hull for approval, the President worked out the details of how he would approach the Soviet Union. On Monday, October 9, he outlined his plan to Morganthau.[2] In this Bullitt was to play a major role. FDR was making foreign policy independently of Hull with the help of Bullitt, Hull's subordinate, but FDR was concerned with preserving the formalities, if not the substance, of the chain of command. His problems at the London Economic Conference had taught him that much the hard way. Earlier, when Morganthau had told FDR that Bullitt had "pumped" him about Russia, FDR had replied "rather excitedly, 'Bullitt has absolutely no right to do that. He should work through the Secretary of State and not go over his head

the way Moley used to.'"[3] On Tuesday FDR wrote Hull out-
lining the plan and asking his approval of the letter of Kalinin.
Since, as FDR reminded Hull, Morganthau was leaving the following day at noon there was no time for Hull's typical pro-
longed consideration.[4] FDR was taking pains to keep Hull
informed and to ask his approval for decisions which Hull in
fact had little power to influence.

At 7:30 that evening Bullitt called Morganthau to inform
him that he had received the go ahead from FDR, and to start
implementing their plan. "After great difficulty, I [Morganthau]
located Mr. Skvirsky in New York through his secretary and
asked him to be at my office Wednesday morning at 10:30."

The following morning after Skvirsky arrived, Morganthau
told him that "'several weeks ago I told you that for the time
being all negotiations were off pending consideration by the
White House. You asked me if this was a friendly move and I
said yes. I will now give it to you'. . . . His face lit up with a big
smile, Bullitt made his entry on the stage as arranged by the
President himself, sat down, and said to Skvirsky, 'I have a piece
of paper in my hand unsigned. This document can be made into
a invitation for your country to send representatives over here to
discuss relationship between our two countries.'" Bullitt told the
Russian that "'we wish you to telegraph the contents of this piece
of paper by your most confidential code, and learn if it is acceptable to your people. If it is acceptable, will you have your people
send a draft of an answer to us and we will let you know in turn
if this proposed draft will be acceptable to the President. If both
drafts are acceptable, the President will sign this piece of paper,
and both letters can be released simultaneously from Moscow
and Washington. If they are not acceptable, will you give me
your word of honor that there never will be any publicity in
regard to this proposed change of letters and that the whole
matter will be kept a secret?' Mr. Skvirsky assured Bullitt that
that would be the case."[5] Bullitt described Skvirsky's reaction:

"Mr. Skvirsky was obviously much moved by the text of the copy, read it extremely slowly, and after collecting himself, said:

'This, if I understand it correctly, means preliminary negotiations and not recognition.'

I [Bullitt] replied: 'That is precisely what it means.'

He said: 'You know that my government has several times refused to enter into preliminary negotiations.'

I told him I was aware of that. He said that his Government had insisted invariably on direct conversations following recognition. I replied that conversations could not be more direct than between representatives of the Soviet Government and the President himself; that such negotiations must precede any further steps. Mr. Skvirsky promised to send the text of the copy at once and said that he hoped to have a reply by Friday."[6]

The heart of FDR's message to Kalinin was the third paragraph.

> The difficulties that have created this anomalous situation are serious but not, in my opinion, insoluble; and difficulties between great nations can be removed only by frank, friendly conversations. If you are of similar mind, I should be glad to receive any representatives you may designate to explore with me personally all questions outstanding between our countries.[7]

Having initiated contact with Russia, FDR turned his attention to lining up domestic support and in this capacity the enthusiastic Smith Brookhart provided much assistance. Brookhart had never understood the commercial issues, and remained confused on the matter as late as September 27, when he wrote Senator George Norris that "I am sure I would have nearly all the cotton surplus and all the livestock surplus disposed of if the RFC and its officers had backed me up with the necessary credit."[8] Brookhart had been proselytizing

94

among the anti-recognition advocates including labor leaders and members of the clergy, and in this capacity he had several meetings with Father Edmund Walsh, the founder of the Foreign Relations School at Georgetown University and a leading spokesman against the recognition of Russia.[9] FDR and Brookhart soon won Father Walsh over to the Administration's program for recognizing Russia. On Friday, October 13, Father Walsh transmitted to FDR's appointments' secretary, Marvin McIntyre, a list of groups "that he was prepared to place . . . behind the administration's program for Russia."[10] When FDR met with his last visitor that afternoon, Raymond Robbins, an early advocate for recognition, he emphasized to him that the two points he thought of real consequence in the coming negotiations with Russia were "'freedom of worship and guarantees against propaganda.'"[11] This is the first reference to religion as a major issue. Up until this time Kelley's State Department letters and memos are completely devoid of this issue, and Moore and Bullitt included it only briefly in the papers they prepared for Hull in early October. Religion was a new issue introduced into the negotiation preparations by FDR.[12] On the following Monday, October 16, FDR sent Bullitt a memorandum that asked for a promise in writing from the Russians to grant freedom of conscience for Russians and foreigners, freedom of worship, liberation of religious prisoners, and the cessation of anti-religious propaganda. In a handwritten message across the top FDR said to Bullitt, "Confidential. Please speak to me about this. FDR."[13] Later on November 1 Monsignor Keegan also delivered the same memo to FDR.[14]

The U.S. could not insist upon such a position because it was an interference in the internal affairs of the Soviet Union, but FDR with instinctual ingenuity altered the issue to a demand for religious freedom for Americans in Russia. When FDR later told Father Walsh, "'Leave it to me Father, I am a good horse dealer,'" he was referring to the approaching negotiations with Litvinoff, but the best testimony to the validity of this self-assessment was in his adept domestic political handling of this religious issue.[15]

Religious leaders recognized and shared with FDR his dislike for the utter materiality of the communist philosophy, and FDR was able to convince them of the value of making a symbolic gesture in the form of a demand for the religious rights of Americans in Russia. FDR sincerely thought such a gesture would be worthwhile. Not only would the insistence upon religious freedom for Americans in Russia be a statement about the spirituality of man and the nature of the United States, but there was even some hope that such a gesture would be a first step in changing Russian attitudes towards religion. As a writer in the Catholic journal *America* dramatically phrased it shortly after recognition: "It may yet prove the opening wedge in the godless ring of steel."[16]

A notation in Bishop Spellman's diary is an indication of FDR's successful accommodation with religious leaders. "Jack Kelly and Mr. Galeazzi whose names will never appear in history did much to get President Roosevelt to insist that American citizens at least should worship God as they wished in Russia."[17] Many Catholics who were strong supporters of FDR certainly did not want to break with him over this issue, and FDR found a way that they could accept the recognition of Russia. Father Walsh's outspoken antipathy towards the recognition of Russia was temporarily, at least, placated by the inclusion of the religious issue in its altered form.

FDR had also found himself an issue in which he fully believed. There was no hypocrisy involved on FDR's part. Both Eleanor Roosevelt and Grace Tully, his secretary, have recalled the particular pride with which FDR looked upon the negotiating of the agreement that protected the religious rights of Americans in Russia.[18]

96

The issue that concerned the labor movement was communist propaganda, and FDR secured the acquiescence of organized labor to his policy of recognition by his willingness to make an anti-propaganda pledge an issue. When FDR's exchange of letters with President Kalinin was announced, President William Green of the A.F. of L. publicly stated that "Labor had insisted that this government refuse to recognize Russia until it disavows the policy of the Third International, set up by the Communist party which controls Russia, of promoting world revolution through force and violence. We still have faith in the President believing that he will make that a condition of recognition."[19] Although the labor movement was never fully reconciled to the idea of recognizing the Soviet Union, they were in the end willing to go along with FDR. Later, when Litvinoff was in Washington and FDR's government was negotiating with him, President Green tried to get a "very brief appointment" with FDR to lay before him "the viewpoint of the Fed. of Labor on the Russian situation," and he sent to Hull an inch thick compilation of communist activities; but as the cover letter for the compilation makes evident, Green, in the face of necessity, was prepared to defer to FDR's judgment.[20] "It is not deemed necessary to offer argument for Labor has every confidence in the President and the State Department that in the negotiations for Soviet recognition everything possible will be done to safeguard the United States and its free institutions, including the Trade Union movement of the United States."[21]

On Monday, October 16, FDR was again visited by Colonel Cooper of the American-Russian Chamber of Commerce. The Chamber was a serious enterprise whose board of directors were mostly presidents and top executives of such companies as American Express, Curtiss-Wright, American Locomotive, General Motors, Remington Rand, Westinghouse Air Brake, and others. However, by this time FDR considered commercial dealings to be lower order issues. He had used trade and loans to initiate contact with Russia and to acclimate the American public to its government's dealing with the Soviet Union, but once they had served their purpose FDR's attention left them and turned towards resolving the political issues. It was time to bring the "Russian question into our front parlor instead of back in the kitchen."[22] FDR made this clear to those concerned, including Colonel Cooper who upon recognition stated, "I know that from the beginning of his consideration of the subject of recognition it has been President Roosevelt's determination that trade considerations were of secondary importance. . . ."[23] FDR was to give little further attention to the issues of loans and credits, of the American claims against the Soviet government, and of Russia's status as a monopoly buyer; the very issues that during this period Kelley considered the most important.

While Cooper was visiting FDR, Charles Stuart, another member of the Chamber was visiting with Bullitt, and he left with him two documents he had prepared as Chamber positions.[24] The first document explaining why the Chamber thought that recognition was necessary for Russian trade, was essentially an argument for including a trade agreement as part of the recognition process.

> The Commissar of Foreign Trade is always one of the ablest of the "party." The Board of Directors is composed of members of exceptional ability as well as men who are able to assist in determining the broad policy from a political as well as commercial standpoint . . . the policy is to obtain bids in the several countries and either to purchase on price, or on price in conjunction with better credit terms. Political considerations, it must be emphasized, are under any and all circumstances, a major guiding factor. Thus, in the past two years, there

98

has been a complete swing away from America. The causes . . . are: First, our failure to recognize Russia; Secondly, the better prices and credit terms obtainable in other countries, especially where the Governments undertake to guarantee the safety of the manufacturer when selling to Russia; Thirdly, irritation produced by the raising of forced labor issues, the Anthracite Coal dispute and attitude, etc.[25]

Stuart went on to explain the reasons why recognition would not automatically generate a huge volume of Russian business for American firms, but "there is a large amount of business that may be secured, however, and it is for this amongst other reasons that any recognition should have coupled with it, a trade arrangement satisfactory to both countries."[26] The trade agreement could provide for financing this business by either importing "a measure of those few products which Russia is prepared to export" or "by the direct granting of long term credits in some way financed by the United States Government."[27] Because the second alternative was the most feasible Stuart took pains to explain why he thought Russia was a good credit risk. A Soviet Budgeting Department in Moscow existed to:

Measure exports against imports and at all times to maintain figures and facts which related the income to outgo, deferred obligations, world conditions, present and future being carefully considered. Theoretically a contract is not entered into unless they can see their way clear to meet the obligations created. I have observed them hold in abeyance the purchase of badly needed equipment over a period of many months until the way was clear.[28]

The Russian Government is extremely sensitive on this subject and has long been fully aware that default in any direction would quickly lead to breakdown of its credit structure throughout the world. To the writer's knowledge, on several occasions the Soviet Government has leaned backward in meeting obligations in relation to which there was ground for contest,—doing this in order to avoid any question of willingness or desire to fairly do its part."[29]

Stuart's second document was a plan to set up a commission to handle the trade relations between the two countries secured by the trade agreement. Stuart suggested the appointment of a special Trade Commissioner for Russian Trade, with a staff of sales engineers, and an assistant in Moscow whose particular function it would be to "in every way encourage pleasant trading relations, the development of business and assist in the carrying of business to a satisfactory conclusion."[30] The commission should not be "a buying and selling organization in the sense of Amtorg or Arcos. Such a set-up would be costly, cumbersome and a bad precedent."[31] Stuart wanted to effectively promote this idea, which if implemented would provide American firms with a little more leverage in dealing with Russia, and in doing so he chose to illustrate his case by emphasizing the purchasing power of that country.

Purchasing as well as selling is in the hands of a central organization. Russia, with such a trade set-up is able to throw a tremendous purchasing and likewise selling power in such direction as may seem politically and commercially expedient. It is possible for the central trade organization not only to develop competition as between countries, but through its vast controlled purchasing and selling power, to make its own terms with seller or buyer in any given country. We all know that a mining group in the United States producing five million tons of coal is naturally able to influence to an extent the price situation in relation to its purchases, but the purchasing power of such a mining group becomes insignificant

100

when compared with the purchasing power represented by the entire mining group of Russia.[32]

The American-Russian Chamber of Commerce was a lobbying group for American business, and they understood that American companies were not going to make sales to Russia that they first did not consider salutary to themselves. The Chamber was concerned with finding a means to provide the individual firm in America with market knowledge and advice that could result in better terms of sale for their goods while not offending the buyer, the Soviet Union. In Stuart's plan the Trade Commission's "primary objectives" would be to make trade information readily available to American firms. The Trade Commission would see that information and instructions regarding the terms of the American-Russian trade treaty were published and distributed, that a copy of all contracts between Amtorg and American firms be filed with the Commission, that in the event of dispute the Commission would use its good offices and that statistics of exports and imports were developed to ensure that the relation between them is kept in balance.[33]

The above objectives were suitable, Stuart felt, if the United States in its aid to American businesses seeking commerce with Russia simply met "the conditions established by other countries through guarantee of sales." Most European governments were guaranteeing 75% of the sales made by their businesses to the Soviet Union. However, in the event that the United States government chose to finance sales to Russia, Stuart suggested that certain broad classifications of transactions should have specified periods of financing.[34]

The idea of one central authority to handle trade with Russia had been floating around FDR's administration almost from the time of inauguration. FDR himself had said to Morganthau in early May, "'If you get the opportunity, Henry, you could say that you believe but have no authority to say so, that the President would like to send some person to Moscow as Trade Commissioner."[35] In June George Peek spoke of a "plan to put American-Russian trade relations under the direction of a new and noninvolved person—a hardheaded businessman with experience in the field of international trade, who has no sentimental or promotional tie-up with the Soviet Union."[36] The Attorney General in the same month sent the Secretary of Commerce a memorandum on a proposed Foreign Trade Development Corporation intended for the development of trade with Russia.[37]

As a result Stuart's idea were not falling on uncultivated ground. In fact, Stuart oversold his case, and his ideas had more impact than he imagined. When Kelley read Stuart's documents two things stood out: the huge purchasing power available to the Soviets and their use of that power for political purposes. On that same day, Monday, October 16, Kelley wrote his "Principles to be Observed in Developing Trade with Russia," the first sentence of which declared: "All business concerns engaged in trade with Russia, whether export or import, should be associated in a central organization in order that American business interests may be safeguarded in dealings with the Soviet foreign trade monopoly." Kelley felt that "without such an organization individual firms are at a tremendous disadvantage in dealing with a State trade monopoly which is able, by playing off one firm against another, to force down prices and impose onerous conditions of sale."[38] Kelley stated that although such an organization might be formed under the U.S. Chamber of Commerce or the American Manufacturers Export Association, a finance corporation or a bank would be more suitable because "such an institution would have as its object not only to enable American manufacturers to accept orders from Russia and to provide them with the necessary financial facilities for this purpose, but also to enable Russia to sell non-competitive export products in the United

States and thereby create a basis for the payment of credits to Russia." It must be remembered that while Kelley was writing this, he was struggling most to prevent a loan to Russia.

Having established that a bank should be created to finance and control both exports and imports, Kelley then argued that this bank should control ALL government trade financing. "Assuming that the central organization is a bank, Governmental loans should be made to the bank and not to individual exporters." Kelley also had strong ideas about where control should reside. Although the bank "should be a private institution, provision should be made for Governmental participation in the direction and control of its activities."

Kelley also had well thought out the functions the bank was to perform. Unlike Stuart's proposal, where market information was the primary purpose and where the length of financing was the extent of the specific controls proposed, Kelley wanted his organization to control all aspects of Russian sales. "Credit should be extended to Soviet purchasing agencies by American firms only on the basis of a definite agreement concluded for an appreciable period of time between the central organization and the Soviet trade delegation, in which would be stipulated the terms of credit for various categories of goods, the rate of interest, place of legal settlement of disputes, etc. Such an agreement should also provide for the use of American shipping in transporting goods sold on credit." The bank as Kelley envisioned it would also have a mechanism to make sure these provisions were complied with. "Firms accepting conditions less favorable than those stipulated in the agreement would be denied credit facilities."

Kelley felt this kind of control was necessary because trade with Russia was not simply a commercial transaction but a political danger. "The Soviet foreign trade monopoly is an organ of a foreign government, and it is essential that the Government of the United States should exercise a close and direct

103

supervision over the course of development of the relations between business interests within its boundaries and a foreign government and be in a position to take at any time such action as the national interests may require." Kelley clearly delineated the source of his concern. "To allow a foreign government to deal directly, without supervision and control, over a long period of time with an association of business men who would be more or less dependent on that government for a good part of their business, would mean to afford that government a potential power of interference in our domestic affairs, which would be dangerous even if the goverment in question were most altruistically and sympathetically disposed towards the United States. In this connection it is to be noted that the very fact of a State monopoly of foreign trade renders inevitable the intervention of political considerations in a domain which, under other conditions would be governed by purely economic factors."[39] Stuart's proposal seems to have created a new fear in Kelley because for the first time he appears concerned with the domestic political leverage that could develop through the American businesses who rely on Russia for large purchases. This is a more sophisticated concern than the more histrionic monopoly buyer issue that had been appearing in most of Kelley's recent memos and letters. In the precautions that he was recommending for the trade financing bank, Kelley was exhibiting some real apprehension as to Russia's capabilities for trouble within the U.S. Hull, it will be recalled, came to fear trade with Russia because it could be used to "cause the maximum of proletarian discontent."[40] The fear of the manipulating of American businessmen lent itself to a feeling that businessmen required the supervision of the State Department in their dealings with Russia. As Hull said in another context, "With few American citizens and no diplomatic officials to consult in Russia, the American businessman yielded too readily to Soviet demands."[41]

Kelley's resolve to maintain strong governmental control of all trade with Russia was strengthened a couple of weeks later when in answer to his request, the American Consul in Berlin reported that the attempt of German industry to form a centralized organization to trade with Russia was a failure due to "the unwillingness of Russia to have any dealings with such an organization."[42]

VIII

Preparing for
Maxim Litvinoff

FDR'S PUBLIC ANNOUNCEMENT OF IMPENDING DISCUSSIONS WITH Russia had the effect of creating a good deal of turmoil among the State Department leadership. Under Kelley's guidance, all except Bullitt had developed great reservations about recognition. It was clear that FDR had not accepted the State Department's advice and was moving ahead towards direct discussions with Russia. It was equally clear that FDR was still not confiding in the State Department and was giving very little guidance as to how the negotiations would be handled. This was most disconcerting to Kelley, who went industriously to work establishing requirements which the Russians would have to meet before recognition. Kelley doubted that the Russians would accept his conditions, and if the U.S. steadfastly held to them, recognition would be forestalled. His fear, which he successfully transmitted to the State Department leadership, was that the U.S. would succumb to Russian persuasion.

Kelley's fears were misplaced. Although FDR was not confiding in the State Department even to the extent of specifying his requirements, he was in fact permitting the State Department to define how the issues were to be handled. Understandably, this was not at all clear to the State Department. When the negotiations were over, FDR had held out for and secured every one of Kelley's positions on matters of principle. Nevertheless, during the preparations FDR's intentions were extremely opaque, which greatly increased the anxiety of the members of the Department who were against recognition.

On Wednesday evening, October 18, at 8:00 P.M. after some final adjustments of the translation of President Kalinin's message, Bullitt and Skvirsky exchanged signed letters. Kalinin's letter stressed the global importance of U.S.–Soviet relations and said that the People's Commissar for Foreign Affairs, Maxim Litvinoff, would be traveling to Washington for discussions with the President.

FDR gave Bullitt the papers to hold "and to deliver them personally at the White House at two o'clock, Friday afternoon. The President said that he would announce the exchange of letters at his regular press conference at four o'clock, Friday afternoon, October 20, and would make it clear to the newspapermen that this was not recognition and would request them to see to it that their stories should give no basis for headlines involving the word 'recognition.'"[1]

At 1:55 on October 20 as directed, Bullitt delivered the documents he was caring for to the President. The President had just come from lunch with Secretary of the Interior Harold Ickes who was pleased with the move towards Russia. FDR later told Ickes that "the old line State Department men fussed over the proposition of how to approach Russia," which was FDR's rather benign interpretation of the State Department's desire to prevent recognition by insisting that the obstacles to friendly relations be first eliminated by negotiations through regular State Department channels.[2]

Just prior to the news conference scheduled for 4:00 P.M., Morganthau, Under Secretary of the Treasury Dean Acheson, and all of those involved with the legal justification of the government's purchase of gold, "piled over" to the White House for a conference with the President. This issue is not directly relevant to the question of recognition, but it is important because it clearly defines FDR's attitude towards the gold value of currencies, an issue which after recognition becomes enormously significant as a major point of contention between the State Department and the Russians. At l0:45 that morning FDR had to specifically order Under Secretary Acheson to purchase gold, because Acheson was opposed in principle to the reduction of the gold content of the dollar. He felt that it would be a breach of faith with the holders of government securities, and this was particularly true now because the Treasury was just completing the sale of a new issue. Acheson still objected during the afternoon meeting, expressing his doubts to all, including the President, as to the legality of the move. Acheson's resistance to FDR's desire to devalue the dollar would in fact shortly lead to his removal from office by FDR.[3] FDR's desire to devalue the dollar stemmed from his determination to raise the price of commodities to relieve the economic suffering of the farmers. There was so much public pressure on the issue that the news conference was expected to concern this, and when FDR announced the exchange with the Soviet government it was considered by the press to be a public relations coup.[4]

The White House had earlier announced that the President would make an important statement at the afternoon news conference and the crowd of reporters awaiting the President was extremely large. After sixteen years of official disregard and unofficial hostility toward the Soviet Union, FDR's announcement had great news impact. The half page headline of *The New York Times* read, "Roosevelt Acts To Recognize Russia With Invitation To Conference Here; Litvinoff Coming To Discuss Issues."[5]

The news was having the usual profound effect at the State Department. Russian "authority" Samuel Harper, a friend of many of the State Department regulars, was visiting Washington on October 20 and "dropped into the Eastern European Division in the afternoon, asking what the developments were with respect to recognition. I [Harper] put the question thus bluntly because I knew that the State Department people were not very enthusiastic about extending recognition." Harper's recollections provide a glimpse of Kelley's personality that is not available from his State Department memos. "My friends looked at me in an odd way," Harper continued, "and asked what I knew and what I was doing in Washington. I could not understand why they adopted the tone they did, and continued to tease them in a semifacetious way. Finally, losing patience, the chief of the Division, Robert Kelley, asked me if I could possibly sit quietly, with my mouth shut, for fifteen minutes. He seemed serious, as well as much excited; so I acquiesced. At the end of fifteen minutes he handed me the press release—Roosevelt's message to Kalinin—suggesting that the Soviet government send someone to Washington to talk with him, not with the State Department, about normalizing relations between the two countries. I felt sure that the division heads of the Department, even those connected with areas covered by the Soviet Union, had not known of this step by the President many hours before the public was informed."[6]

Although Bullitt had kept Hull, Phillips, and Moore informed of major developments the word had apparently not filtered down to Kelley. Many years later both Kelley and Phillips told historian Robert Browder that "during the exploratory stages before the invitation was dispatched, the Department was not cognizant of many of his [Bullitt's] activites."[7]

That evening Kelley and Packer dined with Harper at a Russian restaurant in Washington. Harper "wanted to know who had arranged the Roosevelt communication outside of, and perhaps above, the Department. They could not tell me, for it was still a secret; so I said that I would not ask them but would guess. I spoke one word—'Bullitt'—and the very effort of my friends to look frigid convinced me that my guess was right."

Harper thought that Kelley "was often too legalistic," although "there was no one in this country who had studied Soviet legislation and literature more thoroughly than had Kelley." Harper thought Kelley considered him "too idealistic, because I felt the Soviet experiment could not be understood without a little warmth of soul." "As we ate Russian dishes, I suggested that they give their Russian souls a little chance to function, and break through the rigidity of department protocol. It was a good dinner, but it did not have the effect I had hoped it would."[8]

The Department of State's response to the news was immediate. With the President acting on his own to establish contact with the Russians and with his statement to President Kalinin that he would personally discuss with his representative all problems outstanding between the two countries, the prospect for the longevity of the anti-recognition policy was gloomy. Assistant Secretary of State Caffery reacted by telling reporter Joe Baird during the afternoon before the President's release of the story at his news conference "that state department had learned of exchanges of messages between Cuban revolutionists and Moscow communists."

The Cuban revolution had continued to drag on through September and October, and in the unsettled situation there had been more activities by communists for Welles to report. In his telegrams to Washington Welles included some examples of communist and radical literature along with the usual reports of marches and demonstrations.[9] In mid-October following a report by Cole in Riga regarding the claims of the Communist International about the Cuban revolution, Kelley repeated these claims in his Daily Report For Eastern Europe.[10]

> The Legation at Riga reports the most recent issue of the COMMUNIST INTERNATIONAL, the official organ of the Communist International, attributes the principal credit for the overthrow of Machado to the Communist party of Cuba, which had prepared this movement and on the whole led it.
>
> The publication also states, quoting from the program of the Communist International, that in the new situation the task of the Party is to organize the laboring masses for decisive struggle for a revolutionary worker's and peasant's government.[11]

Now, four days later, faced with a strong initiative by FDR that portended recognition, Caffery leaked what he considered to be damaging information regarding Russia's role in fomenting the Cuban revolution to reporter Baird.

> American officials have received evidence which they construe as meaning that the Komintern, or International Communist Organization, in Moscow is directing communist leaders engaged in fomenting labor disorders in Cuba.
>
> Certain officials are further convinced that recent radical labor agitation in the Cuban interior has been directed by communist agents sent to the island from the communist school of propaganda in New York.
>
> The belief that the Komintern has its hand in the Cuban situation is based on certain cablegrams passing between

Havana and Moscow which have come to the attention of American officials.

Caffery told Baird that "he was willing for us to use it but not to attribute it to the department." The United Press "decided wisely to lay off since we could attribute it to no one. . . . Coming just ahead of a development in Russian thing, it looked suspiciously as if a plot being hatched to spike Russians, because one strong point of Bullitt and others is that communists must lay off propaganda in United States."[12]

Although not kept fully informed, Kelley had known the direction in which events were moving and had been preparing long formal analyses of the areas he considered to be problems between the United States and Russia. When confronted by the news on the 20th, Kelley immediately released most of that avalanche of paperwork.[13]

> No. 1 Russian Governmental Indebtedness to the Government of the United States, 28 pages.
>
> No. 2 Russian Governmental Indebtedness to American Citizens Dollar Loans Floated in the United States, 35 pages.
>
> No. 3 Private American Claims Against Soviet Russia, 45 pages.
>
> No. 4 Question of "Communist Propaganda," 183 pages.
>
> No. 5 Treaty Rights Essential to the Welfare and Protection of American Nationals in Russia, 17 pages.

On Saturday morning, October 21, Secretary of State Hull gave an interesting press conference. He began by announcing he had nothing to announce and then added that he did know when the Russian discussions would begin because that would be a matter of Litvinoff's initiative. Hull was either publicly sulking or it was his intention to convey to the reporters that he disagreed with FDR's policy on Russia. "A correspondent here said that it would be very interesting if the Secretary could tell him, even for background purposes, just how these negotiations are to be carried out. Mr. Hull in reply said that he would have to refer the correspondents to the White House on that question." The White House was publicly supporting Hull, and the correspondent said that he had already spoken to Mr. Early of the White House and had been told that "the President's cable was sent through the medium of the Department of State." Hull replied "that all Departments of the Government use our wires for transmitting messages." Another reporter asked if the cable had been sent "through the medium of the unofficial Russian observer in Washington. Mr. Hull again said that he would have to refer the correspondents to the White House on that subject. Asked if he expected to sit in on the conversations with M. Litvinoff, Mr. Hull said that he would not undertake to make any predictions at this time." The only news Hull did not refer to the White House was that Moore "had been assigned the task of completing all of the preparatory legal and similar work that would be needed in the conversations and negotiations with Mr. Litvinoff. Mr. Moore will be assisted by several other officials in the Department, including Mr. Bullitt."[14] The press was not deaf to Hull's signals.

On his way to work Monday morning, October 23, Hull ran into the Chief of the Division of Western European Affairs, Jay P. Moffat, in the elevator, and asked him "to come into his office for a few moments. He thereupon pulled from his inside pocket a clipping from the Hearst press yesterday indicating that once more he was being relegated to a secondary position in the Government and citing as instances thereof the fact that the President was going to negotiate Russia himself, that the debt negotiations had been transferred to the Treasury and that his policy on disarmament had been over-ruled at the White House." Hull told Moffat that as far as Russia was concerned "he had known every incident that had taken place, that Judge Moore had done most of the research work with Bullitt to assist him, although the latter had made every effort to get his name in the paper daily. . . . He could not understand the injustice of these attacks and wondered if there were a part of the deliberate policy of the paper or of the venom of the individual correspondents." Later Caffery told Moffat that Secretary Hull "had remained perturbed all morning. . . . Apparently the Secretary honeycombs the papers and is far more sensitive to personal press attacks than I [Moffat] had anticipated."[15]

Hull was also preparing for the Pan American Conference at Montevideo, Uruguay, and in his words, "the next few weeks were busy ones in the State Department."[16] Faced with the necessity of negotiations with the Russians, Moore spent the next week determining which items were relevant and significant. Because he was "prepared to make an effort to overlook nothing of consequence" he became quite concerned with the problems of other countries and the problems of other departments in dealing with the Russians.[17] He also investigated and discarded deportation, extradition, immigration, islands in the Artic, and Armenia as topics of negotiations.[18] He looked into the legal problems of civil suits in Russia involving Americans, of whether recognition was revocable, and of whether recognition was retroactive.[19] The only area he ignored was "anything specifically relative to credits that may be extended to the Soviet and the exportations we may make to Russia, since that subject seems to be aside from the scope of the task assigned to us.[20] FDR did not regard loans and trade as the types of items worthy of this kind of negotiation, being in his view mundane

115

considerations to be ground out by technicians afterwards. The strength of FDR's feelings on this point is indicated by the fact that this was his only attitude on the approaching negotiations that was transmitted to Moore who was operating "without having the benefit of any definite instructions or expressions from the President."[21]

In Moore's preparation for the negotiations two interests, reflecting his recently forsaken prior occupation, dominated his approach to the issues: a solicitousness for the prerogatives of Congress and a sensitivity to political repercussions. Throughout the preparations Moore filled his working papers with caveats as to what the President could agree to. "In drafting the document we have kept constantly in mind the fact that the treaty making power and the legislative authority of our Government can not be infringed and thus have made several of the stipulations to be exacted of the Soviet Government unilateral instead of bilateral."[22] Moore felt this applied to most of the major problem areas and, as an example, he applied this reasoning to propaganda in the following way. "The Russian Representative will probably ask for a bilateral stipulation relative to subversive propaganda . . . the answer is that a bilateral stipulation might well be regarded as invading the authority of the Senate."[23] "It seems to me that inasmuch as the authority of the President is limited . . . we should go no further than seek to commit the Soviet in the strongest possible terms against any interference in the continental United States or any of its possessions or in any country, as for example Cuba, where it has responsibilities."[24]

Moore's concern with the political impact of the negotiating issues appears in many of his working papers, but the best indication of Moore's well-developed sensibilities along these lines was his belief that a part of his job was to read a broad cross section of the press daily. Newspapers throughout the country "are perhaps as largely accumulated and read in my [Moore's] office as anywhere with additions having been made to the volume at least once and sometimes more than once every day."[25] Moore's boss probably considered this an important function.

During the same first week after FDR's announcement, Kelley concentrated his efforts on the major issues. Of the three types of American claims covered in the first three of his works released on the 20th, the first, dealing with the money actually lent by the government of the United States to the government of Russia and consisting of $193,000,000 in principal and $135,000,000 in unpaid accrued interest, was the strongest.* The others, being claims of individual American investors, had significantly less validity as impediments to recognition. These other claims were handled by Moore who felt that the minimum American position should be a Claims Commission with binding provisions.[26] Kelley warned that if they were referred to a Claims Commission "they will never be settled" but was content to let Moore handle the issue, devoting his own efforts to "Recommendations and Considerations in Connection with Question of Russian Governmental Indebtedness to the Government of the United States."[27] His Opus 1 was a statement of the facts regarding the money owed the American government, and this memo was his advice as to how to act upon those facts. Released on Wednesday, the 25th, while still under the shock of FDR's move, this memo was a potpourri of arguments for maintaining the debts as obstacles to recognition.

In the first paragraph of the memo, Kelley allows that about $5,000,000 of the debt was turned over to representatives of the Kolchak government which was never recognized by the United States and consequently should properly be eliminated from the total. The implication is that the remaining debt, after

*This interest was updated on November 2 by the Treasury Department to $145,000,000.

117

such a fair examination, must be truly owed. In fact there were many questions regarding this debt, particularly the fact that the representatives of the old government continued to control and dispense the Russian government's assets in America after the Soviet regime came into power. Josephus Daniels wrote FDR on October 21, "You remember Mr. Bakhmetieff, the representative of the Kerensky Government, was in Washington—remaining long after the Kerensky Government had fallen. There was a feeling, you will recall, that part of our money advanced to the Kerensky Government never reached Russia."[28] This difficulty was omitted from Kelley's memo, but the State Department was well aware of the problem and Moore took the position that "it is highly probable that Mr. Litvinoff will make some claim arising from the fact that Russian property and credits were used in this country by the representatives of the Provisional Government after the Soviet came into power. . . . Should it be brought forward by him, it seems to me the obvious reply would be that the President can make no contract relative to any such claim."[29] Moore also felt that the $5,000,000 specifically excluded by Kelley because of its use by the Kolchak government could not be excluded because "it does not seem that any waiver can be made except by Congress."[30]

Kelley's second paragraph and the heart of the memo declared that "the Soviet government should be required to acknowledge liability on the debt" and in order to support the justice of this view Kelley called upon the most fundamental principles of international law and financial practicality as authority. This appeal to international law was deeply rooted in the American State Department of the period, the culminating expression of which was the Kellogg-Briand pact outlawing war. The approach bore little relation to the actualities of international affairs, but was no less deeply felt because of it, and it was a strong element in Kelley's obstacles to recognition. Kelley argued that

118

"no principle is more firmly established in international law than the principle that a change in the internal constitution of a State does not affect the public debt of the State, and that a new Government succeeds to the financial obligations contracted by previous Governments." Disguised as an appeal to law, Kelley, in demanding Soviet acknowledgement of the debt, was pursuing a political end, just as were FDR and the Russians in seeking recognition. But Kelley's political goal was the prevention of recognition by making the unpaid debts as important to FDR as they had been to his predecessors.

As for the legal principle involved, there could not have been a more inappropriate time to make a case "that a new Government succeeds to the financial obligations contracted by previous Governments," since most of the governments of Europe had just defaulted on loans made by their own governments. Furthermore it was a little late to be establishing legal precedents specifically regarding Russia since the Soviet government had already failed to pay the debts of its precedessors to every other creditor government with which it had established diplomatic relations; and these debts dwarfed American claims. There was no principle left to uphold, and Kelley acknowledges as much in his last paragraph. Here Kelley suggests that since the U.S. had loaned money only to the Provisional (Kerensky) government, while the other creditor nations had loaned money to the Tsar's government, the Russians could "honor the indebtedness of the Russian Provisional Government witout modifying any position it may have taken towards the indebtedness contracted by the Russian Imperial Government." Kelley is suggesting that the Russians not be forced to uphold the most firmly established principle in international law but rather operate under the principle that a government could choose which of the preceding debts they wished to pay. Kelley was willing to sacrifice this great principle in order to maintain the issue of the debt owed the U.S. as an impediment to recognition.

119

Kelley's third paragraph argued that since the U.S. advanced the Russian government funds "to aid in the prosecution of the war against Germany" the Russian debt should be treated on the same basis as other war debts. Here Kelley has suddenly remembered the defaults on the war debts, and he has also remembered how strongly the country and Congress felt about them. By classifying the Russian debts as war debts, the animosity of the Congress against any compromise could be counted upon, and there was in fact pending in Congress a very strong bill denying any aid to any country that had defaulted. This issue alone could go far in preventing the loans and credits that Kelley most despised.[31]

On Thursday, October 26, the day after releasing this polemic against financial assistance to Russia, Kelley released his sixth opus on the value of "Russian Government Property in the United States," but Kelley's major efforts were being devoted to the propaganda issue.[32] Hull, who thought Kelley "a thoroughly capable and useful official," described Kelley's endeavors thus: "Kelley and his assistants made a close study of every treaty Soviet Russia had signed with other governments. They particularly concentrated on the treaty of 1925 between Russia and Germany, which was the most favorable of all the treaties Russia signed. We paid special attention to the agreement whereby Russia would promise to refrain from internal interference in the United States." Hull was much impressed that the "Eastern European Division prepared this draft by taking a phrase here and a sentence there from twenty-six similar treaties Russia had signed with other countries, ranging from Germany to Afghanistan. When it was finished, there was not a single word in the draft that had not already appeared in some treaty to which Russia had affixed her signature and seal."[33]

By Friday, October 27, Kelley had made enough progress on his draft anti-propaganda treaty to submit it for consideration along with an explanation for its necessity. Entitled "Considerations and Recommendations with Respect to the Question of 'Communist Propaganda,'" this 5-page memo was to a large degree a condensation of his 183-page Opus 4 and was divided into 6 paragraphs. It is worth quoting the main points of each of these paragraphs because this is as comprehensive but relatively succinct expression of Kelley's understanding of the Soviet government as can be found.

1. The Soviet government and the Communist International are both controlled and directed by the leaders of the "All-Union Communist Party (of Bolsheviks)," who are the real rulers of Russia.

2. The leaders of the Communist Party in Russia have as their ultimate aim the establishment of a communist society throughout the world which they believe can be accomplished only through the overthrow by force of the existing political and social order throughout the world.

3. In the period immediately following their advent to power in Russia, the Communist leaders carried on their international revolutionary activities directly through the Soviet government. Subsequently, when the Soviet government began to enter into relations with other Governments, most of the activities of this nature was transferred to the Communist International. . . .

4. The Governments of various countries have attempted without success to obtain from the Soviet government an undertaking which would result in the cessation of the activities directed against them by the rulers of Russia. The Soviet government has readily agreed that it would not, through its representatives . . . interfere. . . . Responsible spokesmen of the Soviet government have repeatedly declared, however, that the Soviet government can not and will not undertake

121

to restrain the Communist International, which it claims is an international labor organization quite distinct from itself, from engaging in international revolutionary activities.

5. The essential difficulty, therefore, connected with obtaining from the Soviet government an undertaking which will bring about a cessation of the activities directed by Moscow against other Governments lies in the facts that these activities are carried on through the instrumentality, for the most part, of the Communist International and associated organizations.

6. The rulers of Russia, for the most part through the Communist International and associated organizations, are carrying on activities against the interests and Government of the United States in this country and in other countries, particularly in Latin America. This Government desires to bring about a cessation of these activities and to that end should obtain from the Soviet government an undertaking that it will cause these activities to be discontinued. . . . It is believed that an agreement, employing the phraseology of the attached draft, not only would obligate the Soviet government itself to refrain from carrying on and directing activities in the United States and other countries against the Government of the United States, but would also place an unequivocal obligation upon the Soviet government to restrain the Communist International and other organizations in Russia which have as an aim the overthrow by force of the Government of the United States from interfering in the internal affairs of this country.[34]

The key to understanding much that followed after recognition is Kelley's wording of the treaty, which was believed to bind the Communist International unequivocally from attempting to interfere in American domestic affairs. In taking credit for this,

122

Hull illustrates the extent to which all considered the treaty to be "ironclad." "I insisted, however, that the agreement be much broader than the usual agreements the Soviet Government signed, which bound only the Government itself not to conduct propaganda and left all individuals in Russia free to do so, including the Communist International."[35] The prohibitions were so broad that Kelley frankly had doubts whether the Soviets would ever sign this type of treaty. Always much impressed by words, Kelley wrote "the Soviet government can not give an undertaking which will bring about a cessation of these activities unless the Communist leaders are prepared to abandon such activities. Hitherto the leaders of the Communist Party have not been willing to discontinue their world revolutionary activities, and such undertakings as the Soviet government has assumed have, if not formally, at least in application, been restricted to the activities of the Soviet government." Kelley explained that "the experiences of other countries in their endeavors to obtain a cessation of Moscow's interference in their internal affairs justify doubts as to whether such an obligation would be accepted." And if the Soviet leaders refused to sign, Kelley spelled out the conclusion that should be drawn. "If the Soviet government is not willing to give an undertaking of this nature, the conclusion would seem to be warranted that the Communist leaders in Russia are unwilling to abandon their revolutionary aims with respect to the United States."[36]

Kelley considered all this to have a real bearing on contemporary America. In Opus 4 he pointed out the relevance of communist propaganda to the Roosevelt administration, stating that "the manner in which the American Communist Party has carried on a determined struggle to cause the failure of President Roosevelt's recovery program is a sufficient demonstration of the fact, if demonstration is needed, that the efforts of the American communists to achieve their eventual and immediate purposes have not ceased."[37]

123

Also during the first week after FDR's announcement Bullitt, Phillips, and Hull were involved in another little drama. Russia was Bullitt's opportunity, and he was doing everything that he could to take advantage of it. Hull was scheduled to be in South America while Litvinoff was in the United States, which would effectively leave Moore and Bullitt in charge of the negotiations for the State Department. Moore was a friend and not a competitor for Bullitt's already well-established ties to the President. Bullitt could expect to play a major role in the negotiations with a real chance to be the first ambassador to the Soviet Union. However, during the week Phillips was urging Hull "to find ways to get the [Pan American] Conference postponed."[38] Hull wanted to attend at the head of the American delegation and at first rejected Phillips' arguments but by the following Monday, October 30, "he was most anxious to get out of it."[39] Phillips urged postponement based upon the "dreadfully involved situations in Cuba, Leticia, and Chaco, and for many other reasons" but Bullitt, interpreting this as a move against himself, complained to Morganthau on Friday, October 27 that "Phillips was trying to maneuver things so that he, Phillips, would be in charge when Litvinoff came over."[40] There was certainly a sound basis for Bullitt's wariness of Phillips. Phillips had been repulsed by Bullitt's behavior after Bullitt's previous attempt to negotiate with the Russians in 1919 and had been violently opposed to Bullitt's return to the State Department. Furthermore, Phillips felt strongly that the Russians should have approached the U.S. rather than the U.S. making the first move. Bullitt was the man who approached the Soviets first, and regardless of how totally Bullitt accepted Kelley's information and statistics, he remained the pro-recognition man in a Department full of anti's.

As a result of Phillips' urgings, Hull went to the White House twice on Monday to persuade the President to postpone the conference, but FDR remained unconvinced and would not consent.[41] Unable to delay the conference, Hull postponed his own departure by a week in order to pursue to completion "a collection of important problems at the State Department."[42]

After a week of preparation the State Department was ready on Monday for a comprehensive meeting of those involved with the preparations for the upcoming negotiations. Bullitt, Kelley, and Legal Advisor of the Department of State, Green Hackworth, met at 9:30 in Moore's office. Moore had put together on the previous Saturday a memorandum to be used as the basis of the meeting. Kelley's position on the debts of the Kerensky government and on propaganda are by this meeting already incorporated as the State Department's positions.

During the meeting the validity of some of the expected Soviet positions were considered and Bullitt exhibited his usual sincere inflexibility. When the subject of Soviet counter-claims was brought up Bullitt totally rejected any thought of acknowledging their validity. The counter-claims referred to the damages that the Russians insisted had been inflicted upon their country by the American military expedition a decade and a half earlier. The Russians had asserted that these were legitimate obligations for which they were due compensation. Bullitt had definite views on this matter, and the conversation went like this.

> Mr. Kelley: Claims of this sort fall into two categories, as we might say, political and private. In France we had to pay private claims against American troops.
>
> Mr. Bullitt: I think we ought to get all counter-claims wiped out.
>
> Mr. Kelley: I feel that if there is any chance of an agreement here, the Russians will be willing to drop them.
>
> Mr. Hackworth: I don't think they have any, anyhow.
>
> Mr. Bullitt: There should be a specific waiver of counter-claims, public and private.[43]

125

As a counter-argument to the American loans to the Kerensky government the Russians could be expected to bring up the large funds held in American banks after the revolution that were disposed of by the deposed Kerensky government's representative. Because of this the State Department was concerned about the possibility of recognition being automatically retroactive back to the beginning of the Soviet regime. Those funds, long since gone, would become legally the property of the Soviet government after recognition. If the issue of the disposition of those Russian funds could be successfully separated from the issue of the debts incurred by the Kerensky government, it would remove a major argument against the validity of those debts. The State Department's approach was to treat the handling of these funds as a separate issue: have the Soviet government accept the validity of the American loans as well as having the Soviet government accept whatever disposition had been made of the Soviet assets in America from the revolution until the present.

> Mr. Kelley: It seems essential to me that the Russians should be obligated to accept disposition which has been made of Russian Government property.
>
> Mr. Bullitt: I think one has to consider, in the present state of international law, it is very much better to get anything that may conceivably come up covered by specific provisions before recognition, in which case we know we will not have any trouble; otherwise, lawsuits will be going on for twenty years.[44]

During the meeting Moore wanted to omit the commercial factors entirely but Bullitt insisted on bringing them up.

> [Moore:] I do not think it is up to us to incorporate anything in the proposed document about possible credit being extended by our Government to the Soviet, or possible exportations to Russia.

126

Mr. Bullitt: I think that matter is going to come up quickly and almost inevitably when we begin discussing Russian debts to the United States and provisions for paying, and I think that ought to be decided before recognition is extended. The Russians are going to say, "We can't promise we are going to pay this right off." The moment they come to discussing actual methods of paying Russian debts to the Government of the United States, they are going to say, "We won't make payment directly, but by loans or guarantee to the United States Government. We will put on an extra four percent to the interest rate and that extra four percent will be used to pay the debt of the Russian Government to the United States." That is probably going to be brought up as a method of payment by the Russians.

[Moore:] I don't believe that at this moment we can incorporate anything on that subject in the document we are to prepare.

Mr. Bullitt: No, but I think we ought to have it "by the ears" to be brought into the discussion. I have attempted to get Mr. Morganthau to formulate his ideas, but he hasn't got down to any actual formulation.[45]

Bullitt had much interest in this area and as his basic approach he had swallowed whole Kelley's recommendations regarding the handling of trade financing. Bullitt had ideas for "control of private loans to Russia and commercial activities" and had grabbed hold of a complicated scheme to make "credit advances to Russia through American blocked marks in Germany."[46] The idea was that Americans would give Russia the short-term credits owed them by Germany, and in exchange receive from Russia long-term notes. Russia would use these short-term debts to offset the short-term Russian debt to Germany then falling due. Because of German monetary and political behavior the chances of Americans directly collecting

127

on their short-term notes from Germany were problematic, so
the scheme had the advantage of extending long-term credits
to Russia with money that was already at risk. And because
these German obligations were held by American citizens, the
U.S. government could extend credits to Russia without having
to loan any of its own funds.

Actually Bullitt did not have this issue "by the ears"; it was
more the case that he had it by the tail and with one hand only.
Bullitt was using outdated information regarding Russia's debts
to Germany and the actual situation was already grossly different from what he thought it to be.[47] Bullitt was also un-
informed about Germany's debts to America. In developing
information regarding these German debts Bullitt had talked
with banker James Warburg, whom he had worked with during
the preparations for the London Economic Conference in the
Spring. In response to a request by Bullitt, Warburg had gone
to the trouble of wiring New York to secure some specific
figures.[48] Warburg's energies during this period, however, were
narrowly focused upon the singular issue of inflation and his
interest in Bullitt's scheme was casual and transitory. As a result
Bullitt was not well informed about either the German debts
owed to the U.S. or the Russian debts owed to Germany.
Furthermore, Bullitt was largely ignorant of the feasibility of
the plan from the standpoint of American investors. The plan
involved financial obligations that were widely dispersed among
American citizens and institutions and every one of these in-
vestment units had different financial needs, and Bullitt had no
way of telling how many would find his plan suitable. From a
practical standpoint, it was not likely that holders of short term
debt instruments would be interested, in sufficient numbers to
make the plan workable, in exchanging these for 20-year obligations.

Both the State Department and Morganthau thought
Morganthau must be in charge of trade with Russia, and

Bullitt, because of his interest in the subject lobbied Morgan-thau for the adoption of Kelley's plan, but as Bullitt reported at the meeting, Morganthau was not responsive. In fact Morgan-thau had told FDR that "Bullitt was crowding me to organize American business into a semi-government corporation that could deal exclusively with Russia. I [Morganthau] told him [FDR] that my instinct told me that this was not the right thing to do." FDR's response to Morganthau indicates the disdain that he now felt for the issue; he told Morganthau that "you are absolutely right. I want to keep these Russian negotiations on a high plane, and it will be time enough to talk about busi-ness after we have come to every other decision."[49] FDR was not approving Morganthau's specific approach over Bullitt's. As far as FDR was concerned it was not the appropriate time even to be handling the issue. Morganthau, however, was try-ing to make himself useful to FDR by becoming involved, and on October 24 at a meeting of the Executive Council he requested the members to furnish him "a list of all articles, items, or commodities that said member's department may desire sold to or purchased from Russia."[50] He continued to meet with representatives of the American-Russian Chamber of Commerce and by November 1, he announced to FDR that he "had some swell figures on Russia."[51] What these were is not known but Morganthau, aided by State Department reports of Russia's unfair trade practices, was working towards the con-cept of a barter corporation as the proper way to handle trade between the two countries. Actually Morganthau was just dab-bling. His commission had been a newspaper report revoked by FDR two days after it was extended, and he was receiving no positive direction from FDR, who was simply not interested in the issue. Besides his own job as head of the FCA during this period, Morganthau was heavily involved in purchasing, under FDR's direction, commodities and gold.[52] It is this later topic which dominated his interest and would in fact soon result in

129

his appointment as Under Secretary and then Secretary of the Treasury.

After the State Department's meeting on Monday, Moore asked Kelley and Hackworth to prepare a working document by Wednesday evening, so that on Thursday morning a meeting could be held with the Secretary and Under Secretary.[53] Meanwhile on Wednesday, November 1, Kelley issued his seventh opus. Reflecting his desire to control America's trade with Russia, this was a 229-page report entitled, "Estimate of Maximum Value of Possible Annual Imports Into the United States of Merchandise of Russian Origin."[54] If one were concerned with how Russia would repay an American loan, as Hull was, this sort of information makes a good argument for where the upper loan limit should be established. Two days later, on Friday, November 3, Kelley issued his eighth opus and the last in the series. This was a 227-page report entitled, "Statements by Litvinov on Matters of Foreign Policy That Are of Interest To the United States." The contribution of this report to the forthcoming negotiations can be judged by the heading of the first major section:

> I. Statements showing the fundamental Revolutionary Aim Underlying Soviet Foreign Policy and the Hostility, Inherent in Communist Doctrine, of the Soviet Government Towards the Non-Communist Governments.[55]

In the subsection entitled, "Statements of the Soviet Policy Towards Trade Relations Between the Soviet Government and Non-Communist Countries," Kelley goes into some detail as to how he thought of trade between Russia and other countries. "As has been pointed out, the policy of developing and maintaining economic relations with non-communist countries is an important phase of the Bolshevik regime's general policy of recognizing the necessity for the continuation of a period of 'peaceful co-existence' of the communist and non-communist political and economic systems 'right up to the day when history does its work,' i.e., until the coming of the world proletarian revolution." Kelley took the theoretical pronouncements of the communists at their word. "The Bolshevik leaders have been careful to point out, however," Kelley explained, "that the adoption of this policy was only a tactical maneuver executed in order to assist their regime to survive until the proletarian revolution should extend to other countries. Capitalism, being induced by the hope of profits to deal with Russia and increase Russia's productive power, would become its own 'gravedigger.'"[56]

On the following Monday, the day before Litvinoffs arrival, Hull, Phillips, Bullitt, and Morganthau met FDR at the White House for a "dress rehearsal" to coordinate how they would approach the negotiations with Litvinoff. Hull reported that "we went over the subjects to be discussed with Litvinoff, and agreed that the two most important were precautions against Soviet propaganda and illegal activities in the United States, and freedom of worship for Americans in Russia."[57]

This was FDR's decision and he chose these two areas because the remaining public opposition to recognition focused around them, and not because he thought either one had much bearing upon American life. A superb politician, FDR understood America better than his advisors and knew these issues were important in generating public acceptance of recognition and not in strengthening religion in America or in immunizing American politics against communist propaganda. He knew these institutions were sufficiently strong from their own internal momentum to make both these agreements totally irrelevant to American life. As much as he believed in God and liked the idea of an agreement that helped Americans practice their religious beliefs while in Russia, he derided the idea that it would have any significance for religion in America. Shortly after the announcement of the exchange of letters with Kalinin, Henry Wallace visited FDR to talk about the recogni-

THE DECISION TO RECOGNIZE

tion of Russia, because he was concerned about the religious question. "Henry Wallace," FDR told Morganthau, "is very much worried about our recognizing Russia on account of the religious effect it will have in this country." Morganthau recorded the conversation because it was the first time FDR had ever expressed a personal opinion regarding Wallace to Morganthau, and Morganthau was "surprised that he was ready to discuss him so freely." FDR found Wallace's idea so novel that it went beyond normal restraint. FDR's conversation had a tone of amused ridicule and he called Wallace "a kind of a mystic."[58] It is in his estimation of the import of these issues to American life that FDR most differed from his State Department. Although Hull, Phillips, Bullitt, and Moore shared FDR's concern for the domestic political aspects of these issues, they felt, unlike FDR, that these issues, particularly propaganda, were of real consequence to American institutions.

IX

The Recognition
Negotiations

BEFORE SAILING FOR AMERICA LITVINOFF TOLD REPORTERS THAT
so far as he was concerned he "could reach an agreement with
President Roosevelt in a half hour," and upon his arrival in
America *The New York Times* reported that "he indicated that the
question of diplomatic relations would be the only one he would
discuss with President Roosevelt now and that discussion of
other questions would be taken up later if recognition is
accorded."[1]

At 6:00 P.M. on November 7 Litvinoff was escorted by Hull
to the White House for an official reception by the President,
and the next morning the first negotiating session was held in
Hull's office. Hull, Phillips, Moore, Bullitt, and Kelley attended
for the U.S. Litvinoff came alone. Litvinoff insisted from the
beginning that his intention, previewed by his statements to the
newspapers, was to recognize first and then negotiate. "It was

133

fairly apparent from the start that the latter's idea of establishing normal relations is to obtain unconditional recognition, and then an effort to follow to remove all serious difficulties by negotiations."[2] Under Secretary Phillips thought that "the Secretary opened the conference in a very friendly manner and touched generally on the principal points to be discussed. There are four of these: (1) Religious freedom for American nationals in Russia; (2) a clear understanding of the rights of American nationals in Russia who have been placed under arrest by the Russian authorities; (3) Governmental and private debts against Russia and (4) Russian propaganda in the United States. Most of the day was spent on the first point. . . ."[3] Morganthau thought that "Hull gave the impression that the religious issue is the most important one, and that it was very much uppermost in his mind. He talked about nothing else for the whole first hour. Hull said if we just started diplomatic relations between Russia and the USA without first coming to an agreement on the religious issue, the Roosevelt Administration would be overthrown at the next election. . . . Judge Moore kept asking for a formal statement in regard to the religious issue which would not detract from the dignity of the USSR. Litvinoff kept answering that he could not give any statement, informal or otherwise, as it would be binding on his country and, therefore, he did not wish to make any statement." Litvinoff said that "'No American nationals have ever complained against religious restrictions while in Russia.' Litvinoff said very emphatically, 'We can not set up a privileged class.'"

When the topic of discussion switched to the debts owed to America by Russia, Litvinoff and the Americans reached the same impasse. "Litvinoff suggests that claims and counter-claims be handled through diplomatic channels after recognition. Hull says we have a congressional election every two years. We will have to face criticism if we do not handle the question of debts and religion simultaneously with recognition. Litvinoff said that we have not discussed debts in 16 years with the U.S.A. Now if we have recognition at least we are making some progress!" Litvinoff's alternative position regarding the debts was complete cancellation. Neither could Litvinoff and the Americans agree on the matter of propaganda. Morganthau thought that "Hull's attitude throughout was very hesitating and apologetic. Litvinoff is decisive and firm. Litvinoff disclaimed all responsibility of the Third International. He said the Third International has no governmental standing. He said, 'We are not asking for anything. We have no request to make of any of your organizations in the U.S., so why ask us about some of our organizations?' The conference broke up for lunch at the White House."[4]

At the end of the luncheon Litvinoff, who was seated to the President's right, reached inside his coat and "pulled out a couple of booklets of Russian stamps which he proceeded to show to the President. . . . They were all new issue stamps, some of which have not yet reached this country."[5] Litvinoff gave these stamps to the President, and his assistant Oumansky, who also came prepared, gave some stamps to both Interior Secretary Harold Ickes and Morganthau. This was the only successful interchange of the day.

When the talks resumed at four o'clock Morganthau now thought that "Hull was very decisive." Because the morning session did not disclose how Litvinoff "would treat requests for specific agreements. . . . It was decided to make a test on this point and accordingly at the afternoon session there was handed him the proposed agreement touching religious matters which is embodied in the document the President has seen."[6] Hull's new approach to this issue was to tell Litvinoff "that reports are coming from Russia to the effect that our nationals are being denied proper protection in the exercise of what according to our conceptions are their religious rights and inquired what quarantee for removing this serious difficulty could be furnished. In that connection Mr. Litvinov was handed the draft of the the agreement, which in our opinion should be furnished, and he was asked to say whether it met his approval. He read it and said in substance that the Russian laws are sufficient for the purpose indicated and that he had no authority to say that they would be changed. He also observed that he could not tell how a particular court might interpret the laws or how they might be administered from time to time, but that he was certain that they would be interpreted and administered fairly."[7] The Americans asked Litvinoff to consider the draft and to give them his views in writing, but Litvinoff took the document and immediately wrote beside each point what the current Soviet laws on the matter were. The Americans were upset by the changes written beside the points in question. The Americans were also upset because they wished specific guarantees beyond the letter of the current laws. The prospects after the first day seemed quite bleak. Moore wrote Hull that "Mr. Litvinov's meaning evidently is that he expects naked unconditional recognition." Moore told Hull that it was unthinkable that an unconditional recognition "would satisfy the American public or fail to produce a dangerous reaction," and he began considering precautions to be taken if the talks failed. "Should the negotiations break down a method should be sought showing that the failure resulted from the inability of our Government to obtain satisfactory agreement against subversive propaganda and to safeguard the religious independence of our nationals."[8] This emphasis again reflected FDR's stress on the political issues and his disregard for the importance of the economic ones.

The following morning the talks were begun at 11:00 in Hull's office. Unlike the previous day, when the main concern had been religion, propaganda was now the principal topic. "Most of it revolved about Soviet propaganda in the United States and the responsibility of the Soviet Government towards the Third International. The Secretary pointed out forcibly that Stalin was a director of the Third International and that, therefore, government responsibility was involved in the activities of the Third International in the United States. Litvinov denied this allegation absolutely and refused to discuss it. He was absolutely intransigent."[9] Moore's summary of Litvinoff's positions on the major points covered in the discussion showed no progress anywhere from the American point of view.

"1. *As to religion*. He in effect rejected our agreement proposal by amending it so as to conform to the present Soviet law. . . .

2. *As to propaganda*. He was very resolute in declining to make any agreement that would place the Soviet Government under the responsibility of limiting the activities of the Third International. . . .

3. *As to espionage* . . . [Litvinoff] was unwilling to enter into any agreement to protect our nationals against being penalized for violating regulations which may never have been brought to their attention.

4. *As to crimes* . . . he said that the fact that American nationals had not been severely dealt with heretofore is sufficient indication, without any change in the law that they will not be thus dealt with hereafter."[10]

Because of his "great anxiety" as to the possibility of failure Moore wrote Hull that "the impression I formed yesterday was confirmed this morning, namely that Mr. Litvinoff expects to obtain recognition without making any commital whatever. He is unwilling to go an inch further than to say that the Soviet laws as reasonably interpreted and administered afford American nationals and the institutions of our Government all the protection they can desire and that so far as concerns our financial demands and the Soviet counter claims their consideration must be postponed until diplomatic relations are established. He is thus not willing to make any of the agreements which we so carefully prepared during the ten days preceding his arrival." Moore reminded Hull that "Mr. Litvinoff, in answer to a question I asked him this morning, made a categorical

reply leaving no doubt that he desires recognition without placing the Soviet Government under any promises or pledges of
any character whatever." With the failure of the talks looking
more imminent with every session, Moore's concern for the
domestic public relations aspects was increasing. "It seems to
me of prime importance," he continued, "if recognition is not
granted and the negotiations broken off, that we should find
some proper way of having it understood that this occurred
because of the refusal to furnish assurances relative to such
questions as those pertaining to propaganda, religion, espionage, et cetera, rather than the financial questions were
pivotal."[11]

The program called for a conference between the President
and Litvinoff at 5:00, but Hull called it off because he "felt the
importance of reporting to the President the stalemate which
had been reached in the Russian negotiations."[12] So at 5:20
Hull, Phillips, Moore, Bullitt and Kelley reported to the President their lack of progress, and FDR responded by scheduling
a meeting with Litvinoff for noon the following day.

At 11:30 the next day, Friday, the negotiators gathered at
the White House to review and to await Litvinoff. As Phillips
recorded, "Litvinov came in at 12 o'clock and the President re-
viewed the whole situation with him. It was one of the most
remarkable performances I have ever seen. Somehow the President succeeded in changing the whole atmosphere. He did it
by a combination of humor, sincerity, clearness and friendliness—a combination of all four, which brought the first
response that Mr. Litvinov has given out since his arrival in
Washington." Phillips wrote that "Mr. Litvinov agreed to consider the proposition on propaganda which we had presented
to him and which he had previously refused to consider. He
agreed substantially to our proposition of religious liberty for
Americans in Russia, but, of course, we got down to no details
or phraseology. At the end of the conference the President said

138

that he would like to have a man-to-man talk with Mr. Litvinov this evening at 9 o'clock, which would be much more informal, so he told Mr. Litvinov, than any conference which included the Secretary of State and Under Secretary. He wanted, he said, to be able to call Mr. Litvinov names if he felt like it and he certainly hoped that Mr. Litvinov would feel free to call him names too. Litvinov laughed heartily."[13]

FDR had just dismissed the top level of the State Department from assisting him in his negotiations. Phillips recorded that after Litvinoff left the room "the President said he was somewhat frightened at the idea of a man-to-man conversation on so many points on which he was not fully versed and I recommended that Bullitt be present. The President readily accepted this idea."[14]

One can either interpret this as signifying that the breach between Phillips and Bullitt had ceased to be important, or that Phillips, aided by the President's delicacy, was putting the best face on a difficult situation. The fact that FDR would want to deal privately with Litvinoff is not surprising. FDR always approached any international negotiations as being a horsetrade between the two men who had the power. What is worth noting is where he turned for assistance. Before asking for Bullitt he had eliminated Hull and Phillips from the discussions on the unconventional grounds of excessive formality. Only Bullitt and Moore were left, and the title of Assistant Secretary, it could be argued, entitled Moore to FDR's unusual blackball as well. In fact, it wasn't necessary. FDR had chosen Bullitt and Phillips knew it. The State Department negotiators had gotten nowhere on their own. Bullitt had been portraying himself to FDR as being the pro-recognition man in a State Department opposed to the idea. Now that Litvinoff was responding in a manner quite contrary to that achieved and reported by Hull, Bullitt was the only choice. Phillips was about to assume control of the Department as Acting Secretary, as this was Hull's last day in Washington before his departure for Montevideo. In asking Phillips who he recommended FDR was following the proper procedure and preserving form, not asking advice.

There is one other point worth noting here, and that is what the grounds FDR used for eliminating Hull and Phillips indicates about FDR's attitude concerning the State Department. The implied stereotype is of well-tailored functionaries, and it was so much a part of the common culture that he could use it in front of the men he was dismissing as a reason for their dismissal.

FDR was quite adept at this sort of thing. Directly after this meeting FDR joined his cabinet and "paid," in Secretary of the Interior Ickes' opinion, "a lovely tribute to Secretary of State Hull. . . . The President said that Hull was the one man not only in the United States but in the whole world who could go to Montevideo with any hope of bringing back any tangible results in the way of better understanding among the countries on this hemisphere."[15] Having forced Hull's departure, FDR was putting the best face on it.

That evening Postmaster General James Farley dined with the President, and FDR related to him with relish an incident from his afternoon conversation with Litvinoff. "'I [FDR] said guarantee of religious freedom must be given Americans before anything could be done. And then, Jim, I threw one straight from the shoulder at him. You'll enjoy this. I told Litvinov that I knew he had his opinion of me, and that, in turn, I had my own ideas of him. Then I followed that up by saying I was willing to wager that five minutes before his time would come to die, and he was conscious of it, that he would be thinking of his parents and wanting to make his peace with God. Jim, he looked at me closely, but didn't say a word.' Roosevelt threw back his head and laughed."[16]

Walter Duranty of *The New York Times* wrote an article after the afternoon meeting with Litvinoff that pretty well reflected the attitude of the President about the previous negotiations at the State Department. "The earlier conversations were so cluttered up by a mass of documents that the two parties didn't get near enough to see the 'whites of each other's eyes.'"[17] At a press conference held while the State Department was holding its first session with Litvinoff two days earlier, FDR had told the reporters:

> As you all know—and this is for background—on anything of that kind, both sides arrange three or four hundred pages of material of all sorts, details and figures, and then they start to go through this large volume of things and they use the process of elimination. The first part of it is rather mechanical, it is rather a mechanical procedure, keeping in very close touch, personally at all times. Of course, there is no use sitting in when going into the details and figures.[18]

FDR had obviously seen some of Kelley's reports, but he was vastly underrating the power of those papers.

Later that Friday evening, FDR, Litvinoff, and Bullitt met from 9:00 until midnight. The negotiating position taken by FDR during the discussions with Litvinoff is spelled out in a handwritten memo that FDR gave to Bullitt sometime during the negotiations.

> *Memo for W.B.*
> As I have tried to make very clear:
> 1. My original letter said "discussion to reach a satisfactory solution of the *problems* involved" also "all questions outstanding between our countries."
> 2. That certain questions which I have at great length explained to Mr. Litvinov *must* be so clearly stated that the announcement will satisfy at least a majority of our people.
> These are:
> 1. *Assurances* against propaganda.

2. *Assurances* for freedom of worship by Americans in Russia including right to have their own clergy.

3. Assurances for public trial and notice of arrest.

4. As to debts, claims and counterclaims. These are clearly one of the "outstanding questions" in regard to which a "satisfactory solution" must be reached. A mere agreement to discuss them in the future does not fulfill this.

All this is so clear that I honestly think that Mr. Litvinov should come to an agreement, especially in view of the excellent corroborating reply from M. Kalinin.

Yours,
Franklin D. Roosevelt[19]

Once FDR made clear that the bargaining position taken by the State Department was in fact his own and that he would require no less, it changed the whole character of the negotiations; but not by itself. Litvinoff had come for recognition, but faced with these demands in the hostile atmosphere of the State Department there would have been no purpose in granting such concessions. The other side of FDR's bargaining technique was an expression of amity on his part and on that of the country he represented, which could be permanently gained if his conditions were accepted. Unlike the State Department, FDR and Bullitt brought to the conversations a real desire to accomplish recognition, and although intransigent on their requirements, they held out the picture of a sincere and beneficial relationship. Both men were capable of much personal charm, and Bullitt could point to a career of strong pro-recognition sentiment. He could also point to negotiations with Lenin which, because he chose to stand on principle, led to the smashing of his early State Department career. Influenced by FDR's approach and taking Kelley at his word, Bullitt was convinced that the signing of these agreements would result in friendly relations. In fact two years later, under much different conditions, Bullitt would be much offended when Litvinoff told him and Kelley that there was no such thing as "really friendly relations" in international affairs.[20] FDR, to a large degree following Bullitt's advice, had set Litvinoff on a difficult road, but the promised quality of the relationship once recognition was granted made the road worth taking.

The next day, Phillips, after listening to Bullitt's description of the meeting of the previous evening recorded that "it becomes clearer to me that Mr. Litvinoff has no intention of allowing the negotiations to fail. The situation in the Far East is much too tense for Russia to give the impression to Japan that there is any lack of cooperation between Russia and the United States. Every day that the conversations continue we are in a stronger position and Mr. Litvinoff in a weaker one. It seems to me that he will be obliged to accept substantially our terms of recognition."[21] There is an aura of too pat prescience about this entry not to wonder if it was penned after the fact, but regardless, it correctly indicates the course of the negotiations.

FDR had no prearranged plan for conducting the discussions and was making adjustments as he went along. At a news conference after the first meeting on Friday FDR was asked "if, after the discussion tonight, discussions will be resumed at the State Department or here?"

> THE PRESIDENT: I don't know.
> Q. Nothing definite?
> THE PRESIDENT: It is just pure guesswork on my part but I suppose the natural thing will be the State Department.[22]

After the second meeting on Friday night Litvinoff told reporters that arrangements had not yet been made for the next meeting, and Bullitt said that arrangements would be made on Saturday.[23] The arrangements that were made the next day

143

scheduled Litvinoff back into the State Department in the late afternoon for more conferences with the regulars. At this meeting Litvinoff made it clear that he did not intend to negotiate with the State Department.

Coming as arranged to Phillips' office at 4:14 in the afternoon Litvinoff was met by the Under Secretary, Moore, Bullitt, Hackworth, and Kelley. Phillips "referred to the various proposals which the President had handed him in writing during the conference last evening, in the hope that he would be prepared to discuss them. On the contrary, Mr. Litvinov refused to discuss anything this afternoon and it was quite clear that he preferred to deal only with the President. The meeting broke up after forty minutes of futile talk."[24]

Phillips marvelled at how FDR elicited Litvinoff's first positive reaction, but his standard of comparison was the State Department negotiations which consisted of a half dozen diplomats, all mistrustful of Russia and communism, who were demanding concessions from Litvinoff, many of which they doubted would be granted. Although there are no transcripts of any of the discussions, it is clear that the negotiations at the State Department were far different in tone from those at the White House. The fundamental perception of Russia shared by all in the State Department, including Bullitt, was Kelley's, and even if he remained silent, Kelley was the dominant presence.

After the Saturday meeting the newspapers were told only that Litvinoff would return for another conference on Monday. As a result of the failure of the Saturday meeting to make any progress the news releases stressed for the first time that immediate agreement should not be expected and that delay was due to American insistence upon assurances in a number of areas prior to recognition. Although agreement seemed to be further away than planned, the news releases emphasized that progress had been made and that the prognosis still remained optimistic. *The New York Times* reported on Sunday that:

While this is not believed to constitute a serious impediment to recognition, it shows not only why the negotiations have lasted longer than generally expected, but why they may extend long enough to prevent M. Litvinoff's contemplated departure from New York Wednesday. . . . Despite all this, there is every expectation in official circles that recognition of Russia will follow the current negotiations.[25]

Walter Duranty's column in the Sunday *Times* was headlined "Litvinov Facing A 'Horse Trader'" and reported that "Roosevelt Is Viewed as Being Shrewd Bargainer in Stand for Soviet Assurances."[26]

On Sunday evening Morganthau gave a social dinner for Litvinoff to which a number of guests not concerned with the negotiations were invited. Before attending, Bullitt visited with FDR at the White House and probably brought to Morganthau's dinner an invitation for Litvinoff to return afterwards to the White House for further discussions with FDR. After eating, Litvinoff and Bullitt left the gathering early to meet with the President.[27]

Following Bullitt's advice, FDR remained adamant on the concessions required. The religious issue was probably settled to FDR's satisfaction at this meeting but many differences still remained.[28] Talking to reporters late that evening after the White House conference, Bullitt further pushed back the time when agreement could be expected. Bullitt stressed to the press that progress was being made but "he added, however, that the conversations might not be concluded before President Roosevelt left for Warm Springs, Ga., on Friday. . . . Mr. Bullitt said there was still a 'great deal to be done.' He added that the conversations might be compared to the progress of two book worms, which would start at opposite ends of a shelf but in time would get together."[29]

During the next two days Bullitt alone did the negotiating with Litvinoff, and Bullitt yielded nothing.[30] After recognition, Moffat had a conversation on negotiating technique with Bullitt and recorded in his diary that "some of the incidents were so dramatic that it is wiser not to put them on paper."[31] Bullitt himself reported in a magazine article years later that during the discussions Litvinoff was handed a schedule of steamship sailings "and told to sign or go home."[32] Historian Robert Browder thought this approach so unusual in diplomatic negotiations that he had some doubts as to whether the incident was recalled correctly, but Browder thought, if it was accurately remembered, "the State Department was most certainly resorting to drastic action."[33] This may have been drastic action for the State Department, but for Bullitt it was completely typical. Monday afternoon after talking to Bullitt, Phillips recorded that "the plan is for the President to write a letter to Litvinov, setting forth the minimum of our position and ask him to take it or leave it."[34] Faced with American intransigence, the Soviet government made the decision sometime during these two days while Bullitt was conducting negotiations with Litvinoff, that they would accept the American conditions, and as a result all the problems except the debts were resolved. On Wednesday morning the negotiations shifted from Litvinoff's residence to the White House in order to thrash out a debt settlement. Bullitt arrived at the White House at 10:00 and shortly afterwards at 10:15 Litvinoff arrived. FDR, Bullitt, and Litvinoff discussed a credit settlement until 10:55 when FDR left to attend a press conference called to announce Acheson's resignation as Under Secretary of the Treasury and the appointment of Morganthau as his successor.[35]

When FDR arrived at the news conference, he apologized for being late "because I have been over at the White House talking to Litvinov." Although FDR did report "very distinct progress," when asked if he expected recognition by Friday he

146

replied, "I would not say 'recognition.' Heavens above! . . . I would hate to limit myself to Friday or Monday or any day." FDR may have been understating a bit to create more news impact.[36] While FDR was indefinitely postponing the prospects of recognition, the only remaining unresolved issue facing him was the debts.

Meanwhile Bullitt and Litvinoff "continued to argue for two hours on the subject of debts and claims."[37] All the emphasis was on reaching an agreement on the debt owed with no attempt to settle the specifics of repayment.

The reason for doing this was that it was already clear that the latter course would take quite some time. The Soviets would only pay the old debt as added interest on a new loan, and the basic American idea of exchanging blocked marks had only been superficially investigated. The Americans could tell Litvinoff nothing specific about the nature of the proposed loan, and this hindered agreement on the amount since Litvinoff was understandably reluctant to make commitments without knowing what he could expect to receive in return. In addition, FDR had no interest in the economic details required for working out the American plan. Bullitt later quoted Litvinoff as saying, "I can't understand the President; he hasn't talked about anything but religious freedom to me, and I want to discuss important things like trade relations, etc."[38] FDR felt the specifics of an American loan were mere details and no reason to hold up a grant of recognition based on agreements of so many important principles. If the Americans and Russians could arrive at a mutually acceptable figure for the debt owed, recognition could be granted, and when the Americans had better figures the technicians could work out the specifics for final payment.

The difficulty now remained in getting Litvinoff to agree to an acceptable figure, which like everything else in these negotiations was the American position. In spite of Bullitt's best efforts, the highest Litvinoff would offer was $50,000,000. Bullitt as always used the most force available and thought he "managed to shake him [Litvinoff] a bit by telling him that the Johnson Bill, forbidding loans to countries in default on their indebtedness to the Government of the United States, was certain to be passed in January and that if the Soviet Government should make any absurd offer of settlement such an offer would surely be turned down by Congress and the Soviet Government would be unable to obtain one penny of credit from either the Government or any private corporation or individual in the United States, or their agencies abroad." Finally Litvinoff asked, "'What sum would you consider might be acceptable to Congress?' and added, 'You will, of course, say $150,000,000.'" Bullitt replied, "'No, I will say nothing. I cannot predict what Congress will do, but the President can predict very exactly what Congress will do, and you should address that question to him.'"[39] It now remained for FDR to decide what figure he would be willing to accept from Litvinoff, and Bullitt told Appointment Secretary Marvin McIntyre that five minutes of FDR's time with Litvinoff "would be very helpful." McIntyre asked FDR if he should "bring them over and have them wait in the cabinet room since they were still in the White House," but FDR told McIntyre to have them return at 2:00 P.M.[40]

To prepare FDR for the meeting Bullitt wrote him a memo bringing him up to date on the morning discussion and informing him as to the type of arguments he could expect from Litvinoff. "Litvinov added that he would say to you [FDR] that he had entire confidence in your fair-mindedness, and he was sure that when you looked at the facts about our loan to the Kerensky Government and found that the money had been spent for the most part by Bakhmetieff buying supplies for Kolchak's army, you would agree that the Soviet Government should not be obliged to assume liability for money used by its enemies."

148

Bullitt told FDR that the relevant point in this matter was "that two-thirds of this Kerensky loan was telegraphed at once to Kerensky's Government and used fighting the Germans." As to bargaining strategy, Bullitt told FDR that "I think you should endeavor forcibly to get him to fix at least $100,000,000 as the lower limit. . . . P.S. I think we were a bit too gentle with him this morning."[41]

When Litvinoff returned to the White House at 2:00 he raised the figure he was willing to offer to $75,000,000 to be paid "in the form of a percentage above the ordinary rate of interest on a loan to be granted to it by the Government of the United States or its nationals." "Mr. Litvinov said that he had entire confidence in the fair-mindedness of the President and felt sure that when the President had looked into the facts he would not feel that a sum greater than $75,000,000 was justified." "The President said that he believed confidently that he could persuade Congress to accept a sum of $150,000,000, but that he feared that Congress would not accept any smaller sum."[42] At this point the difference between the two sides on this last of many issues had decreased enough so that both FDR and Litvinoff could feel the closeness of recognition. Litvinoff made a semi-concession of another $25,000,000, and with that the formula acceptable to both FDR and Litvinoff had been found. Litvinoff said that "so far as he personally was concerned, and without making any commitment, he would be inclined to advise his Government to accept $100,000,000 if the President should still consider such a sum fair."[43] The gap that remained between the two positions no longer seemed great enough to FDR to warrant delaying recognition. FDR at this late stage in the negotiations had already secured the concessions that he needed to make recognition a success, and he was anxious to consummate it. Only the size of the debt payment remained as an issue, and in FDR's judgment it was an issue of much less significance than the political issues. As Moore told the nation in a radio address explaining the recognition agreements, "the President's resolute purpose" was to "safeguard the integrity of our Government and the rights of our nationals now or hereafter residing in Soviet territory. That was the primary purpose to which any strictly material question such as the settlement of debts was altogether ancillary."[44] In fact, from FDR's perspective it was not in itself really a good reason for refusing relations. He was still carrying on diplomatic intercourse with France and the other nations that had recently defaulted on their war debts, and later when Russia refused to pay the debt, he would not consider breaking relations. It was an issue that basically bored him; it was an issue on which the Russians had already come two-thirds of the way; and it was also an issue on which Litvinoff, after having conceded so much so quickly, had finally planted his feet. In the past few days, in fact, the Russians had come so far towards agreeing to all the American conditions that it seemed foolish to withhold recognition while haggling over an ancillary issue. And that is the essential point: the Russians had agreed to about everything the Americans had demanded.

Bullitt also appeared at this final hour of the long negotiations to have been feeling the pressure for compromise and to have at last been willing to make a concession on this final point. Through the autumn Bullitt had insisted that no concessions could be expected from the Soviet government after recognition, and consequently Bullitt's advice to FDR to go no lower than $100,000,000 seems to indicate a willingness on his part to accept this figure. As Bullitt advised Hull, "Before recognition and before loans, we shall find the Soviet Government relatively amenable. After recognition or loans, we should find the Soviet Government adamant."[45] Of course Bullitt may have changed his mind after a week of face-to-face negotiations, but we know that on this issue particularly he was not operating under any new conceptions. Bullitt reported to FDR that "I urged Litvinov not to fix the lower figure at $50,000,000 as his Government would surely insist that that should be accepted as the maximum figure once the sum had been stated."[46] Under the pressure of Litvinoff's resistance on this one final issue preventing an almost completely successful negotiation and the accompanying acclaim that would accrue to himself, Bullitt seemed at the end ready to make a compromise, even if in the swirl of conflicting emotions he did not fully acknowledge this to himself.

After recognition Litvinoff was to remain in Washington to discuss "with Mr. Morganthau and Mr. Bullitt the exact sum between the limits of $75,000,000 and $150,000,000 to be paid by the Soviet Government." As indicated by the vagueness of the method of repayment there was much to be done, because the American government did not know what it wished to propose. Bullitt liked the idea of using blocked marks held by American citizens, but he had no real idea what it entailed and that uncertainty was reflected in the "gentleman's agreement" which specified that the loan would be granted by "the Government of the United States or its nationals."[47]

All that remained now was the final drafting of the documents, and the next morning Moore, Hackworth, Kelley, Bullitt, and Phillips met to begin this last task of the negotiations.[48] Faced with the reality of recognition, Kelley's first response was to arrange for the Army to remove the records of the Provisional Russian Government from the Russian embassy before recognition was signed and the embassy was turned over to the Soviets.[49] That evening while the Army trucks were being loaded with records at the Russian embassy, FDR at the White House was hosting the annual Cabinet dinner. The musicale following the dinner lasted until about 11:00 and as the guests were leaving Woodin, Phillips, Bullitt, Morganthau, and Litvinoff assembled in the President's study. FDR soon joined them and "after a few pleasant preliminaries, the President began to read the exchange of notes and the various enclosures thereto." Litvinoff objected to specific wordings, and after some discussion the documents formally establishing diplomatic contact were simultaneously signed by FDR and Litvinoff at 12:46 A.M. "It was a dramatic moment" and in Phillips's opinion "the President was in great form and evidently happy at the final results."⁵⁰ FDR fancied the idea of recognition beginning on the 16th, so he decided the official moment of recognition would be 10 minutes before midnight. Towards the end of the celebrating when "Litvinov was about to leave, the President said to him: 'There is one other thing; you must tell Stalin that the antireligious policy is wrong. God will punish you Russians if you go on persecuting the church.'" Litvinoff related this story to Tugwell "immediately afterwards (he told others too, for they in turn reported it to me [Tugwell])." Tugwell felt that he "ought not to put this remark in quotation marks, because I cannot be certain of its literal accuracy; but I am certain that it is almost exactly what he said." Tugwell had previously discussed the subject thoroughly with FDR and had concluded that FDR thought that "recognition would be helpful to religious Russians in various ways any imagination can conceive." "Litvinov was taken aback. It was altogether unexpected. . . . Litvinov related this incident to others in a puzzled way. He spoke of it because he thought it had no diplomatic significance and so could be talked about; but also he was astounded and curious. He wound up by asking: 'Does he really believe in God?'"⁵¹

FDR detained Phillips after all the others had gone to ask his opinion of Bullitt. FDR had decided to appoint Bullitt ambassador and was again consulting Phillips as a gesture to preserve form. Phillips recorded that he "praised his work highly."⁵²

The next morning Bullitt and Litvinoff met FDR at the White House and were joined by FDR's house guest, Norman

Davis, who wished to confer with Litvinoff on disarmament. Litvinoff discounted the worth of the four or five power conversations suggested by Davis, on the grounds that Japan would not accept any reductions and would block acceptance of international control.[53] After this discussion Litvinoff was connected by telephone and short wave radio to his family in Russia. Complete details of this conversation, full of regards and well wishes from every perspective were immediately made available to the press.[54]

At 2:00 FDR announced to his cabinet that he had recognized Russia. He "appeared in great spirits," and Farley reported that FDR told them that "he felt the agreement would be very pleasing to the people of this country, and that those who had opposed recognition on religious grounds would no longer do so. . . . 'Generally speaking,' he concluded, 'I feel I have driven a good bargain, not only for this country, but for the world, and that it will go a long way toward preserving the future peace of the world.'"[55] Interior Secretary Ickes, after listening to FDR's explanation of the agreements, recorded in his diary that "as near as I could make out, the President got everything that he wanted out of these conversations."[56] Phillips "raised the question as to who would take charge of the debt negotiations since Acheson was no longer available at the Treasury. Secretary Woodin, who sat opposite me [Phillips] smiling but helpless and who leaves tomorrow on his two or three months' furlough (of course not to return) volunteered the information that there was no one in the Treasury who could undertake this work. The President, therefore, threw it in my lap in spite of my protests that it was Treasury Department business rather than State Department business."[57] Following the cabinet meeting FDR went to the press conference previously arranged to announce the results of his negotiations with Litvinoff.

153

"There must have been 200 newspapermen in the circular study of the Chief Executive," Duranty of *The New York Times* wrote, "when he made his historic announcement, and the way he did it gave an interesting illustration of the character of Franklin D. Roosevelt, his sense of drama—hope the word 'showmanship' is not 'lèse-majesté'—and his profound knowledge of psychology. Everyone present was on tiptoe waiting for news about the results of the negotiations with M. Litvinoff. Mr. Roosevelt smiled pleasantly at the crowd, cast an affectionate eye round the walls at his splendid collection of colored prints of old New England scenes and stated in a conversational tone that he had gratifying news from the iron and steel industry about the working of their NRA code."[58] Calmly enjoying himself FDR pronounced this to be "a very important matter."[59] "There was something like a gasp of suspense from his hearers."[60] This false beginning greatly enhanced the impact of the announcement of recognition which immediately followed. "Last night" FDR began, "just before the magic hour of midnight, the United States agreed to the resumption of normal relations with Russia. You will find, when you go out, a large and voluminous document—a great many pages—and I am going to do something very mean—I am going to ask you to read it before you write your stories."[61] FDR then proceeded to read the agreements, either in whole or in part, to the reporters.

When FDR finished reading and explaining, Press Secretary Steven Early briefly spoke to the President. FDR then announced that "the State Department calls my attention to a very serious error on the title page of this document. They have spelled Commissar with one "s" instead of two. So will you please correct it. (laughter) I think you have everything."[62]

Within an hour and a half after the end of the news conference FDR had left the White House to begin a Thanksgiving vacation in Warm Springs, recognition and amicable relations with the Soviet Union happily secured behind him.[63]

154

Among those not previously committed to oppose any dealings with a communist government the recognition was almost universally regarded as a complete success. *The New York Times* directly under its headline printed a box captioned, "Points Conceded by Russia." The introductory sentence stated that it "was said in informed quarters to include virtually every concession the Soviet Government has ever made to any country."[64] The New York *Herald Tribune* said that even those irreconcilably opposed to any contact with communist Russia would have to concede "that in his negotiations with Mr. Litvinoff President Roosevelt has secured from the Soviet Government every concession and every guarantee of respect for our rights which one government can ask of another as a preliminary to diplomatic intercourse."[65] *The Wall Street Journal* called FDR "a master bargainer" who had "persuaded Moscow to accept in substance the condition laid down by Colby and Hughes a decade and more ago, plus renunciation of Russia's putative claims for indemnity on account of our military operations against the Bolshevik regime in 1918." The editorial approved of the de-emphasis of the old debt. "The question of our Government's loan to the Kerensky government is tactifully left to future negotiations; if there is a mutual but unexpressed recognition that that is a dead loss, we are merely writing off a mischance."[66] *The Washington Post* said that the recognition agreements had in a "masterly manner" disposed of the past and cleared "the way for the realization of mutual benefits in the future" without leaving open any loopholes for serious disagreement. "The United States concedes nothing of any real significance and the Soviet Union avoids the risk of international embarrassments."[67] FDR even received good reviews from the Catholic press. As much as the Catholic press had been against recognition, the President emerged as a defender of "the value of religion in society against communist propaganda."[68] George Flynn in his study of the subject concluded:

155

"The Catholic Press, while divided on the merits and terms of recognizing Russia, was unanimous in its praise of President Roosevelt's personal behavior."[69] FDR's purposeful avoidance of the economic issues while concentrating upon religious freedom was an attempt to show the Russians that capitalistic America could not be understood if simply reduced to dollars and markets. In the way in which he conducted the negotiations FDR was making a statement to the Russians about the nature of American society and in a broader sense he was criticizing and attempting to educate the Russian leaders as to the importance of spirituality in human existence. This aspect of the negotiations was recognized by many religious leaders and found expression in the Catholic press. There was considering the almost total hostility to the idea only a few months previously, surprisingly much favorable commentary after the negotiations on the recognition and the accompanying agreements. One favorable article entitled, "What Russian Recognition Means," in the December 2, 1933 edition of the journal *America* saw FDR's point exactly. "Wasn't it sufficient to dangle before the eyes of these credulous, child-like citizens of the New World the bright vision of reciprocal trade advantages and find them all falling down in adoration of the Golden Calf?" The article saw the chief meaning of the recognition as coming from the clauses pledging religious freedom to American citizens in Russia. "A principle of human right, inherent in the nature of man's spiritual being, is vindicated in the most thrilling diplomatic duel of modern times."[70]

The recognition was judged by Democratic leaders and FDR's advisors to be a political success. Key Pittman, Chairman of the Senate Foreign Relations Committee, wrote FDR that "you have accomplished, in my opinion, in your invitation to Russia and in your negotiations with Litvinov the greatest diplomatic victory in my memory."[71] Speaker of the House Henry Rainey told the press that it was the "'greatest thing in the world that had happened to bring about world peace.'"[72] Bernard Baruch wrote Louis Howe that "there is unanimous approval at present of the President's Russian policy," and Felix Frankfurter wrote FDR from England that "your Russian recognition shows how, with careful handling even the most passionate feeling evaporates, or, at the least, that action sensibly grounded silences even noisy opposition."[73] From Mexico Josephus Daniels wrote FDR that "nothing along international lines has cheered me quite as much as the magnificent way you handled the Russian conversations leading up to the recognition of Russia."[74] Former Under Secretary of State Frank Polk, who was representing Americans who held defaulted Russian bonds, a group whose interests did not fare well in FDR's approach to the negotiations, wrote FDR that "I feel I must send you a line to express my hearty congratulations on the way you have handled the Russian recognition. It was bound to come and you not only secured far more than anyone thought you could secure but you also did it in a way that will go far to silence those irreconcilably opposed to recognition."[75]

Even in the State Department there was the feeling that recognition was successful and that it was a settlement beneficial to the U.S. Moore summarized his feelings in a radio address to the nation. "Not in any boastful spirit, but taking the facts as outlined, may it not be confidently said that the President by his successful termination of the negotiations has lengthened the list of fine achievements marking the few months since his inauguration."[76] Moffat wrote in his diary, "Well, the news about the Russian recognition is out and on the whole I am inclined to feel we drove a harder bargain than had been anticipated." The final agreement "has apparently satisfied even Senator King and Father Walsh. More cannot be said. Only Ham Fish in vocalizing against the agreement."[77] Phillips recorded in his journal that "Philip Carroll, representative of the National City Bank, dropped in to say that he was immensely pleased with the terms of Soviet recognition. Carroll is an intelligent and critical man and I was glad to have his views. It looks as though almost the entire press of the country regarded favorably our negotiations with Litvinov and approves of the terms of recognition. Many papers speak of it as a 'diplomatic triumph.'"[78] In his oral history of these events Phillips recalled, "To make a long story short, Litvinov finally came across with everything we wanted."[79]

On the other hand, the Russian experts were unhappy about FDR's granting recognition on the basis of what appeared to them to be the duplicitous Russian claims of friendship. It must be remembered that Bullitt was the Russian experts' window into FDR's thoughts and motivations, and Bullitt's emphasis on "really friendly relations" served only to confirm the impression of FDR's superficiality. This, compounded by Bullitt's enthusiasm for the melodramatic aspects of any encounter, strengthened the Russian experts in their view that the President's reversal of their policy was the result of simplistic reasoning. They had interpreted FDR as initially moving towards recognition because of political pressure from business, and now they saw FDR granting recognition on the basis of some highly dubious Russian declarations of friendship. Consequently, the view of the recognition negotiations that was ripening in the minds of the Russian experts disdainfully portrayed FDR's Russian policy as the maneuverings of a politician.

In the Riga legation there was strong disappointment over the agreements. Because third secretary George Kennan had specifically suggested language for the consular agreement different than the Russian-German treaty language used, he was particularly upset by this settlement; he wrote that "I viewed the assurances as a whole, I must say, with little enthusiasm." In his memoirs Kennan recorded that "shortly before Litvinov's visit to Washington, the American minister in Riga, Mr. Robert Peet Skinner, had invited from each of us in the Russian Section of the legation an individual opinion on the question of recognition. In replying, I had given it as my conviction that the Russians would not be willing to make any significant concessions on principle on either of these points [propaganda and debts]." Kennan felt that "they would not do it in order to obtain American recognition; and they would not do it as a gesture of appreciation for recognition once obtained. Most of my colleagues had, I believe, expressed similar views." Kennan concluded that "what happened subsequently confirmed their correctness."[80]

In the same vein as the Riga delegation's criticism, there has been much written over the years denigrating the concessions given by the Soviets, but Phillips's estimation best sums up what had occurred during the negotiations. The U.S. had demanded much, and the Soviets had conceded everything necessary to secure recognition. In studying these agreements in 1953, historian Paul Browder found "considerable evidence to indicate that the Soviet Government regarded these commitments as unusually broad concessions."[81] It is worth briefly examining each agreement.

The religious question was one totally of FDR's creation. It was an issue with the potential to create among many otherwise domestic political allies a continuing resistance which FDR preferred to placate, and it was an issue with which he was truly sympathetic. In Labor Secretary Frances Perkins's words, freedom of worship seemed to FDR "a natural moral guarantee."[82] He reconciled the issue both for himself and others by coming to believe in the efficacy of guaranteeing religious freedom for Americans in Russia as a significant statement about the nature of the United States and in a broader sense about the nature of humankind, as well as a first step towards improving the climate within Russia for all to worship as they saw fit. This was an issue with symbolic meaning, not substance. Samuel Harper thought the American insistence upon the issue amusing. "I had to smile when I read that our embassy staff in Moscow must have the opportunity of religious teaching for their children, for my observations led me to doubt if they would be much concerned over this right."[83] Litvinoff must have been astounded when the idea was first proposed and became the dominant issue in the early sessions. He protested to the State Department negotiators that "'no American nationals have ever complained against religious restrictions while in Russia.'"[84] Later Litvinoff complained of FDR's infatuation with the issue to the exclusion of economic issues he considered more important.[85]

On the afternoon of the first day of negotiations Litvinoff took the list of asked for religious concessions and wrote beside each issue the Soviet position; agreeing to some, altering some, and refusing some. Regardless of this negative early response, when the negotiations were over Litvinoff had conceded on every point asked for by the U.S. Had the issue been left in the hands of the State Department, however, it may well have never been resolved. Moore and Kelley understood that the form of the Russian letter on religion would be, as in the propaganda agreement, a compilation of the language taken directly from Soviet laws. They objected because "this has been found extremely difficult for the reason that the laws do not touch several important points." The main objection, and one that could have been furnished only by Kelley, was that certain of the laws quoted by Litvinoff "are not understood to be in effect throughout the territory of the Soviet Government."[86] Kelley and the State Department wanted an original statement specifically covering every point as a guarantee. When FDR and Litvinoff established that the form of Litvinoff's agreement would be a listing of the issues, with each issue followed by the guaranteeing Soviet laws, it eliminated the need to find the exact specific wordings within the Soviet laws and made irrelevant this particular objection. The objection to the breadth of

160

the domain of the laws within the Soviet Union remained, however, and Moore, Kelley, and Phillips all were quite dissatisfied with the President's refusal to contest the issue. Phillips's understanding of the objections of his subordinates was typically superficial. "We think that an original statement from the Soviets to us is necessary, if only to give the appearance of new concessions."[87] On Monday, November 13, the day that the State Department was worrying about the religious issue, Moore wrote Hull in Uruguay that "at this moment I feel a good deal of apprehension that we may not insist that definite agreements on the major questions shall be furnished coincident with recognition."[88] Such was the structure of the State Department that an issue that had diplomatic meaning only because the President so endowed it, could remain a problem to the Department even after the mind of the man who created it had been completely satisfied; and FDR's mind was satisfied. On Saturday on his way south to Warm Springs, FDR stopped in Savannah, Georgia, to deliver a speech as honorary chairman of Georgia's bicentennial year. After stating his "sincere" belief "that the most impelling motive" behind the negotiations "was the desire of both countries for peace and for the strengthening of the peaceful purpose of the civilized world," FDR specifically referred to only one of the many agreements that resulted from these negotiations, the protection of religious freedom. FDR told the people of Savannah that "there must be satisfaction to know that from now on any American sojourning among the great Russian people will be free to worship God in his own way."[89]

Litvinoff had begun the negotiations adamantly refusing to sign any kind of anti-propaganda agreement, but when the negotiations were over he had signed the broadest and most complete agreement that the Soviet government had ever accepted. The propaganda issue was to Kelley the most significant topic, and drawing from 26 other treaties, he redrafted this agreement until he felt he had created so strong a prohibition against propaganda that he doubted the Soviets would agree to it. It was, compared to anything else the Soviets had ever signed, a major concession on their part, and the State Department considered it an ironclad guarantee.

Because the agreement did not refer to any specific organization such as the Comintern, there was no reason inherent in the wording of the agreement that prevented a bilateral pledge. The Americans would not accede to this, however, and in reply to the four paragraphs of detailed specifications pledged by Litvinoff, FDR responded with one carefully worded sentence. "It will be the fixed policy of the Executive of the United States within the limits of the powers conferred by the Constitution and the laws of the United States to adhere reciprocally to the engagements above expressed."[90]

FDR with his sound political instincts did not fear domestic communism, but he recognized the political value of the propaganda issue and responded to it within that narrow breadth. FDR constituted propaganda as one of the two principal issues, but unlike the entire policy making level of the State Department, he never developed any feel for it. At the press conference announcing recognition, FDR did not even bother to mention what specific guarantees were contained in the propaganda pledge signed by Litvinoff. All he said was that "there are four paragraphs stating that fixed policy" without even a casual allusion as to what that fixed policy was to be. In contrast, FDR began explaining the religious agreement by stating, "I will read this to you because I think it is an important thing," and then he went on to read in its entirety his letter to Litvinoff.[91] Then he also read a large part of Litvinoff's letter to himself on the matter. In fact FDR read to the reporters a significant portion of every agreement except the one on propaganda.

162

On the two political issues, propaganda and religion, that FDR had designated as primary, the Soviet Union had acceded to all that the Americans had demanded. On the other issues, the Americans were equally successful.

The Soviet agreement concerning consular rights for the protection of Americans in Russia was framed by Litvinoff according to the demands of the State Department. The provision in the agreement for a most favored nation status with a specific reference to the Russian-German treaty of October 12, 1925, was lifted directly from page 12 of Kelley's Opus 5 published on October 20, 1933. The selections of Article 11 and the Final Protocol from that 1925 treaty for inclusion in the body of the pledge mirrors Kelley's selection of these two articles for citation on page 13 of Opus 5.[92] These provisions provided for prompt notification of American consuls after the arrest of an American citizen, which knowledge Kelley thought essential to the implementation of the only effective means of protecting American citizens, "sheer diplomatic pressure."[93] Kelley thought "the existence of treaty provisions often operates against rather than for the interests of foreigners in Russia, since such treaty provisions may, under certain circumstances, only serve to tie the hands of the foreign state in exerting pressure through retaliatory measures."[94] The choice of the rather abbreviated format of the Russia agreement was Kelley's and was not due to the superficiality of FDR's approach as Kennan in Riga presumed.[95] A statement against economic espionage in the form quoted in Opus 5 was also signed by Litvinoff as a separate agreement. As in the other issues, the Soviets gave the Americans what they wanted in regards to consular rights.

The three remaining agreements signed by Litvinoff were concerned with economic issues. One agreement signed by Litvinoff eliminated the problems the State Department had with the recognition being retroactive. Litvinoff agreed that the Soviet Union would accept the "judgments rendered or that may be rendered by American courts" and "acts done or settlements made by or with the Government of the United States, or public officials in the United States, or its nationals, relating to property credits, or obligations of any Government of Russia or nationals thereof."[96] In addition to accepting whatever dispositions had been made of Russian property in America since the beginning of the Soviet regime, the agreement also specified that the Soviet government would waive its claim to all remaining assets of prior Russian regimes in America. These assets would be assigned to the American government and it was intended that this assignment would be all inclusive. Hull explained it to the Attorney General this way. "It was the purpose of the assignment in question to release and assign to the United States not only all amounts to which the Soviet government was entitled as the successor to former governments of Russia, but also all amounts to which the Soviet government considered it was entitled in any manner."[97] The value of the Russian property listed in Kelley's Opus No. 6 was $8,000,000, but this was acknowledged to be a tentative figure and estimates of the value ranged within the State Department up to $15,000,000.[98]

There do not seem to be any definitive documents specifying whether this money was to be included in the $150,000,000 or in addition to it. Kelley would claim in February that the assignment was in addition to the debt settlement but three years later he would tell the Secretary of the Treasury that it was part of the $150,000,000.[99] Regardless, assignment and acceptance of the disposition of the prior Russian government's assets in America were two more issues in which the Soviets completely acceded to American demands.

An agreement specifically waiving Soviet counterclaims against the American expeditionary forces in Russia was Bullitt's personal issue. Litvinoff signed an agreement waiving Siberian counterclaims but would not specifically waive the rest.

In Kelley's words the Russians "would not waive Archangel, although they would not press it, but in the Agreement it would be a mutual settlement; that is, what they would pay to us would be in settlement of all claims."[100] Since Litvinoff had agreed not to press the counterclaims as an economic offset, his objections to signing an agreement specifically waiving all compensation for damages by the American military expedition was obviously political. Perhaps the Soviets felt that if an agreement waiving all counterclaims was signed it would be an admission that another country had the right to send, on its own determination, troops to Russian soil. Litvinoff's waiver of Siberian counterclaims stated that it was done only after an examination of the records revealed the attitude of the "American government toward the expedition into Siberia, the operations there of foreign military forces and the inviolability of the territory of the Union of Soviet Socialist Republics."[101] The waiver of the demand for compensation for damages in Siberia may have been made as a gesture against the Japanese who were a threat to Soviet territory during the time of the Siberian expedition and who were again a threat during the time of the recognition negotiations. In any case without Soviet records all this is conjecture. The Americans did secure Soviet agreement to consider all their counterclaims as fully settled and disposed of, and the waiver regarding Siberia was committed to writing. Except for the debt issue, the single American failure to secure everything desired was the Soviet failure to commit all the counterclaim waivers to writing.

After granting all the many concessions that the U.S. required why did the Russians quibble over the last $50,000,000 that would have completed the agreement they were so eagerly seeking? The answer, of course, is that they were not quibbling; the amounts were of real significance to the Russians. The depression had greatly reduced the foreign exchange available from exports which was much needed to pay for the products required for the economy's rapid industrialization. In order to stay within its rapidly shrinking means, the Russians were drastically reducing their foreign debt.[102] The $150,000,000 represented a significant percentage of the entire Soviet foreign indebtedness of 1934. The Russians were making a substantial gesture. The money had incomparably more utility to the Russians than it did to the Americans. FDR in fact had probably chosen the figure of $150,000,000 because he felt it would sound good to Congress and not for any economic reason. There was much talk in the papers about what a fine trader Litvinoff was, but in actuality the Soviets had given the U.S. everything it asked for. It was a significant concession by the Soviets which went completely unrecognized by the Russian specialists in the State Department.

FDR and Bullitt had conducted most of the discussions with Litvinoff, and only they were aware of the exact nature of what had been agreed to during the negotiations. Yet they seemed quite content, even anxious, not to preserve any written record of the negotiations, satisfied to be served by memory. As Moore told the American people, "There were no stenographers present and no reports made and thus, so far as the conferences are concerned, there will be a bare outline and not a full picture exposed to the eyes of the future historian."[103] In keeping with this spirit there is a March 3, 1934 memo that states "Mr. Kannee forwards envelope of miscellaneous papers and clippings re Litvinoff conferences and states that those were left on the mantle in Mr. McIntyre's room during the conferences. Mr. Kannee states that he put them in Mr. McIntyre's desk and called them to the attention of Mr. Bullitt who said, 'leave them there, they are not important.'"[104] In addition to the decision of FDR to forego written records, some particular attitudes emerged from the negotiations that would also have great bearing upon later events.

166

A most significant consequence of the negotiations was its contribution to FDR's complex relationship with the State Department. Although FDR had made curtsies to correct procedure by ostensibly working through Hull, and then after his departure, through Phillips, he had in fact completely worked around the State Department, reaching down and using Bullitt in a very personal way. FDR knew that the Department had been against recognition and he had run the negotiations out of his own vest pocket. The result was that it enhanced his bias that the Department consisted of ineffectual paper shufflers. At the top, the State Department was indeed ineffectual because FDR, having chosen to be his own Secretary of State, had appointed weak individuals. Misplanted congressmen such as Hull and Moore gave support to FDR's stereotype by the quality of their leadership. Under Secretary of State Phillips, because he was in fact a fine example of the stereotype, added credence; but Chief of the Eastern European Division Robert Kelley and his subordinates, who together bore the brunt of FDR's disdain, were not at all the socially adept but ineffectual men of FDR's stereotype.

In the same manner that the negotiation enhanced FDR's belief in the power of personal diplomacy, the negotiations also enhanced his belief that the problems posed by the resistance of reluctant officials were of little significance. FDR had begun by underestimating the capabilities of the area specialists and the conduct of the negotiations only confirmed his predisposition. Although FDR knew that the State Department had been against recognition it did not greatly concern him. He even remained quite content in permitting the State Department to define which issues required resolution before granting recognition. FDR did not comprehend the skill and singlemindness with which Kelley was waging his battle against Russian communism. Kelley was not a cookie pusher but rather a brilliant

167

bureaucrat whose papers well served his policy by enraging a decade of Secretaries of State and Presidents at the thought of recognition. In demeanor an objective scholar, Kelley was at heart a passionate ideologue. FDR seriously underestimated the man whose ideas would survive his own and become the basis for American post war policy regarding Russia, and whose thoughts even today have much to do with American attitudes towards the Soviet Union. As illustration of Kelley's effectiveness, Morganthau by the time recognition was extended had come to believe that trade with Russia should be done only on the basis of a barter agreement, in large part because he was influenced by a long list of unfair Russian trade practices that had been supplied him by the State Department.[105]

FDR's personal involvement in the conduct of the negotiations and the great desire of the Russian government for recognition had rendered unimportant the organized hostility of the Russian experts regarding the Soviet Union. Unless FDR remained personally involved that hostility would not remain unimportant, and FDR was about to delegate the issue to the care of Bullitt and the State Department. As a consequence his plans for improved relations between the two countries would pay the price for his underestimation of his bureaucracy.

If FDR underestimated his bureaucracy he overestimated Bullitt, who was the weak reed upon which FDR relied to carry his negotiations to their final fruition. FDR's complete confidence in Bullitt, who emerged from these negotiations with enormous prestige, was a most important consequence of the recognition negotiations. Bullitt had been the personal envoy who had handled FDR's secret approach to the Russians. Bullitt had been the pro-recognition man in a State Department strongly against recognition, and Bullitt had very successfully handled much of the negotiations with Litvinoff alone. Bullitt took personal credit for many of the successes of the negotiations, and shortly after recognition he "described some of the high points of the negotiations with Litvinoff" in a long talk with Moffat. After this discussion Moffat was convinced that Bullitt deserved "the highest of marks for the technique was largely his and if he does as well at Moscow as he had done to date, we shall have cause for congratulations."[106] FDR officially confirmed his opinion of Bullitt's abilities by naming him as America's first ambassador to the Soviet Union.

Only the less important economic issues remained to be negotiated, and after Bullitt's bravura performance FDR gladly entrusted these matters to his hands. This was not the first time that FDR had listened to Bullitt in the matter of intergovernmental debts. In January 1933 Bullitt had convinced FDR to send him abroad as his personal representative to tell the heads of foreign governments privately that FDR would expect the repayment of the entire principal on the war debts, but that he would, in return for other concessions, forgive the interest.[107] Although the trip ended up with Bullitt in the papers on both sides of the Atlantic, and with a demand for his arrest under the Logan Act from the floor of the Senate, FDR had been willing to listen to Bullitt then with regards to intergovernmental debts, and now after Bullitt's totally successful negotiations with Litvinoff, FDR was willing to listen to him again. Bullitt's preliminary work with blocked marks gave him an expertise in the area that FDR gladly deferred to. The casual opinion of banker James Warburg had confirmed Bullitt's confidence that the scheme was workable but Bullitt had not yet really even begun to understand the issue.[108] In this regard there was one other relevant aspect of Bullitt's personality that played a role in his approach to this issue and which led to much of the subsequent confusion. Bullitt was not what could be called a natural financier, although he was certainly not shy about holding and expressing strong opinions in such matters. All Bullitt's travelling and indeed his whole manner of living was supported by his inheritance, which allowed him to

169

live exactly as he chose, but Bullitt always remained casual regarding money and was sometimes chided by his brother regarding his understanding of finances. "He [William Bullitt] took no interest in the acquisition of money and once wrote to me [Orville Bullitt], 'I don't know anything about investments and I have no idea what you are holding now in the way of stocks or bonds or what is in my account.'"[109] Even more disparaging of Bullitt's financial faculties was his brother's remark to him in a discussion in early 1933 about the decision of the U.S. to go off the gold standard. Orville Bullitt told his brother that "he had no right to an opinion as he had never even been able to balance his checkbook."[110]

Another important result that came out of the negotiations was the belief that the Soviets had signed an ironclad guarantee on the propaganda issue. That fact had little significance for FDR, but it had enormous importance within the State Department, and particularly for Kelley and Bullitt.

The recognition agreements did not in the least assuage Kelley's suspicions regarding the Soviet Union, nor did it increase his confidence in FDR's policies. Kelley simply did not approve of recognition as a governmental policy. As an administrative procedure, Kelley found FDR's manner of handling recognition equally disturbing. Although FDR had allowed the State Department, which meant in effect Kelley, both to define the issues to be resolved and to specify the language of the agreements, he had at crucial times personally taken control of the proceedings while specifically avoiding any consultation with his area specialists. He had bypassed Kelley in first making contact with the Soviet Union and he had bypassed Kelley when he personally stepped in after the negotiations with Litvinoff had bogged down in the State Department. The result was an alienation of feeling among the diplomats of the Eastern European Division from FDR and his Russian policy. From their view FDR's policy was naive and unrealistic and they were displeased with this breach in the defenses that they had so laboriously thrown up against the Soviet threat. The alienation from FDR's policy was so strong throughout the division that George Kennan in Riga was profoundly disturbed when he read the recognition agreements. Kennan assumed that the government's failure to hold out for the detailed sort of consular agreement that he had been working on had probably been due to FDR and the superficiality of his approach to Russian policy. The agreement was in fact Kelley's work, but for the young Kennan "the implication was unmistakable." FDR had seized upon the impressive sounding but ineffective language only to convey to an uncritical public an appearance of vigilance in protecting American interests.

Kelley was most professional in his conduct, and he certainly did not present himself as being in opposition to his government's policies. His actions were always concerned with defending the United States against the continuing threat he saw emanating from the Soviet Union. As a consequence his overwhelming distrust guaranteed that diplomacy could never be successful in bridging any part of the gap that already existed. Kelley's was a static approach to world politics that automatically forced events to fulfill preestablished conclusions. Kelley had believed that the Russians would not accept his agreements and the early State Department negotiations were conducted in a manner that ensured that the Russians would not accept them. Yet FDR secured every political guarantee that Kelley had been seeking, including the 26 treaty composite anti-propaganda pledge that Kelley had worked so hard in drafting. FDR had introduced the freedom of religion issue and had garnered from it all that he had intended, yet Kelley's microscopic concentration upon words and legal phrases missed FDR's point entirely and left him dissatisfied and apprehensive concerning possible trickery in future Russian interpretation. Kelley's compulsion to act first to prevent the Soviet chicanery that he was

171

sure would occur in the absence of his defenses, guaranteed difficulty in any interaction with the Soviet government. In light of this it should be recalled here that the one action Kelley despised more than recognition was the extension of financial aid to promote trade.

X

Monticello in Moscow
and Stalin's Kiss

WITHIN A FEW DAYS OF RECOGNITION IT WAS REALIZED THAT IT
would not be possible to resolve the issues of the "gentleman's
agreement" before Litvinoff left the United States. The Americans really did not have a good understanding of the financial
aspects of their own proposals. To a large degree FDR had relied upon Bullitt, and Bullitt was a long way from having the
issue "by the ears." The final negotiations would have to be
postponed because the Americans had so much work to do.

On Friday, November 17, Ivan Divilkovsky, Secretary to the
Commissariat of Foreign Affairs, and one of the two men accompanying Litvinoff to America, met with Kelley and asked
him a number of specific questions regarding the disposition of
the money lent to the Russian Provisional Government. Four
days later Kelley used Skvirsky to transfer to Divilkovsky most

of this information although some was not available in the form
requested and "whether it could all be obtained from available
records could not be ascertained without extensive research."[1]

Interfering with debt negotiations were the ceremonial details that came to the fore immediately after recognition was
announced. On Friday night Litvinoff posed for Movie-Tone
news and was walked to the Russian embassy by Kelley.[2] On
Saturday morning Litvinoff gave a luncheon at the Mayflower
Hotel for the members of the Cabinet. Phillips sat beside Litvinoff at the luncheon and they had a "pleasant talk" about the
"splendid" houses proposed for the American embassy in Moscow.[3] That afternoon after the luncheon Bullitt called Warburg
and told him "that he was now ready to take up definitely the
Lee, Higginson conversion and could I [Warburg] come down
at once to talk to Litvinov." Warburg replied that "in the first
place, I could not come down before Tuesday night, and in the
second place, I would have to talk to Murnane." Murnane was
one of two men at Lee, Higginson & Co. who was familiar with
these German credits, and when Warburg tried to get in touch
with him he learned that he was in Europe. Warburg soon also
determined that the one other man he considered knowledge-
able on the debts was somewhere in Cleveland. Unable to reach
either of the two men he considered experts, Warburg called
Bullitt back and reported that there would be some delay in his
being able to secure good advice on the matter.[4] The vagueness
surrounding the details of the American position on the debts
remained sufficient to preclude the early solution that had
been hoped for.

Litvinoff was reported by the newspapers to have met with
Morganthau briefly before the luncheon and later with Bullitt,
but the schedule of negotiations was determined on Monday
morning when Litvinoff visited the State Department.[5] *The New
York Times* reported of this Monday meeting that "the matter of

the consuls took up most of the conference at the State Department with William Phillips, Acting Secretary. Representatives of both governments consider that establishment of the respective embassies and location of the consuls is something which can be accomplished very quickly, whereas the difficult questions of debts, trade agreements and a possible non-aggression treaty must be worked out gradually, and certainly not before M. Litvinoff leaves the United States, probably on Saturday."[6] In recording the topics discussed Phillips did not even bother to include the subject of debts.[7] This exchange was all that was accomplished towards negotiating the size of the Russian debt payment while Litvinoff remained in Washington. There was no point in discussing the debt until the question of American financing of the repayment vehicle was investigated, and at the moment the Americans were unprepared to supply such information. Because the Americans were still so far away from determining the final shape of their blocked mark arrangement, the State Department was quite content to postpone all talks until they had better examined the problem. After Monday there were no further attempts to settle the debt problem before Litvinoff sailed. On Tuesday Litvinoff and Bogdanov, Chairman of Amtorg, met with Bullitt and Morganthau at the Treasury, but the meeting only lasted for 20 minutes, and the following day Litvinoff sent FDR in Warm Springs a farewell letter and personally called on Phillips to say goodbye.[8] Phillips announced to the press: "'Due to the intricacy of the questions to be explored, it has been impossible to reach definite conclusions before the departure of Mr. Litvinoff.'"[9]

Bullitt had lunch with Phillips on Wednesday and went over with him "the various details in connection with the establishment of the Embassy in Moscow."[10] Bullitt as the new ambassador to the Soviet Union was caught up in the logistics of this problem and the travel scheduling that solving it would entail.

He planned to leave soon on a scouting trip to Moscow and then after returning to the U.S. to gather his full staff, to journey again to Russia.

Before leaving, Bullitt visited with FDR in Warm Springs. Washington was awash in talk of loans and schemes of trade. The November 18 recognition editorial of the *Washington Post* was almost completely devoted to these issues and the *Post*'s lead editorial the following day was entitled, "Russia's Foreign Trade."[11] Encouraged by the State Department, Bullitt was seeking from FDR an unequivocal delegation of authority on these matters. Bullitt was successful in this endeavor and he returned to Washington "with certain debatable matters cleared up. The State Department is to undertake all matters, whether of trade or of finance, relating to Russia. It is settled that there are to be no credits advanced, no commercial activities encouraged until after the two countries have come to a definite agreement in the matter of debts and claims."[12] If Bullitt had compromise on his mind on the last day of negotiations he certainly did not now. Russia's behavior was again highly suspect and responsive only to force, a "fact" that Kelley never failed to emphasize.

On Wednesday, November 29, Bullitt sailed for Russia to make the arrangements necessary for establishing the new embassy in Moscow. Bullitt had the idea that both he and Litvinoff would meet in Europe and together they would make a triumphant entry into Moscow. Litvinoff, however, spurned the opportunity to talk to Nazi leaders and passed quickly through Germany and into Russia thereby making such a plan impossible. Nevertheless, Bullitt's reception into Russia was certainly not ordinary. Representatives of the foreign office met him at the border, welcoming him on behalf of Litvinoff, and he was given an informal dinner at the station restaurant. Afterwards Bullitt and his party "boarded a private car placed at their disposal by the government and proceeded to

176

Moscow." The Associated Press reported that "it was the first time in the history of the Soviet Government that any foreign Ambassador had been met at the frontier or shown any attention whatsover before arriving in Moscow."[13]

When Bullitt reached Moscow he was met at the station by Troyanovsky and other officials and taken "to the Hotel National, where the American flag was suspended over the entrance." The Russians intended to please Bullitt and they knew their man and the value he placed upon symbolic gestures. "The apartment reserved for me [Bullitt] was the same which I was occupying with my mother when Austria sent her ultimatum to Serbia."[14] Bullitt was particularly pleased when the Communist Party Press, "which hitherto has been uniformly hostile to Ambassadors unearthed remarks of Lenin about me from his 'Testament' and various speeches. Apparently he really liked me and expressed his liking many times. In view of Lenin's present position in Russia, which is not unlike that of Jesus Christ in the Christian church, this is a bit like having the personal endorsement of the Master recorded in St. Mark. Divilkovsky, for example, said to me, 'You cannot understand it, but there is not one of us who would not gladly have his throat cut to have had such things said about him by Lenin.'"[15]

Later, Bullitt would put some flowers on Jack Reed's grave, a gesture that, although unnoticed by both the Russian and American press, Bullitt felt "did not pass unnoticed by the authorities in the Kremlin."[16]

Bullitt's first task was to find suitable quarters for the American embassy. Bullitt was offered the Supreme Court Building or the house of the Central Executive Committee. He chose the house of the Central Executive Committee but was displeased with its size and continued a search for more space. After much looking Bullitt felt he was "compelled to suggest that we should be given the first of the magnificent new buildings which are being planned for Lenin Avenue, which will run from the

Theatre Square past the Kremlin to the Palace of the Soviets. . . . The Moscow Soviet was naturally very reluctant to hand it to us and we obtained it only by a personal order of Stalin."[17] Bullitt, having a more grandiose conception for the embassy, however, concluded that "no permanently satisfactory quarters for the embassy and consulate could be established except by building," and so set off inspecting building sites. "There was one which was not offered to us, but which we offered to ourselves: a bluff covered with beautiful woods containing a lake overlooking the river and the whole city of Moscow in the center of the great city park. It is a situation which suggests Monticello, and I can conceive of nothing more perfect for an American Embassy than a reproduction of Monticello in that setting with houses for the entire staff of both consulate and embassy arranged along the sides of the property. We were not modest in our demands, but asked for the entire bluff containing some fifteen acres of ground. The Moscow Soviet continued to offer us other building sites, any one of which would be adequate but none of which compared in interest or beauty to this site."[18] After Litvinoff told Bullitt that the Moscow Soviet "had definitely decided it would not give us the building site in the center of the town's park," Bullitt personally asked Stalin for the site, telling him that in his mind's eye he could see "an American Embassy modelled on the home of the author of the Declaration of Independence on that particular bluff overlooking the Moscow River." Stalin replied, "'You shall have it.'"[19]

Two days after arriving in Moscow Bullitt presented his credentials to President Kalinin "and as a very special politeness Litvinoff broke all diplomatic precedents and gave me a copy of Kalinin's reply a day in advance."[20] Duranty's column in *The New York Times* reported that "something new in diplomatic procedure—at least as far as Soviet relations with other countries are concerned—happened today when William C. Bullitt, United States Ambassador, presented his credentials to

President Mikhail Kalinin at noon in the Kremlin. Instead of the customary arid expressions of greeting and good-will Mr. Bullitt made a warm speech emphasizing not only the desire of the two countries for peace, but for mutual friendship. M. Kalinin rose to the occasion and replied with equal warmth. . . ."[21] The Soviets also expressed some kind words for the President. Bullitt reported to FDR that "not only Kalinin and Litvinov, but everyone else in the Soviet Government was delighted by the remarks which you and I prepared in Warm Springs. . . . He [Kalinin] asked me to say to you that he was following with the closest attention everything that you were doing in America, and that he and everyone else in Russia considered you completely out of the class of the leaders of capitalist states; that it was clear to them all that you really cared about the welfare of the laboring men and the farmers and that you were not engaged in protecting the vested rights of property."[22] Kalinin told Bullitt that he hoped he "would travel in every part of the Union of Soviet Socialist Republics." Bullitt said he would need a plane to do that, and that he might be able to arrange to have a personal plane in Moscow if Kalinin "would permit me to use it without restrictions." Kalinin told Bullitt that there would be no restrictions on his movements.[23]

The Soviet leadership spent much effort in winning Bullitt's friendship. On Friday Litvinoff gave Bullitt a formal dinner which "nearly all the members of the Government" attended. "It was a superb banquet with food and wines of a quality that no one in America would dare to serve nowadays, and many toasts were drunk to you and to me and to the United States."[24] There were so many dinners and conversations with the members of the Government that Bullitt felt it "unnecessary to record the whole series of dinners and conversations."[25] The high point was a dinner at the Kremlin given by "Voroshilov, supreme commander of both the army and navy." Voroshilov's aide called for Bullitt and "conducted me through lines of

179

soldiers to Voroshilov's residence in a palace in the Kremlin. There I found awaiting me Mr. and Mrs. Voroshilov, Stalin, Kalinin, Molotov, Litvinov" and many others.[26] "Litvinov said to me as I looked over the room, 'This is the whole "gang" that really runs things—the inside directorate.' I was introduced to Stalin after I had shaken hands with Kalinin and Molotov, but made no effort to continue conversing with him before dinner. . . . After we had consumed a tremendous hors d'oeuvre, consisting of every conceivable kind of caviar and crab and other Russian delicacy and every conceivable kind of vodka and other aperitif we sat down. . . . As soon as we had settled ourselves at the table Stalin rose, lifted his glass and proposed a toast. 'To President Roosevelt, who in spite of the mute growls of the Fishes dared to recognize the Soviet Union.' Everyone drained his glass to the bottom and sat down again with considerable laughter at Stalin's reference to Ham Fish. I then proposed the health of President Kalinin and thereupon a series of toasts was begun which continued throughout the entire meal. The next one was Molotov's to me in which he proposed 'The health of one who comes to us [not] as a new Ambassador but an old friend.' . . . Stalin proposed my health several times and I did his once and we had considerable conversation across Madame Voroshilov." During the evening there was a great deal of talk concerning the probability of an attack by Japan. "Stalin, on introducing Egorov to me, said, 'This is the man who will lead our Army victoriously against Japan when Japan attacks.' . . . Just before the meal ended Stalin rose again and turning to me said, 'There is one thing I want to ask of you, the second line of our railroad to Vladivostock is not completed. To complete it quickly we need 250,000 tons of steel rails at once. They need not be new rails. Your rails are so much heavier than ours that the rails you discard are good enough for us. Your railways, I understand, are reequipping themselves and will have many old rails to dispose of immediately. Cannot you arrange for us to purchase the old rails? I do not ask that they should be given to us, but only that our purchase of them should be facilitated.' I replied that I should be glad to do anything I could in the matter and asked where the rails should be delivered, to which Stalin replied, 'Vladivostock.' . . . Stalin then said, 'without those rails we shall beat the Japanese, but if we have the rails it will be easier.'"

After the dinner adjourned to an adjoining drawing room "Stalin came over and sat down beside me and we talked for some time. He said he hoped that I would feel myself completely at home in the Soviet Union; that he and all the members of the Government had felt that I was a friend for so long, that they had such admiration for yourself [FDR] and the things you were trying to do in America that they felt we could co-operate with the greatest intimacy. I told him that you sincerely hoped that war might be prevented in the Far East and that the Soviet Government might work out its great experiment in peace. He said, 'I know that that is what President Roosevelt wants and I hope you will tell him from me that he is today, in spite of being the leader of a capitalist nation, one of the most popular men in the Soviet Union.' . . . As I got up to leave, Stalin said to me, 'I want you to understand that if you want to see me at any time, day or night, you have only to let me know and I will see you at once.' This was a most extraordinary gesture on his part as he has hitherto refused to see any Ambassador at any time. . . . After I had said good-bye to Voroshilov and the others, Stalin went to the door of the apartment with me and said, 'Is there anything at all in the Soviet Union that you want? Anything?'" Bullitt then asked for the fifteen acres in the city park which Stalin granted on the spot. "Thereupon, I held out my hand to shake hands with Stalin and, to my amazement, Stalin took my head in his two hands and gave me a large kiss! I swallowed my astonishment, and, when, he turned up his face for a return kiss, I delivered it." Taking seriously the No-

181

vember professions by Bullitt and FDR of intimate and friendly relations, the Soviet leadership had spent so much effort in wooing Bullitt that he found the evening "unbelievable in retrospect" and would have had "difficulty in convincing myself that it was a reality" if he had not dictated it immediately upon returning to the Hotel.[27]

The following morning, the day of departure from Moscow, Bullitt had a serious and important talk with Litvinoff, who began by asking "whether the Government of the United States would have any objection to the Soviet Government joining the League of Nations." When Bullitt asked why the Soviets were considering such a reversal of its established policy Litvinoff confided that Russia and France intended to make a defensive alliance, and that France was pressuring the Soviet Union to join the League so that the treaty could be brought before the League as a "regional understanding." Although the Soviet Government didn't feel an attack by Germany was imminent, they did greatly fear an immediate attack by Japan and if such a war dragged on Germany or Poland or both might then decide to enter the fray. Bullitt and Litvinoff discussed "ways and means of preventing" an attack by Japan and "Litvinoff suggested that in addition to the supplying of the steel rails, of which Stalin had spoken to me the previous evening, the most effective means of forestalling an attack would be the institution by the United States of proposals for non-aggression pacts between the United States, the Soviet Union, China, and Japan." As Phillips had done in the U.S., Bullitt "explained to him the difficulties in the way of any such proposal. He [Litvinoff] then said that he felt that anything that could be done to make the Japanese believe that the United States was ready to cooperate with Russia, even though there might be no basis for the belief, would be valuable."[28] That afternoon Litvinoff gave a "tremendous reception" for Bullitt and that evening Bullitt left for home.[29] He left with highly romanticized images in his mind of the Soviet leaders. Of Kalinin he had "read that he was a simple-minded old peasant, but he is far from simple-minded. He has a delightful shrewdness and sense of humor."[30] He thought that Molotov had "a magnificent forehead and the general aspect of a first-rate French scientist, great poise, kindliness, and intelligence."[31] He thought that Voroshilov was "one of the most charming persons that I have ever met. He has an immense sense of humor and keeps himself in such perfect physical condition that he looks like a man of 35."[32] Stalin impressed Bullitt as "a man not only of great shrewdness and inflexible will (Lenin, you know, said of him that he had enough will to equip the entire Communist Party), but also possessed of the quality of intuition in extraordinary measure. Moreover, like every real statesman I have known, he has the quality of being able to treat the most serious things with a joke and a twinkle in his eye."[33] Much taken with the men of the Kremlin, Bullitt conversely gave much credence to their expressions of friendship and admiration for himself and his staff. "The men at the head of the Soviet Government today are really intelligent, sophisticated, vigorous human beings and they cannot be persuaded to waste their time with the ordinary conventional diplomatist. On the other hand, they are extremely eager to have contact with anyone who has first-rate intelligence and dimension as a human being."[34] Consequently Bullitt was much impressed when Kalinin "said to a number of people . . . , 'That is the first Ambassador I have met who is also a human being.'"[35] He was pleased when Stalin told him "that we should have received politely any Ambassador that might have been sent us by the Government of the United States, but we should have received no one but yourself in this particular way."[36]

During the toasts at the dinner given by Voroshilov, Litvinoff whispered to Bullitt, "'You told me that you wouldn't stay here if you were going to be treated as an outsider. Do you realize that everyone at this table has completely forgotten that anyone is here except the members of the inner gang?'" Bullitt impressed, concluded, "That certainly seemed to be the case."[37] The Soviet government, having seen real possibilities in Bullitt's talk of friendly relations, certainly knew their man, and Bullitt was completely overwhelmed by the treatment he received. The entire Soviet government had done everything they could to court and flatter Bullitt in expectations of establishing a working relationship with the U.S., but they were too successful. Bullitt's conclusion was that "it is obvious that the Soviet Government values so highly the moral support it may receive from the United States in the matter of preventing war with Japan that there is almost nothing we may not ask for and obtain at the present time." Bullitt had already become convinced of Russia's desperate need for American financial assistance and in Russia he became convinced of that country's great need for American moral support. "I am convinced" he wrote FDR, "that there is almost nothing that the Soviet Union will not give us in the way of commercial agreements, or anything else, in return for our moral support in preserving peace."[38]

After leaving Russia in late December Bullitt went on to Berlin and Paris for other talks. During his stay in Moscow Bullitt had conducted no negotiations as to the final amount of the debt to be paid, but the great solicitousness shown him by the Soviets would serve to strengthen whatever unbending and righteous negotiating position he took when he again addressed that subject.

XI

======

Robert F. Kelley—
The New Positions

FDR HAD BEGUN BY KEEPING THE ECONOMIC ISSUES OUT OF THE
State Department's purview, but the vagueness surrounding the
issue after recognition gave the Eastern European Division an
opportunity to move the issues back into its own domain. At the
cabinet meeting on the day after recognition, Phillips had immediately and instinctively objected when FDR threw the debt
negotiations into his lap. Phillips protested that it was outside
the domain of the State Department and that it was a Treasury
Department function. This soon changed. Within a week the
Eastern European Division, acting through Bullitt, was insisting
to the President that the entire spectrum of economic issues be
placed under the exclusive control of the State Department.
Bullitt successfully gained FDR's delegation of authority for the
State Department and then almost immediately afterwards

185

THE DECISION TO RECOGNIZE

departed for Moscow leaving the matter behind in the hands of Kelley and his staff.

The State Department assumed the task of developing the sketchy proposals for the transfer of blocked marks into a vehicle for Russian payment of the debts. A working committee composed of Moore, Kelley, Hackworth, and John Wiley, who was to be Bullitt's second in command at the new embassy, began investigating what a three-corner transfer of credits would entail.[1] On December 5 Wiley reported to Moore who in turn reported to Phillips that "in seeking means to enable the Union of Soviet Socialist Republics to begin payments on the amounts due the United States in settlement of claims, an examination has been made into the availability of American money frozen in Germany as an offset to Soviet maturities in the Reich. In order to obtain substantial payments from the Soviets, it has been hoped that a substantial amount could be found in order to release Soviet gold and foreign exchange now obligated to Germany. . . . It is proposed to exhaust every avenue of private credit before considering the possibility of the employment of either Government funds or guarantees."[2] Following Bullitt's suggestion the committee contacted John Hancock of Lehman Brothers to investigate the Standstill Agreement and the problem of Frozen Industrial credits.[3] Franklin Field of the Bank of Manhattan was asked to investigate discreetly the availability of the Lee, Higginson credits.[4] James Warburg also visited the State Department twice on the matter. Wiley soon concluded that Warburg's "sanguine assurances that he could hand over the Lee, Higginson credit for us to play with was perhaps inspired more by friendliness than fact." Warburg's lack of real interest in this scheme is reflected in his comments made years later as he looked through his papers and tried to reconstruct his involvement in these events. "I have no idea what this scheme was that Bullitt and Wiley and I discussed. Lee, Higginson did have a large credit to the German government which it had

186

sold on the market here—that I remember. How the hell you would transfer it to Russia in connection with an RFC operation I haven't any idea."[5] However, "based somewhat on Jimmie's optimism," the State Department had developed its original plan to sit "in the background like some benign maiden aunt and platonically arrange for banks and other interested parties in the United States, on their own initiative, to turn over German obligations amounting to from one to 200 million dollars direct to the Soviet Government in return for the latter's long term obligations. This transaction having been concluded, then, and then only, would a revolving credit be set up for the further-ance of American-Soviet trade. For this second operation an Edge plan bank or other financial set-up was contemplated."[6] The original concept that Bullitt had in mind when negotiating with Litvinoff called for dealing with the debt repayment ve-hicle and with trade credits as two separate financial undertak-ings. As indefinite as the Americans were in their minds about exactly what they were suggesting as a debt repayment vehicle, they were even less clear in their minds on the specifics of trade credits due to FDR's insistence upon postponing consideration of the subject until after recognition in order to keep the nego-tiations on a "high plane." This vagueness allowed Kelley much room to maneuver in developing and specifying the nature of the American position on these matters. Regardless of what FDR and Litvinoff had in mind regarding Russian trade, Kelley had in mind from the beginning an Edge Act government controlled bank.

Franklin Field presented three proposals to the State Depart-ment for the sale of the remaining $2,200,000 of Lee, Higginson credits held by the Bank of Manhattan and he said he believed that "other holders of the $50,000,000 held by large banks in the East would agree to these terms." Field also told the State Department that he thought the banks "would be unwilling to accept longer than five-year obligations." The State Department

187

felt "that Field's proposals represent only starting points for subsequent bargaining. However, they are not encouraging from the point of view of long-term principles."[7] And these Lee, Higginson credits would be the easiest to work with since they were the only German obligations which were not very widely dispersed.[8] The State Department felt that these difficulties made the role of a maiden aunt untenable. A telegram signed by Kelley, Moore, and Phillips informed Bullitt that "we are considering the possibility of setting up a financial institution with combined public and private capital which could purchase American owned German obligations in the open market and accept long term Soviet obligations therefore."[9] The State Department was suggesting this new government bank not to control trade but to provide for a debt repayment vehicle. In order to assist with the financial planning Bullitt was asked to "ascertain whether Soviet obligations falling due in Germany are payable in marks or in other foreign currency and what types of paper can be utilized by the Soviet Government without German consent in meeting these obligations. It is suggested that a discussion with the Soviet trade representative in Berlin upon your return from Moscow might yield some information which would be of assistance."[10]

Phillips accepted the necessity of the bank, and on December 9 he wrote a memorandum explaining the subject. "It seems probable that, in order to work out a plan of buying American credits in Germany to be transferred to the Soviet Government to be used to offset the Soviet debts to Germany, it would be necessary to organize a bank of some character to be financed by our Government and private bankers in this country." In fact Moore had that morning been sent to talk with Jesse Jones "about the possibility of the R.F.C. subscribing to the stock of such an institution." However, the concept of the bank was not a static idea and it had already evolved one more step, adding to the proposed functions of the bank another set of responsibilities. Phillips wrote that "in the event a corporation as indicated should be set up, the prospect is that it would go further than merely handling the credits mentioned and take charge and have to do with trading transactions between industries in this country and the Soviet Government." Now for the first time the State Department had found a possible way for implementing the Edge Act Bank that Kelley desired for controlling Russian trade, but it was still at this point strictly a State Department idea. "Of course, all that we are thinking of here would be subject to the President's approval and it is not, at this moment, certain what the R.F.C. will advise or be willing to do."[11]

By December 21 the plans for the Bank had been investigated, and the State Department formally requested Bullitt's consent. "Study and investigation since my telegram of December 8 have convinced us that the transfer to the Russians of American-owned German obligations can only be effected through the intermediary of a financial institution . . . would you be in favor of recommending to the President that authority be requested of Congress to set up an Edge plan or other bank with Government funds and a charter sufficiently broad to effect the German-Soviet transaction and the financing of trade with the Soviet Union."[12] If Bullitt felt compelled to get deeply involved in staff work in order to establish himself before recognition, he certainly felt no such compulsion for such involvement now. He wired back, "If no other method should be practicable I should favor setting up bank."[13] With one short sentence Bullitt readily delegated the determination of a major financial decision to Kelley. He asked no question nor requested any list of particulars. It was simply a straightforward acquiescence to the experts, and one of much future consequence.

Wiley also wrote Bullitt to explain the new bank. "I [Wiley] convinced myself that if anything was to be accomplished in the way of effectively prying loose American-owned German obligations, the Edge plan bank would have to be established as an initial step in order to have an independent agency able to purchase these maturities in the open market; leaving, of course, the revolving or other commercial credit project in abeyance until the consummation of this first transaction."[14] Reflecting Kelley's suspicions, all the State Department personnel involved were already resolved to settle the debt issue before granting any trade credit.[15] This approach served Kelley's purposes because it made trade credits not dependent upon recognition, which had already been secured, but upon a satisfactory settlement of the debt, the only area that had not yet been completely resolved and so remained vulnerable.

The new idea of providing one institution to handle both the debt repayment vehicle and trade credits was a marvelous bureaucratic maneuver. It meant that Bullitt's current mandate from FDR, delegated through him to the State Department, could be used to bring the long-term trade financing apparatus permanently under the effective control of the State Department and consequently under the control of Kelley. The State Department had in fact already been involved over the past decade in hindering the long-term financing necessary for increased trade.

One aspect of the prior Republican Administration's policy of attempting to guide American investments in foreign countries was the classification of "loans to governments not recognized by the United States" as objectionable.[16] Whatever the success of the State Department in preventing other classifications of objectionable loans, in the area of preventing loans to the Soviet Union they were diligent and successful. In his study of the subject, *The Diplomacy of the Dollar*, Herbert Feis said of the State Department's behavior in this area: "Both before and after our recognition of the Union of Socialist Soviet Republics, the State Department discouraged all public credit operations for the Soviet Union."[17]

On January 7th the ship carrying both Bullitt and the new Soviet ambassador to the United States, Alexander Troyanovsky, sailed into the port of New York. In New York Harbor Troyanovsky smiled for pictures until his face was "tired" and talked to reporters, telling them that "he held himself ready to do all in his power to further friendly relations between this country and his own." He expressed himself "happy to come here and eager to meet 'your honorable President, Mr. Roosevelt, clearly a courageous and a wise man'" and he read a short prepared speech that declared: "'We are attached to each other by many common purposes at the present time. We must join our hands and work together to attain these purposes for the well-being of our peoples and the prosperity of all humanity.'"[18]

Troyanovsky had overnight reservations in New York at the Ritz Tower, but he decided to proceed immediately to Washington with Bullitt. Upon disembarkation, Troyanovsky and Bullitt and their parties "went directly to Pennsylvania station and boarded the 10:30 train for Washington." That evening Kelley and Jefferson Patterson of the Protocol Division officially greeted the Russians as they arrived in Washington.[19]

Bullitt had secured in Europe a Soviet list of obligations in reichmarks falling due in 1934 as the State Department had requested, and he also returned with Litvinoff's statements regarding possibilities for future trade.[20] Litvinoff had "expressed the opinion that the United States could not 'take more than $60,000,000 worth of goods from the Soviet Union in any one year, and that if we wanted an export trade with the Soviet Union of more than this amount we would have to extend long-term credits."[21] The Russians made it clear that a large increase in Soviet purchases in America would have to depend upon extension of long-term credits. The Soviet estimate of the amount of Soviet exports that the U.S. could absorb was in the ball park with the figure that Kelley came up with in his Opus

191

7. Although Litvinoff and Kelley agreed on the data, the conclusions they drew from it were completely opposite. Litvinoff thought it a reason to extend credits whereas Kelley considered it a reason to deny them. In any case Litvinoff's position was the position taken by the Soviet Government during the winter of 1933-1934. In late December *The New York Times* quoted Stalin as saying:

> Our more rapid development of foreign trade depends on conditions and the amount of credit. We have never failed to meet our obligations. We might have claimed a moratorium like the rest of them, but we did not because we did not want to break confidence. And confidence, as everyone knows, is the basis of credit.
>
> What I mean is that the volume of our trade with America for the time being must be measured by the degree of confidence America puts in us and this by the volume of credit.[22]

The day after his arrival in Washington Troyanovsky presented his credentials to FDR. Speaking briefly he emphasized the new friendship between the countries and the need for world peace. He concluded by saying "I shall consider it my highest task to do everything in my power toward the creation of the closest bonds of cooperation and friendship between our two nations."[23] When FDR and Bullitt met the same day, their discussion as reported by *The New York Times* concerned "the choice of a staff and of quarters in Moscow."[24] These were things that fascinated both Bullitt and FDR. Financial details bored them. In a 25-page personal letter to FDR reporting on his trip to Moscow, Bullitt devoted only half a page to trade and omitted the debt problem entirely. FDR wrote Bullitt an unusually long reply concerning the minutia of logistics, in which he advised Bullitt to "organize your expedition as if you were setting out on a ship which was to touch no port for a year." FDR advised

192

him that being cut off from civilization he was going to be "more or less in the position of Commander Byrd." FDR explained how Bullitt should handle the five "chief physical problems" of his expedition and FDR was quite specific regarding how some of these problems should be treated. "You should take in with you all typewriters and other office machines and supplies which may conceivably be necessary and should concentrate in the hands of the commissary all purchases of food and other supplies which it may be necessary to purchase in Moscow or to import from Poland or Latvia." FDR advised Bullitt that "you should establish a commissary department either under an expert Naval Quartermaster acting under the directions of this disbursing officer or directly under the disbursing officer." FDR told Bullitt, "You should, I think, set up a small operating room and a room for non-contagious patients and an isolation ward for contagious diseases." And FDR advised Bullitt that because of the "extraordinarily close contact with all the members of your little community, you should exercise exceptional care in selecting men of congenial character and should keep a weather eye out for uncongenial wives."[25] The routine and technical problems of debt and trade were left to the State Department staff.

Bullitt was confirmed as ambassador by the Senate on January 11, and spent much effort on the logistical problems that so fascinated him and FDR. But the major event occurring during the first half of January was the changing shape of the American approach to debts and trade under Kelley's management. By January 16 Kelley was ready to present his conclusion that "it will not be possible to effect a direct exchange of American-owned German maturities for Soviet obligations, at least in any large amount. The amount of German short time obligations held in the United States has been greatly reduced as a result of the extensive liquidation which took place during 1933, and with possibly one exception such obligations are very

193

widely held."[26] The American concept of a debt repayment vehicle that had been relied upon in the discussions with Litvinoff was now recognized as totally worthless. In addition now the original reason for establishing an Edge Act bank no longer existed.

Besides explaining the problem, Kelley used the occasion to stress a theme that he was again stressing very heavily; the uncertainty of Russia's credit standing. "Furthermore," Kelley wrote Moore, "it has become quite evident that American holders of German maturities are not willing at the present time to exchange them for long term Soviet obligations. They prefer apparently to endeavor to work out the best situation they can in their present holdings rather than to shift to the security of a Government where credit has not yet been established."[27] Moore had already been convinced and he suggested to Kelley a way to strengthen the argument before the memorandum was shown to FDR. Moore suggested that when "mention is made of the credit of the Soviet as not yet being established . . . it might not be amiss to add that the possibility of a direct exchange of American demands against Germany for Soviet obligations had diminished because of the apparent general apprehension of an early war between the Soviet and Japan."[28]

The reason for this emphasis upon questioning the credit worthiness of the Soviet Union was that the failure to find a way to transfer the German credits meant that some other means had to be found to extend to the Soviets the funds on which they could pay the old debts as extra interest. One possibility was a straightforward loan as the wording of the "gentleman's agreement" specified. This was anathema to Kelley and he built a consensus against the idea. In doing this he relied upon the same theme that had worked so successfully on Hull back in the fall. Kelley emphasized the high risk involved due to the unsoundness of foreign loans made without any provision for repayment through increased American imports. By mid-January he was in a position to declare confidently that "the flotation in the United States of a private loan to the Soviet Government or the grant of a loan by the Government of the United States to the Soviet Government is out of the question."[29]

In working with Kelley to prepare the information for FDR on the Edge Act bank, Bullitt also became sensitive to the credit risks involved in long-term credits due to the limited Russian exports to the United States. By the time Bullitt returned to the U.S., Kelley's consensus had already been accepted by the State Department, and within two weeks Bullitt too had already fully accepted it. On January 20th the Philadelphia Chamber of Commerce gave a dinner honoring Bullitt, and he began by telling them what they wanted to hear about the growing markets in Russia for American goods. "Demand in Russia today," Bullitt said, "is enormous, and the standard of living is rising, so that new demand is constantly created. . . . In addition to the demand for articles of personal consumption of all sorts, there is also an immense demand for machine tools, various other products of heavy industry, certain minerals, livestock, and some agricultural products. . . . There are few products of the United States for which there is not at least some slight demand in the Soviet Union." Having whetted the appetite of the audience with his vision of potential markets, Bullitt, reflecting his recent sensitivity to credit risk, felt compelled also to caution his audience. "The question of paying for such products is another matter," he warned the businessmen. "We all agree, I am sure, that we want no more of the strange financing of foreign sales which took place during the 1920's and produced the result that we found we had given away our products when we thought we had sold them. We no longer want to send abroad our products and at the same time send abroad the money to pay for them, and then proceed to make payment impossible." Bullitt then told his audience. "If you ask me, therefore, how much the

Soviet Union can buy from us, I must ask you in return how much in goods and services you are ready to take from the Soviet Union . . . if we desire to sell large quantities of goods to the Soviet Union, we must take large quantities of goods from the Soviet Union in exchange. Credits in some measure are no doubt justifiable, but credits merely postpone the day when goods have to be taken, and therefore credits in excessively large amounts must be avoided." But Bullitt warned that even credits in small amounts were risky because "a further question which must be considered when we think of credits and orderly building up of mutual trade is the question of war. A nation may have every intention of paying its bills and may have ample resources to pay its bills, but if it is attacked it must turn every energy to the prosecution of war and in most cases must delay its normal payments. Unfortunately, it is impossible to say that there is no chance of war in the world today."[30] That the emphasis on risk in the speech was indeed significant is attested to by the fact that *The New York Times* made this the headline for its story: "W.C. Bullitt Warns of Soviet Credits."[31]

The repayment of Americans loans by foreign countries was an issue that in the winter of early 1934 was attracting a lot of congressional attention. Concern about the defaults on the war debts was growing in intensity throughout the country, and Congress was responding to the political power of the issue. Hiram Johnson had introduced legislation in the Senate that would make it illegal for the American government or its citizens to buy the bonds of any country that had defaulted upon prior obligations. The Johnson Act as enacted would contain an exemption, however, specifically designed to exclude the Soviet Union, and Bullitt later claimed that FDR had drawn the final draft of the bill himself.[32] Bullitt and Senator and Mrs. Johnson were FDR's dinner guests at the White House on the evening of February 7, and the conversation lasted until 11:20.[33] During his short stay in America Bullitt was involved in a number of other conversations with the President and others who were involved in matters concerning Russia. On February 1, the day before FDR signed the executive order establishing the Export-Import Bank, Bullitt and Jesse Jones visited the President together. On January 17 Bullitt and Warburg met with the President, and on February 6 Bullitt and Hancock lunched with the President. Lunches with the President, suppers with the President and his household, brief consultations or extended evenings of conversation—Bullitt was almost a constant presence at the White House. In the month of late January and early February during Bullitt's brief return to the United States, he visited FDR at the White House a total of fifteen times, not including the evening he attended a ball as part of Mrs. Roosevelt's party. In contrast, Phillips is recorded as having had five meetings with FDR during this period, Hull three, and Moore only one, and Moore's one meeting and one of Hull's three meetings were also attended by Bullitt.[34] During this period FDR was entrusting the technical details of the economic issues to Bullitt, and Bullitt in turn was relying upon Kelley.

Having built his consensus within the State Department, Kelley was in a position to prevent any separate financing, public or private, in place of the blocked marks scheme, and the general acceptance of his Edge Act bank now provided him the happy opportunity to neatly accomplish this. Because the original blocked marks scheme had failed to be workable and because a straightforward loan was out of the question, Kelley suggested that the trade credit of the Edge Act bank be used as the debt repayment vehicle. The two separate functions of arranging the debt payment vehicle and of extending trade credit would hereafter be combined, with the debt repayment vehicle serving a double duty as trade credit. In Kelley's words, "The most expedient way of affording the requisite financial assistance to the Soviet Government [for debt repayment] is through the

197

extension of long-term credits on Soviet purchases in the United States."[35] This was the final transition in the concept of the functions of the Edge Act bank, and it brought all Russian financing under effective State Department control.

In support of the Edge Act bank playing such a central role Kelley extolled the potential advantages of the bank. "Such an institution can be utilized to put American business interests on an equal footing with the Soviet monopoly of foreign trade. Foreign countries have invariably found that their national business interests have suffered severely from the disadvantage under which individual firms have labored in dealing with a State monopoly of foreign trade, which is able, by playing off one firm against another, to force down prices and impose onerous conditions of sale." Kelley explained, "The Soviet Government, realizing the advantage accruing to it, has fought resolutely every effort made to organize in any way into a central unit individual business concerns in foreign countries."[36] Realizing Bullitt's and FDR's desire for good relations with Russia and Bullitt's personal stake in accomplishing this, Kelley included as a sop an estimate of how Russia would react. "Inasmuch as the extension of long term credit is essential at the present time for the expansion of Soviet purchases in the United States, and inasmuch as the Soviet Government undoubtedly realizes that an arrangement of some sort must be worked out to finance the extension of such credits, it will be possible to set up without provoking the opposition of the Soviet Government an institution which can be used to safeguard American business interests in their dealings with the Soviet monopoly of foreign trade. It is highly advisable that advantage be taken of this opportunity."[37] Kelley made this same claim of no Russian opposition again, almost word for word, in a February 23 memo on the purposes of the bank, that was given to both Hull and Moore.[38] Kelley was surely dissembling. Given the best of will on both sides the proposal was bound to cause real difficulties because in all other countries the Soviets had maintained a total separation between the debts of prior governments and the financing of its trade. Even though the Soviets refused repayment of prior government debts to the Europeans, they were still able to use the lure of their markets to secure government guarantees for trade financing of purchases within each country. The Soviet had every expectation, in the light of the negotiations in Washington and the many agreements acceded to and declarations of goodwill given, that they would do better in the United States, but certainly do no worse, than they had in other countries. The combination would also surely raise Soviet protests because Kelley intended to withhold all trade financing of any kind until the old debt was arranged in a satisfactory manner and because he intended to become involved in Russian trade in a way the Russians had not encountered before. Echoing his intentions of the previous fall, Kelley proposed to control every aspect of Russian trade. "Prior to the establishment of the bank in question it is essential that a detailed agreement be reached with the Soviet Government with regard to the amount of purchases which will be made in the United States, the extent and terms of credit to be granted, the modalities of payment, the rate of interest, the settlement of disputes, the use of American shipping and insurance, etc. . . . Simultaneous with the agreement there must be concluded a final settlement of American claims against the Soviet Union in which shall be stipulated the exact amount to be paid by the Soviet Government and the conditions of payment."[39] In addition, Kelley felt that "such an institution can also be utilized to regulate imports from the Soviet Union, discouraging those which are detrimental to American interests and encouraging those which are non-competitive, in order to create a basis for the payment of credits extended to the Soviet Union."[40]

Kelley had already had one opportunity since recognition to guide the State Department's response to the Russians on mat-

THE DECISION TO RECOGNIZE

ters of trade. On November 29 Skvirsky had, in Phillips words, "raised an exceedingly interesting question" by requesting that a Soviet trade commissioner to reside in New York be given diplomatic status.[41] Phillips "replied that I could not give him an immediate answer inasmuch as this was a matter that would require some consideration." Phillips was reluctant to consent and he told Skvirsky that the U.S. had turned down requests from other countries for diplomatic status for commercial representatives. "Skvirsky argued the point by saying that, inasmuch as trade matters were wholly under the control of the Soviet Government, the Russian case was a proper exception."[42] Most countries had allowed Russia this exception, including France, Germany, Italy, and Great Britain. The significant refusal was Japan's. Phillips concluded that "it is a matter on which I shall have to consult the President," but he first referred the question to Kelley and it was still in the Russian Division when Skvirsky pressed Phillips for an answer on December 14, over two weeks later.[43] The reason for the slowness was that the Eastern European Division was preparing a 14-page study on "The Functions and Duties of a Soviet Trade Delegation (A Torgpredstvo) and the Extent to which the Soviet Government has Succeeded in its Efforts to Prevail Upon Various Governments to Accord Diplomatic Status to the Head of that Delegation (The Torgpred)," plus 7 enclosures totalling 35 pages, and a 5-page summary memo to Phillips by Kelley. On December 18 Kelley gave all this to Phillips as his recommendation to not extend diplomatic status because granting "diplomatic immunities to the Soviet Trade Delegation would increase still further the advantage which the Trade Delegation has over American business firms by virtue of its monopolistic character and political control."[44] Phillips talked with FDR on the 19th and must have secured his consent because on the 20th he informed Skvirsky that the U.S. was turning down his request.[45]

The businessmen that Kelley was so anxious to protect were causing the State Department some anxiety in their pursuit of the Russians. Wiley complained in mid-December that the Russians "are beset by self-appointed impressarios ranging all the way from Boris Said, to Hallgarten & Company and even Sullivan and Cromwell. Indeed, rumor has it that the Chase Bank is feverishly studying a deal with Amtorg. . . ."[46] In mid-January Kelley explained to Phillips that his department has been overwhelmed with correspondence since the publication of FDR's exchange of letters with Kalinin on October 20. "Since that date, EE [Eastern European Division] has drafted special replies to 587 letters, has sent out form replies to 701 letters, and has sent to the Stenographic Section for form reply approximately 256 letters . . . which is by far the largest number of communications handled in a similar period in the history of the Division."[47]

On February 2 FDR signed the executive order establishing the Export-Import Bank of Washington created specifically for Russian financing. In researching the legality of providing a new means of extending credits to Russia, the lawyers for the RFC and the Treasury Department had found the going difficult until the General Counsel of the RFC, Stanley Reed, suggested that they could simplify their task by asking FDR what outcome he desired. "If he wants us to find it legal, we can do it. If he doesn't, we can easily give him an opinion, not." Accordingly Morganthau and Oliphant of the Treasury met with FDR and reported back that FDR had said "of course he wanted us to find it legal."[48] The Export-Import Bank, however, was only superficially FDR's creature. FDR's executive order established a five-man board of trustees and the representative of the State Department on the committee was Robert F. Kelley. Also serving an the board were two representatives of the RFC, the Administrator of the AAA and the Secretary of Commerce.[49] As with any such committee the man with the expertise and the interest is effectively in control, and Kelley had both these qualities in abundance. In addition, he also carried the State Department's delegation of authority from the President regarding Russia. Such delegation from FDR was often scattered to the winds, being given to anyone who walked into his office with an interest, but in this case it was for FDR fairly whole, particularly on political matters.

Further consolidating State Department control, Assistant Secretary Moore and three others were added to the board of trustees on February 13, and Moore was elected Chairman of the Board; and on February 27 a three-man executive committee consisting of Kelley, George Peek, and Talley of the RFC was nominated to handle business when the full board was not in session.[50] Although Peek had been a trustee since his appointment with Moore on February 13, this meeting on February 27 was the first that he attended.[51] Peek did so because he had just accepted FDR's offer to be president of the Bank. However the Bank was only one part of his envisioned empire. The previous day Peek had temporarily won a power struggle with the State Department over control of all foreign trade. Phillips had thought it "the biggest blow the State Department has ever received."[52] As a result, although Peek was president of the Bank his attention was focused elsewhere.

Shortly after the establishment of the Bank in early February, Bullitt was preparing to return to Russia. Not having heard anything regarding the American proposals on debt payment financing in over two and half months, the Russians were becoming concerned. Troyanovsky had inquired of Phillips on January 22 as to when "conversations looking to the settlement of claims" would begin, without receiving any definite response.[53] Now that Bullitt was about to depart, Troyanovsky, who was suffering from rheumatism and unable to leave his residence, began pressing Bullitt to visit him and on Friday afternoon, February 10, Bullitt complied with the Soviet ambassador's request. Upon Bullitt's arrival, the Russian ambassador asked him of the progress that had been made, and Bullitt explained to him that the delay had been caused by the establishment of the Export-Import Bank, which Bullitt hoped would begin functioning during the coming week.[54] With the establishment of the Bank the State Department had secured its desired control over the structure of all future financing, and so in early February it changed its focus from debt repayment vehicles to determining how much debt Russia actually owed. Explaining that his opinion was unofficial and not binding, Bullitt told Troyanovsky that he "considered that a payment by the Soviet Government to the Government of the United States of $150,000,000 was an absolute minimum." This first statement of position since recognition immediately eliminated all room for negotiating the difference between the two positions as set forth in the "gentleman's agreement." Bullitt "pointed out that the dollar had been devalued to 60 percent of its former value and that $150,000,000 therefore, represented merely $90,000,000 at the old rate of exchange."[55] Where Kelley and Bullitt came up with this idea is not known, but it certainly was not common or even unusual practice. In contrast, an examination of the American handling of the European war debts shows that devaluations were treated as irrelevancies.

Secretary of State Henry Stimson's fundamental goal in guiding American foreign policy during his tenure had been the maintenance of friendly relations with the European democracies, and in his last months in office he sadly watched the war debts erode the bonds of goodwill that he had worked so hard to preserve. He was aware that "the $95,000,000 of the British payment is equivalent to pretty nearly $150,000,000, owing to the depreciation of the currency," but as much as he disparaged the bitterness stirred up by the size of the debts, the thought of adjusting the amount of the payment to compensate for currency fluctuations was never considered.[56]

Furthermore, the question of whether in early 1934 there had actually been a devaluation of the dollar against the ruble was ambiguous. The State Department's official justification for increasing the Russian debt based upon currency fluctuation was painfully thin. "While, of course, it is true that the foreign exchange rate of the dollar in November was approximately the same as that existing at the present time, it is also true that, if the gold content of the dollar had not been reduced, the foreign exchange rate of the dollar would certainly have strongly tended to move towards the previous gold parity of the dollar and consequently the Soviet Government would pay off its obligation, not on the basis of the foreign exchange rate current in November, but on the basis of a rate approximating the then gold parity of the dollars."[57] This nice piece of convoluted reasoning, firmly grounded upon might-have-been, relies upon a supposed inviolability of the gold value of the dollar which domestically was the very issue that FDR's lack of concern with in regard to Treasury obligations had directly led to the dismissal of Acheson.

After establishing that the maximum settlement in November was now the minimum settlement, Bullitt went on to discuss interest rates. There were two interest rates to consider. The interest on whatever type of new credit the U.S. extended to Russia as a debt repayment vehicle and the additional interest charge to be applied to the new credit as payment of the $150,000,000 of old debt. Bullitt talked of these two having a combined interest rate of 15% and later noted his surprise that Troyanovsky "did not seem shocked by the example I gave him, which would mean a 15 per cent payment."[58] Troyanovsky, however, was attempting to preserve the spirit of cooperation, and this was also reflected in the way Troyanovsky handled

204

a number of minor issues during the meeting with Bullitt. Troyanovsky told Bullitt that his government was considering taking a minority interest in the Scantic Line, which they did not ordinarily like to do, "but that there was such confidence in Americans at the present time that the Soviet Union might be disposed to do this." Bullitt brought up the topic of the building site in the park for the proposed American embassy and asked Troyanovsky for a "promise that at the end of the expiration of the 99-year lease it might be renewed." Troyanovsky replied that "he hoped to be able to bring to the Department on Monday morning a note stating that the lease would be renewable for another 99 years, at the expiration of the first period." The question of whether the embassy clerks in Moscow should be given diplomatic visas was discussed. Troyanovsky "said he was in doubt as to whether or not he could give diplomatic visas to men who were not to go on the diplomatic list in Moscow. . . . He asked me [Bullitt] about my personal secretary and I said that my personal secretary had merely the status of a clerk. He said that he would like to give him a diplomatic visa. . . . He then said that unless he received instructions from his Government to the contrary before Monday morning he would give diplomatic visas to all our officers and clerks."[59] Troyanovsky asked for an appointment with Bullitt on Monday morning to officially discuss the subject of debts. There are no known records to indicate if the Monday morning meeting ever occurred or if it did, what the nature of the discussion was, but Monday was Bullitt's last day in Washington. On Tuesday Bullitt gathered his expedition and left for New York and then on to Moscow.

The Friday meeting marked the zenith in Soviet-American relations of this period because it included the first attempt at specifics by the Americans in discussing the debts. The American proposal would quickly destroy the goodwill of the November negotiations. What is especially curious is that four days before

Bullitt's departure he was still quite vague about the final shape of the American position, omitting some points entirely and speaking strictly off the record. This iš important because it indicates the degree to which Bullitt was entrusting these details to the staff of the Eastern European Division. It is also important because the final position was purported by the State Department to have been written and approved by the President before Bullitt's departure.[60] Between the Friday meeting with Troyanovsky and his departure on Tuesday the White House logs report only one meeting between Bullitt and the President at 4:00 Sunday afternoon.[61] If the logistics of the expedition occupied Bullitt in early January, two days before leaving it was surely his major concern. The exact details of the position that FDR approved, how those details were presented to him, and how closely they coincided with what was actually conveyed to the Russians will probably never be known. However, it is not that relevant, simpy because FDR did not think the debts important, was not interested in discussing them, and was content to leave the matter in Bullitt's hands. What is relevant is that Bullitt's real understanding of what was occurring with regards to the financial negotiating positions is highly suspect.

Bullitt had spent much time choosing the people for the new embassy. He "handpicked all the officers of the first American Embassy staff, either from personal acquaintances or on recommendations of people he trusted."[62] Kelley had very early impressed Bullitt regarding the quality of the people in Riga and in fact Bullitt's handpicked staff was dominated by Kelley's people.[63] The staff included John Wiley as counselor and second in command, and Loy Henderson as second secretary and third in command.[64] Wiley was not a Russian expert but was a professional friend who shared Kelley's outlook regarding communists and with whom Kelley carried on a personal correspondence regarding the politics of Europe.[65] Henderson was also a professional friend of Kelley's and although Henderson "spoke only a little Russian, he had been studying the Soviet Union for a number of years and had pronounced views on the need for taking great care in our dealing with the Bolsheviks."[66] In time Henderson would become Kelley's greatest disciple. Among the younger members of the staff were third secretary George Kennan, vice consul Charles Bohlen, vice consul Elbridge Durbow, and assistant military attache Lieutenant Thomas White, future Air Force Chief of Staff.[67] Kennan and Bohlen, two men who had much to do in later years with the shaping of American-Russian relations, were products of Kelley's scholarly training process.

On February 20th, while Bullitt was enroute to Moscow, Kelley presented the official American position to Troyanovsky. Kelley proposed that the Russian Government "will pay to your [American] Government, in currency of the United States, the sum of One hundred and Fifty Million Dollars ($150,000,000.00), together with interest, in the manner hereinafter provided, the payment to be completed within twenty (20) years."[68] The justification for the insistence upon the maximum figure in the "gentleman's agreement" was the supposed devaluation, but what is entirely new here is the inclusion of interest to be accrued upon the old debt while any portion of it remained unpaid. Not only was interest of this kind never considered during the negotiations in November, but it was so contrary to FDR's approach to foreign debts that one wonders how the State Department ever managed to secure his consent to it. In every negotiation from his discussions with Britain before his inauguration, to "The Bunny" plan in the spring of 1933, to the refinancing of Finland's debt in November of 1933 while Litvinoff was in Washington, FDR was not only willing to forego all future interest beyond a nominal rate of less than 1%, but he was willing to consider all prior interest payments as principal.[69] Furthermore whatever calculations FDR used in November to arrive at the $150,000,000 of old debt still owed

207

by Russia, it represented an implicit forgiving of $145,000,000 of accrued interest on the Kerensky debt.[70]

Kelley went on to explain to Troyanovsky that the interest rate on the $150,000,000 was to accrue continually at 5% and if any interest was not paid when it fell due than it was to "be added to the principal and shall thereafter bear interest at the same rate per annum." Kelley also explained that both the $150,000,000 and the continually accruing interest at 5% were to be repaid by adding 10% to the payments of whatever "credit or loan" was provided by the U.S. as the vehicle for debt repayment. This meant that the added interest was to be paid at the rate of 10%, and that as a result the 15% total interest that seemed so high to Bullitt when he first discussed it with Troyanovsky would probably be near the lower end of the possible range resulting from this approach. If the debt repayment vehicle bore a very low regular interest rate of 4%, then Russia would be required to pay a total interest of 14%, and if the repayment vehicle regular interest rate was 8%, then the total interest would be 18%. Higher regular rates of interest were possible in Kelley's scheme because the added 10% interest as old debt repayment would be due on all "credits or loans" not only made by the United States government but also by "its nationals, or any agency of either." Kelley intended to apply the added interest to all non cash Russian trade with America, whether it in any way involved government financing or not, and to police this he told Troyanovsky that the U.S.S.R. "will submit" to the U.S. "from time to time, as it may be requested, a schedule of all credits or loans extended to it by nationals" of the United States. To be sure that all commercial intercourse between the two countries was covered, Kelley defined when a loan was considered to have been granted. "A credit or loan is deemed to be extended under the above provisions upon either the opening of an irrevocable credit or the granting of a loan."[71] The only area left ambiguous by Kelley was the specific

208

debt repayment vehicle to be used. No specific loans or credits were established or promised.

The Russian had left the negotiations in abeyance so that the American government could work out the details of a complex transfer to Russia of German short-term obligations held in the United States. It was assumed that these three months were being used by the Americans to work out the necessarily complicated financial details of such a proposal. At the State Department's request Litvinoff had the Soviet consul in Paris provide Bullitt with a list of Russian obligations falling due in Germany. The three months were used to good purpose, although not the purpose the Russians suspected. Kelley used this time to build a consensus for concentrating control of all financial dealings with Russia, governmental and private, in his own hands, and to then alter the basic shape of the "gentleman's agreement." Control of private trade financing was a particularly touchy issue and the State Department knew it, cloaking this aspect of the American proposal from American businesses. Later, while contesting this issue with Litvinoff, Bullitt told the State Department, "If we should warn General Motors that Litvinov had agreed to pay extra interest on all such credits, Litvinov would deny the statement promptly and a public controversy might result the domestic political consequences of which I am in no position to judge."[72]

To leave no advantage unspecified the American proposal included a Soviet waiver of "all demands and claims of every character by it or any of its nationals against the United States or any of its nationals." And finally the proposal also specified that the $150,000,000 "shall not include, but shall be in addition to, any assets that have been assigned or released to the United States."[73] If there was any ambiguity in November as to whether the assignment would be included as part of the payment, or in 1937 when Kelley told Morganthau they were included, there was certainly no confusion on the matter now.

209

Kelley clearly specified to Troyanovsky that they were not to be used as offsets against any part of the debt.

Expecting the American proposal to be a specific vehicle for debt repayment, the Russians must have been astounded when the State Department position was a reworking of the "gentleman's agreement" which was entirely contrary to the assumptions and the spirit of the November negotiations. The attainment of a reasonable compromise satisfactory to both sides would certainly have been difficult under the best of negotiating conditions. Consequently it is impossible even to speculate on the kind of agreement that might have been attainable had the U.S. government made any sort of reasonable proposal, or whether an agreement was even possible. However, the broad yet petty alterations of the basic settlement of November immediately changed the atmosphere in which further negotiations would be conducted, and the American refusal to make any significant retreat from its new positions, combined with an insistence that the change was due to Russian bad faith, made any agreement an impossibility. Troyanovsky responded to the proposal by stating that interest was not mentioned in the "gentleman's agreement" and that Litvinoff would take the matter up with Bullitt when he arrived in Moscow.[74]

XII

===

Ambassador Bullitt

OBLIVIOUS TO THE FAR REACHING IMPACT OF THE CODICILS IN-
troduced into the American proposal, Bullitt pushed on to
Moscow expecting to be treated in the same fine manner he
had experienced on his previous trip. "As our train drew into
Moscow station on March 8, 1934, Ambassador Bullitt, noting a
band on the platform, put on his hat and overcoat and prepared for a small welcoming ceremony. But when he stepped
down from the train, he saw that the band, instead of being
opposite his compartment, was facing the third-class cars. The
musicians were there not to welcome him but to greet a delegation of Communist women arriving for the celebration of Red
International Woman's Day. The only Russians meeting the
Ambassador and his staff were the Soviet Chief of Protocol and
George Andreychin, an old friend of Bullitt's."[1] Bullitt had a
lot of other surprises in store.

Litvinoff was hospitalized when Bullitt arrived and so he was not able to meet with him immediately. On March 14 Litvinoff received Bullitt in the hospital and they had their first discussion of the American proposal. "Litvinoff expressed objection to almost every sentence of the draft. . . . He said that he was prepared to suggest $100,000,000 to his Government but without interest. He was vehement in his objection to interest." Bullitt then lectured Litvinoff on economics reminding him "that the dollar had been cut to 60 per cent of its former value and that the Soviet Union no longer ran the risk of the rise of the dollar to parity, that therefore the sum of $150,000,000 actually represented only $90,000,000." After some discussion Bullitt reached his standard unyielding conclusion. "I gathered the impression that we may perhaps be able to get the full $150,000,000. We should certainly hold out for it at present."

In discussing the second paragraph of the American proposal, "Litvinoff took the surprising position that he had not agreed to pay any extra interest on any credits whatever but only on loans to be given to his Government to be used for purchases anywhere. I [Bullitt] combated this assertion as vigorously as possible reminding him that we had had long discussions of the possibility of using frozen American credits in Germany and emphasizing the fact that the President had never had any idea of a direct loan to the Soviet Government but only of a loan in the form of credits. I pointed out that no loan could possibly be made by the United States to any foreign country at the present time and that we had assumed that he was fully aware that a loan in the form of credits was the only possibility."[2]

If it was the settled policy of the U.S. during the negotiations not to extend loans but only credits, Bullitt should have and would have simply referred to such statements when arguing with Litvinoff. Rather, he pointed to their discussion of German debts to America as proof of his intentions. Although this scheme would have provided the funds of American private citizens for the debt repayment vehicle, thereby rendering the use of government funds unnecessary, from the Russian point of view it would have served as a loan. The transfer of German short-term obligations owed Americans to the Russian government, for use as offsets against Russia's own short-term obligations falling due in Germany, would free Russian money slated for Germany for any other use the Russians desired. In fact during the negotiations Bullitt and FDR were confused as to exactly what their position on the matter was because even the major financial specifications were unknown, and as it turned out even the rough features of their position were a chimera because the plan was unworkable. The American position was based upon memory of a vague untenable plan buttressed only by poor, if indeed there were any, written records.

As will become apparent, the loan versus credit argument is something of a red herring anyhow. The real issue was loans versus restricted credits for the purchase of specific American products approved by the American government on an item-by-item basis with no promise or guarantee as to what the final amount of the government's lending would total.

Litvinoff also objected to the 10% rate for the additional interest, but nevertheless Bullitt at the end of the discussion concluded that "in spite of Litvinov's highly unfavorable reception of the State Department draft I derived the impression that if we maintain our position energetically and forcibly we shall be able to arrive at a solution in large measure satisfactory to us."[3]

Bullitt wired this information back to Washington early in the morning of March 15. For all his posturing Bullitt must have had some doubts because he requested a statement of FDR's position. "An instruction from the President stating his point of view in regard to this matter with vigor would be of great assistance to me in subsequent conversations with Litvinov."[4]

The State Department received this telegram of Litvinoff's response to the American proposal at 10:10 A.M. on the morning of the 15th. This was an initial response by Litvinoff made while still in the hospital, but so finely sprung was the State Department trap to respond to "bad faith" that the first Russian reply refusing to accept the American position was of ample weight to trigger the release mechanism. The following day Moore called a special session of the board of trustees of the Export-Import Bank to:

> place before the members of the Board certain information regarding the conduct of the Russian government which he deemed important in view of the proposed activities of the corporation. He said that when Mr. Litvinoff was in the United States, he discussed with the President the matter of the debts owed by the Soviet government to American nationals. Furthermore, that certain definite commitments had been made by Mr. Litvinoff in that connection. He then stated that the State Department had been advised by Mr. Bullitt, who is in Moscow, that Mr. Litvinoff now objected to everything in connection with the proposed debt settlement, and that he [Mr. Bullitt] had been able to secure nothing but "palaver" from representatives of the Soviet Union. In view of the circumstances mentioned, the Chairman stated that in his opinion definite action should be taken by the Board by which it would go on record as opposing the granting of any credits in connection with Russian exports, unless and until the Russian government had reached an agreement regarding its obligations to American nationals which was satisfactory to the President.[5]

Charles Stuart whose memos in October had helped set Kelley's determination for a central bank to control trade into motion was Vice-President of the Export-Import Bank. Stuart didn't

214

see why all trade financing should be blocked and he spoke against the proposal.

> Mr. Stuart said that this same question had arisen in connection with transactions between Russia and other governments; that the latter had invariably gone ahead with normal trade activities before the debt question was settled; and that recently the English had made a new commercial agreement with Russia, notwithstanding the fact that the obligations from Russia to the English were still unsettled. Mr. Stuart expressed the opinion that awaiting settlement of the debt question would greatly delay our Russian trade.[6]

Stuart simply didn't understand what he was up against and how well Kelley had laid the groundwork and built his consensus.

> The Chairman said that some action like that indicated by him was very necessary, particularly in view of the attitude of Congress regarding the making of loans to nations who are in default in their obligations to the United States. He expressed an opinion that considerable controversy could be avoided if the corporation took a firm stand against advancing credit until some definite and satisfactory arrangement was made with Russia regarding the debt situation.[7]

The motion was then passed unanimously that no credit be extended until the Soviet government submitted "to the President of the United States an acceptable agreement respecting the payment of the Russian indebtedness to the Government of United States and its nationals."[8]

Bullitt and FDR were really the only two Americans who had negotiated the economic issues with Litvinoff. Given that neither one had real interest or understanding of the details of

215

the economic issues, they were both to some degree dependent upon the recollection of the other. Had Litvinoff been able to confront them together some possibility of understanding many have been possible. As the situation stood, Moore and the State Department were in the position of interpreting Bullitt on the issue to FDR and FDR on the issue to Bullitt. On March 17 Moore and Kelley wired back to Bullitt that "the President expressly states that he has never had any thought of a direct loan to the Soviet Government and that there is not the slightest possibility of such a loan being made." Whatever ambiguity surrounded the issue in November, FDR was now, according to the State Department's interpretation, firm on this point, but the other facets of the American proposal were another matter. Moore and Kelley told Bullitt that the "President is convinced that the proposal relative to debts and claims which you are discussing with Litvinoff is reasonable but he is willing to give consideration to any not vital modifications insisted upon by Litvinoff which you may recommend."[9] FDR still had faith in and trusted Bullitt and was content to let the delegation for the resolution of the problem remain with him, which given Bullitt's approach to negotiations, however, meant no compromise was possible.

When Bullitt again visited Litvinoff in the hospital on March 18, Litvinoff again "categorically refused to consider anything but a cash loan." Looking everyplace except where the fault lay, Bullitt came to the conclusion that a proposed Swedish loan of a hundred million crowns had "stiffened greatly Soviet attitude" and was the reason for Litvinoff's intransigence.[10] Not content with directing the American government's response to the Soviet government, Kelley soon found the occasion to chide the Swedish ambassador for this proposed loan by his government. "I said that I was very much surprised to note that the Swedish Government was undertaking to make a loan of a hundred million crowns to the Soviet Government without making an effort to reach a settlement of its claims against the Soviet Government. I thought that Moscow would have good cause for celebrating this achievement, particularly in view of the fact that it constituted the first loan received by the Soviet Government from a foreign Government."[11] The interest on this proposed loan was to be 5 1/2%.

Three days later on March 21, Bullitt again visited Litvinoff in the hospital, and again Litvinoff insisted upon a loan as the debt repayment vehicle, although he said he might accept the stipulation that the entire amount lent be spent in the United States. Bullitt responded with characteristic restraint, telling Litvinoff "that if his position should be unalterable I would wish to cable the President immediately so that the Export-Import Bank might be liquidated at once and all thought of trade with the Soviet Union abandoned." To complement the pressure he was putting on Litvinoff in Moscow, Bullitt wired the State Department to put pressure upon Troyanovsky in Washington. "It seems to me highly desirable that the Johnson Bill should be passed as soon as possible and that the Department should adopt a firm attitude with Troyanovsky and bring to his attention the revulsion of feeling which would be likely to take place in the United States if the Soviet should so soon after recognition fail to continue the policy of cooperation between our two countries." Bullitt's approach to bargaining remained the same as always. "Previous negotiations with Litvinov have led me to observe that his decisive negotiations are often followed by acquiescence and I do not consider the present problem insoluble."[12] A few days later Secretary of State Hull found the occasion to put Bullitt's advice into practice. In response to a question from Troyanovsky as to the failure of the Export-Import Bank to supply credit either to Russia or to American exporters for the financing of Russian-American trade, Hull told Troyanovsky that all the Americans who had negotiated with Litvinoff last November "were greatly surprised and keenly disappointed to learn that Mr. Litvinoff offered a contention and a version of the debt understanding . . . entirely different from anything the American officials thought they were discussing and entirely different from anything they were thinking about . . . that my government officials were so surprised and disappointed at this, to them, new and strange and unexpected contention of Mr. Litvinoff, which showed such a wide misunderstanding, that it would perhaps be best to bring all commercial and financial relations to a standstill until there could be a clarification of these misunderstandings; that this included the deferment of credits by the so-called Russian Export-Import Bank here."[13]

Rather than disputing with Troyanovsky the issue of loans versus credits, Hull complained about the Soviet failure to accept interest on the unpaid old debt. "Our government," Hull said, "could not for a moment justify to Russian creditors in this country a settlement for a given amount of money payable without any interest at the end of 20 years." Hull said "that since a fair rate of interest would double the principal within a 20-year period, it was patent that merely to propose payments in 20 years was equivalent in a large sense to nothing at all."[14] Hull, of course, was right. Interest on the old debt accruing over twenty years would double the total amount paid in settlement of the American claim. By demanding this interest the State Department had significantly altered, in fact doubled, the amount agreed to in the "gentleman's agreement," while righteously accusing the Russians of perfidy. More to the point, the difficulties created by this assiduous concentration on meaningless financial details not only was irrelevant to the implementation of FDR's strategic intention in granting recognition but was actually serving directly to subvert it.

The State Department had so successfully linked the Russian perfidy in not paying their old debts with all other economic intercourse between the two countries that when Voroshilov asked Bullitt about the two hundred thousand tons of used steel rails that Stalin had specifically requested, Bullitt held it too as hostage to the debt settlement. "I [Bullitt] explained to him in detail the impossibility of any credits being granted until the Soviet Government settled its debts to the Government of the United States."[15]

On April 2 Litvinoff made a counter proposal. If the United States would lend the Russians an amount double to whatever the Russians agreed to pay on their old debts, they would use these funds only for purchases within the U.S. They would pay 4% regular interest and 3% additional interest as repayment of the old debt, but no interest would accrue on the unpaid portion of the old debt. Bullitt did not think much of this counter offer, but considered it "a retreat" from Litvinoff's earlier positions. Bullitt had heard a rumor that the Swedish Parliament had refused to vote for the proposed credit to Russia and he thought that as a result Litvinoff would be "more amenable."[16]

Since the Americans were renegotiating positions thought to have been established in November, Litvinoff reopened the question of the validity of the debts incurred by the Kerensky government. He said that the documents received from the State Department in Washington "revealed the fact that the Kerensky Government had received almost none of the funds placed at its disposal by the Government of the United States and that Bakhmetieff and Ughet had used these funds for the support of themselves and various armed attacks on the Soviet Government. He mentioned specifically Yudinich and Denikin. He said that he would have a dossier ready for me on this subject within two or three days which he was sure would appeal to the fair mindedness of the President." This was a bargaining ploy only, and Litvinoff admitted that "he was still ready" to recommend the payment of $100,000,000 he agreed to in Washington if FDR should insist.[17] What is interesting, however, is the State Department response. "Mr. Litvinoff probably knew when he was in Washington how the proceeds of the Kerensky loan were expended, but even if what he states were true the rights of our Government as a creditor would not be weakened, since it incurred no obligation to control the expenditure."[18] This is a different perspective on the Kerensky debts that one receives from reading Kelley's pre-recognition memos. There was in fact a good deal of slipping and sliding on this issue by the State Department. From here forward, the State Department began to emphasize the use of the debt settlement as compensation for private claims against the Soviet government rather than as compensation for the Kerensky debts. In early May the State Department instructed Bullitt that "in case a debt agreement is reached, it is probable that substantially all of the total to be paid will inure to the benefit of the private claimants."[19] And on May 15 the State Department instructed Bullitt that "since there has been much reference made to the 'Kerensky' obligations, Soviet government should realize that amount received on debt would be mainly for the benefit of claims of our nationals although we cannot make any stipulation to that effect."[20] The reason that no stipulation could be made to that effect was that the State Department was ignoring this aspect of the claims entirely and relying totally on the Kerensky debts as the basis of the American position in its communications with the Attorney General's office. After passage of the Johnson Act in early April the State Department had addressed a list of questions to the Attorney General in order to determine the proper interpretation of which nations were in default. The questions concerning clarification of the Act with regards to Russia were based completely on the indebtedness of the Kerensky government.

> Is the present Soviet Government, as the successor to prior governments of Russia, to be regarded as in default, in view of the fact that no payment has been made on the bonds issued to the Government of the United States by

the Kerensky Government, on account of loans made to that government by the United States during the period of the war, the Kerensky Government having been the immediate predecessor of the Soviet Government.[21]

When the Attorney General's decision was made public in early May it was noticed that the opinion was "based upon the designation of the Russian indebtedness to our Government as the *Kerensky* debt." The State Department responded to this by stating: "While the Kerensky debt was mentioned in one of the questions propounded by the State Department to the Attorney General, the latter's answer, which contains no specific reference to the Kerensky debt, is that the Soviet Government is responsible for the obligations incurred by prior Russian Governments. The fact is that some, but not all, of those obligations were incurred during the Kerensky premiership, and that they are at this moment in default."[22] This default under the provisions of the Johnson Bill now became the justification for continuing to maintain the Export-Import Bank loan restrictions.

After receiving Bullitt's summary of Litvinoff's new offer the State Department dismissed it out of hand. The idea that the principal of the new loan would not be repaid for 20 years was "unreasonable, not to say fantastic."[23] The interest rates were inadequate, and even if the Soviets used the total amount of the loan for the purchase of American goods, this was still a loan from the State Department view. This last point was critical. If a lump sum was made available to the Russians to spend as they saw fit in America, they could operate independently of American governmental control, a development that Kelley was dedicated to preventing.

On April 8 Bullitt told Litvinoff of the State Department's response to the Russian counter proposal. Bullitt "told him that his proposal was entirely unacceptable even as a basis of discussion and asked him if he had anything to add to it. He said he had nothing to add." Litvinoff "was angry and adamant. He refused to take the State Department draft as a basis of discussion either now or hereafter, alleging that it was in absolute contravention of his understanding with the President. He said that any fair minded person could judge that the State Department draft contemplated not a loan or a credit but a taxation of Soviet trade."[24] Kelley's blithe assurances in January and February to the contrary, the Russians did indeed object to the mixing of the debt repayment vehicle with trade financing, and even without Russian documents it is not hard to understand why.[25] The Soviet government had not paid any other nation the debts of prior Russian governments, and this had not interferred with the willingness of those other nations to foster trade. The Soviet government had not signed religious agreements, or such broad anti-propaganda documents, or agreed to pay a specific amount of the old debts with any of these governments. They had agreed to do these things with the American government, and the American government was now insisting that all trade, government financed or otherwise, would require an extra 10% payment to make up for the old debt and its continuously accruing interest.

Bullitt "asked Litvinoff if he had considered the consequences of his attitude, pointing out that the credit markets of the United States would be open to nations not in default and would remain closed to the Soviet Union until an agreement has been reached. He said that he was fully aware of this and was not disturbed. He added that the Johnson Bill presumably applied to England, France, and Italy, as well as the Soviet Union and said, 'we shall be in very good company.'"

Also using a gentle touch Litvinoff told Bullitt: "'This means that we shall buy nothing henceforth in the United States. We can cover all our needs in other countries and shall do so!'"

Bullitt referred to the effect this would have on relations between the two countries, and Litvinoff replied that "the relations of the Soviet Union with France, England, Italy and other countries had been amicable without the settlement of debts and claims and that there was no reason why the relations of the Soviet Union with the United States should not remain amicable under similar circumstances."

Bullitt asked him if there were anything else he could offer as a counter proposal and Litvinoff said that he made his maximum offer and so far as he was concerned the matter was closed. Bullitt told him that a consequence of this attitude might be an announcement by the United States government "that no credits of any kind would be permitted for Soviet trade."

Litvinoff "replied that that had already been announced in Washington and added that the public announcement by the Board of Directors of the Export-Import Bank that no credits would be extended to the Soviet Union had been a badly advised threat designed to bring pressure on the Soviet Union. He said that the Soviet Union would never be moved by such a threat."[26]

The resolution of the Export-Import Bank had also been given the same emphasis in the Soviet press. In the "official organ of the Commissariat for Heavy Industry" the Russians editorialized that "it is difficult to imagine that the authors of this resolution are thoroughly aware of the serious threat it constitutes to American-Soviet trade, which, it appeared, had finally, to the mutual advantage of both countries, been placed on the way to a wider development. Otherwise it is impossible to imagine such a resolution being passed by a bank especially created for the encouragement of trade."[27] Actually the Russians were closer than they thought to the true reasons, but guessed that the purpose of the resolution was to force special concessions and warned that the attempt would be fruitless.

This conversation between Bullitt and Litvinoff was particularly bitter, and Bullitt recommended to Washington that the

American government make no move until Litvinoff "has had time to be impressed by an attitude of complete negation on our part." For the first time Bullitt had an inkling that the Russians may not be sufficiently dependent upon American credit that they could be forced to accept American proposals, but the die had already been cast. "I am not sure that a firm attitude by the United States will result in a retreat by the Soviet Government but feel that whatever the result, our present line should be followed to the end." Bullitt told Washington that his attitude in the face of this adversity would be to "cultivate tranquil personal relations and to act as if the question of debts, claims, and trade did not exist," and then immediately following this he recommended abandoning "the idea of opening consulates in Vladivosktok and Odessa this summer."[28]

About a week later Troyanovsky received new instructions from Litvinoff to meet with FDR "to present Litvinoff's view and that of his Government." Seeking this interview at the State Department, Troyanovsky said that "Litvinoff was very much disturbed about the reports he had changed his position."[29] One point which Litvinoff particularly wished Troyanovsky to clarify with FDR was the specific form that the American credits would take. Solving this issue was supposedly the reason for the delay in the discussions over the winter and the Americans had not yet been specific on the matter. At the State Department Troyanovsky singled out the interest on the unpaid debts as objectionable to the Russians and was told "that when the existence of a debt was admitted interest accrued on it until payment unless there was something said or understood to the contrary."[30]

Because of the Russian pressure, Moore sought FDR's approval for what was being done, and again FDR left the matter in Bullitt's hands. Moore wired Bullitt that FDR "has entire confidence in you and you are at liberty in your own tactful way to intimate to Litvinoff how the relations of the two countries may be unfortunately affected by failure to agree, this having reference to construction of buildings, establishing consulates, et cetera." "He concurs in your thought we should await further suggestion as to debts which we believe may be expected." FDR also indicated again that he was not wed to the American position and indicated his willingness to negotiate. In fact, FDR seemed "inclined to go much further" than Moore "in modifying the original debt proposals" and Moore had to "suggest to him the difficulty he would find in doing what" he had "tentatively in mind." By official State Department communication Moore reported to Bullitt that if the Soviets made a new proposal FDR "may indicate some modifications he is willing to accept."[31]

Two weeks later Moore wrote Bullitt that "speaking very personally, I think the President is most anxious that an agreement should be reached, and will take a very liberal view of any proposal you extract from Litvinov. . . ."[32] Such were the dynamics of the State Department that this strongest indication of FDR's willingness to compromise could not be sent by official cable and was unofficially transmitted by personal letter between old friends.

On May 2 Troyanovsky received in the presence of Hull and Moore his interview with FDR, but the President maneuvered the discussion so that the negotiations would still remain in Bullitt's hands. Troyanovsky "was told that the negotiations should not be transferred to Washington but continued at Moscow, particularly in view of the fact that you [Bullitt] and Litvinoff are thoroughly familiar with all that occurred here last fall, and the interview ended with that understanding. The President could not well decline his request out of hand but made it clear to Troyanovsky that what the latter suggests is the slowest method because on every proposal that might be made in Washington we should have to consult you and he would have to consult Litvinoff." In summary, Bullitt was told that "there is really nothing concrete to say except that the President leaves the negotiation in your hands without having made any committal or statement conflicting in any way with what you have done or anticipating what you may attempt to do."[33]

Upon learning the results of this discussion and that Troyanovsky had not presented any new Russian proposals, Bullitt concluded that it would be bad strategy for him to seek to reopen negotiations and that he would wait for Litvinoff to make the next move.[34] After a routine visit a week later, Litvinoff asked Bullitt to remain and discuss the debts. Litvinoff was not happy with the results of Troyanovsky's discussion with FDR, and he told Bullitt that "he had sent Troyanovsky a severe reprimand for having failed to take up with the President the main disagreement in principle." Litvinoff explained to Bullitt that he had ordered his ambassador to discuss in detail with FDR an "'agreement in regard to the form of credits.'" Troyanovsky had reported back to Litvinoff that "the Department had expressed the opinion to him that the question of the form of the credits was merely a minor matter; that the total sum to be paid was the only stumbling block." Litvinoff told Bullitt that "he feared Troyanovsky's faulty knowledge of English rendered him incompetent." After a long discussion Litvinoff made a new proposal in which he tried to fix clearly the variables associated with an American credit. He proposed that in return for the Soviet's payment of the old debt the United States provide a credit "to the amount of X million dollars at the rate of Y percent, the bills of exchange to mature in Z years." Litvinoff "insisted that the amount X should be double the amount to be paid in settlement of debts." He was open as to the amount of interest Y and "insisted that the maturity period Z should be twenty years but indicated he was ready to discuss X, Y and Z provided agreement could be reached in regard to the form of credit."[35]

In reply to this information the State Department failed to confront the specific form of credit, which Litvinoff had indicated was the crucial issue, so Bullitt wired back asking detailed instructions from the Department.[36] Bullitt said that "to obtain from him [Litvinoff] a promise to pay a fixed amount of indebtedness unless he is promised a fixed amount of credits for fixed periods I believe will be impossible. Is the bank prepared to fix definitely the amount and duration of credits to be extended regardless of credits which may or may not be extended by American corporations or individuals and regardless of conditions in the Soviet Union?" "At the present moment it will be difficult if not impossible to tie the Soviet Government to a definite fixed engagement unless the bank is ready to make a definite commitment. If we wish to reach a settlement now we must face this refractory fact."[37] For the first time Bullitt asked the State Department to make a specific commitment, and for the first time Bullitt seriously discussed a compromise on interest rates, but it was already too late to accomplish an agreement. In Washington Bullitt's direct access to FDR made his consent to any proposal essential, and Bullitt had freely delegated those financial affairs that he chose not to handle. In Moscow, as ambassador, he had to look to the State Department for guidance. He had already delegated the financial details to Kelley's control and now Kelley, as chief of Bullitt's division, as the acknowledged expert on Soviet affairs, and as the representative of the Export-Import Bank, became the man in control. After receiving Bullitt's telegram on the afternoon of May 13, Kelley called a meeting of the Executive Committee of the Bank for 9:00 A.M. on the 15th.[38] The Executive Committee consisted of George Peek, Lynn Talley, and Kelley, and after Kelley "briefly summarized the substance of earlier cables interchanged by the State Department and Ambassador Bullitt" the Executive Committee prepared a reply: "Bank is not prepared to fix definitely aggregate amount of credit to be extended to American exporters. Such credits will be negotiated between Bank and exporter based on agreement between respective

227

governments as to character and amount of exports and imports."[39] Diminishing or avoiding entirely the problem this approach would cause with the Russians, the Executive Committee concluded, "Control and placing of orders fully protects Russians."[40]

At noon on May 15 the State Department sent Bullitt the following telegram. "While the Bank is anxious to proceed and can be relied on for immediate large credits, it can not be expected to specify in advance the total credits for any one year or the maximum or minimum of individual transactions. Credits will be negotiated between Bank and Exporter on basis of general agreement with Soviet government covering character and amount of exports and imports. Of course, as heretofore stated, Bank must reserve its right to approve any and all transactions since otherwise it would be placing the business of this country with the Soviet Union under the control and direction of the Soviet Government. Endeavor to provide that in case of war we may suspend shipments."[41]

This was an open issue when the discussions were suspended in November, and now in May the State Department had at last clarified its position. In return for Russian payment of claims, the U.S. would guarantee no specific amount of credits. If the first American proposal had clearly stated that this was the nature of the intended debt repayment vehicle, it might have made the shifting of the onus of failure to the Russians more difficult. As things stood Bullitt simply accepted these instructions and the next day he called on Krestinsky and Rubinin of the Soviet Foreign Office who were filling in until mid-June for the absent Litvinoff. Bullitt began by presenting the original American offer to the Russians, proposing "that we should attempt to define our exact points of disagreement." Krestinsky refused, saying "that it was impossible to discuss details such as total indebtedness and interest rates so long as there was no agreement on the basic question of the form of credit." Bullitt then presented the State Department's position to the Russians, and "after a long fruitless discussion Krestinsky said: 'Please inform your Government that we will have nothing to do with financial standing of American corporations for credits in which the Export-Import Bank will participate. Either a credit at the bank for double the amount of debt payment or a flat agreement by the bank to discount 100% Soviet obligations to twice the amount of the debt payment is a sine qua non for any settlement."[42]

This in effect ended the period of hope. The gap between the two sides was now clearly defined and manifestly unbridgable. The negotiations struggled on, but all goodwill had been dissipated on both sides and no old debts were ever paid. In American minds, Litvinoff had reneged upon his agreements just as Kelley had predicted, and having forecast Russian behavior Kelley became stronger than ever. Bullitt came to believe that the failure of the Russians to live up to their word resulted from the fact that the immediate danger of war with Japan had passed, and now the Russians did not need the Americans any longer. "The nub of the matter is this: If the Soviet Government should again become convinced that an attack by Japan was likely or imminent we should probably find Litvinov willing to reach an agreement on the basis of our proposals. So long as the Soviet Union feels completely secure I believe that no agreement acceptable to us will be acceptable to the authorities in Moscow."[43] The thought that the American proposals were a change from what had been agreed to and that the Russian behavior was a direct result of that change never entered Bullitt's mind, nor for that matter did it occur to many other Americans. It certainly never occurred to anyone in the State Department. The only American concerned with these events who seemed to have such a thought was Charles Stuart, the Vice President of the Export-Import Bank. In late July after being made aware of the "gentleman's agreement" and being brought up to date on the State Department negotiations, he wrote a report on the matter for George Peek. His opinion was that the American interest rates "may be regarded as excessive" and that the Russian "scheme is fantastic" (totally unrealistic), but "I do not see that we can necessarily accuse them of actual bad faith if we are unable to arrive at figures" that are mutually acceptable.[44] Stuart, however, was at the periphery of these events. Bullitt was at the center, and he had no doubts as to Litvinoff's lack of integrity. He wired Washington that "as I am compelled by my official position to maintain amicable relations with Litvinov it is somewhat difficult for me to accuse him of bad faith."[45]

In spite of Litvinoff's bad faith, Bullitt was still resolved to maintain the best face on the situation. "In the handling of relations between countries so widely separated in ideas, structure and distance as the United States and the Soviet Union," he wrote, "it seems to me of vital importance that minor vexations should not be permitted to produce an atmosphere in which a mutually beneficial cooperation cannot thrive. In Moscow we are subjected to a hundred such irritations daily and it is, I feel, our duty to endure them with equanimity and to preserve our wrath for major issues. We cannot forget that at any time the lines of major policy of the United States and the Soviet Union may run parallel."[46] Bullitt's intentions were high, but he didn't have the personality to maintain that kind of resolve. One constant source of irritation to him was his dream of Monticello in Moscow. His building plans ran into a thousand Soviet obstructions, including the necessity of a permit for each individual tree that would have to be cleared for the construction.

> With difficulties piling up, Bullitt tended more and more to believe that Litvinov was acting on his own and was not giving a full account of the discussions to Stalin. His face flushing and his eyes popping, Bullitt told me [Charles Bohlen] one day of his suspicions that Litvinov

was double-crossing him. . . . Bullitt went to the length of enlisting the old Bolshevik Radek to check on what Litvinov was telling Stalin. . . . He told Bullitt that Litvinov's reporting was without any noteworthy distortions. Bullitt, however, continued to make a sharp differentiation between Litvinov and the other Soviet leaders and thought that a lot of the troubles were due entirely to the Commissar's intransigence.[47]

When Litvinoff returned to Moscow in mid-June he accepted the situation with apparent equanimity, considering a successful resolution hopeless. Litvinoff told Bullitt that "he and his Government were entirely ready to let the matter drop immediately and permanently." Litvinoff said, "'there is no misunderstanding' and asserted that the Government of the United States was attempting to back out of a verbal agreement." When Bullitt delivered one of his usual warnings regarding dire consequences to "close collaboration" Litvinoff said, "'I do not take the matter so tragically.'" He told Bullitt that, since all nations had defaulted, "no one will be able to make propaganda against the Soviet Union if we do not pay one dollar on a debt we did not contract" and that collaboration could be carried on regardless of the debts.[48] Bullitt then told him how he thought the American government would characterize the position of the Soviet government should the debts remain unpaid.

> We shall make no payments either to the American Corporations or individuals whose property we have seized. We shall make no payments on our indebtedness to the Government of the United States and we shall buy nothing in the United States. We shall, however, expect the Government and people of the United States to work with us loyally and intimately.[49]

Bullitt, of course, was right. Litvinoff and FDR may have considered the economic issues dispensable, but they were in fact crucial to the further development of political relations. The failure to reach a settlement of these issues poisoned the well for both sides. Over the next year Bullitt himself became increasingly disillusioned with the Soviet Union. "It soon became evident," he wrote of these events, "that the Soviet government had signed the agreements only to obtain recognition and had no intention of keeping them."[50] Bohlen records that "eventually, Bullitt became so bitter an enemy of the Soviet Union that he favored a Franco-German rapprochement."[51]

Moore also came to the conclusion that Litvinoff's mission was deceitful in intent from the beginning, as Kelley had always warned. "It is now quite apparent that Litvinov when he was here was not serious about any phase of the negotiation except recognition, and that he is now indifferent to all the assurances he gave in respect to other phases."[52] Phillips felt that Litvinoff was "going back on all his oral pledges with respect to reaching a settlement of debt owing the United States and American nationals."[53] Putting the best face on these events after the alliance with Russia in World War II, Hull recalled "a careless or indifferent observance by the Soviet Government of some of the agreements entered into."[54] In fact Hull and his Department considered the failure of the debt negotiations a manifestation of Soviet bad faith. But Bullitt, Moore, Phillips, and Hull were men of the current era. There was a time capsule quality to the lessons learned during the first six months of 1934, and these lessons would later serve as a fundamental experience in Russian relations for the young men who were the new generation of Russian experts. They would all remember this early lesson years later when they attained positions of influence within the government.

Bohlen entitled the chapter in his autobiography of this period "The Shattering of Illusions." "Like Bullitt," he wrote, "I, too, suffered disillusionment during that first year." Bohlen considered it probable "that Litvinov's shifts of position and concentration on specific details such as 'loan' versus 'credit' reflected . . . a change in the Soviet government's attitude on foreign policy" resulting primarily from a diminished fear of Japan.[55] The lesson learned was "the importance of precision in dealing with the Soviet Union and of leaving nothing to chance or to the generalized belief in the good faith of your partner."[56]

Kennan also believed that Litvinoff had been insincere in his negotiations with FDR in November, and that the Russians had never intended to pay the old claims. "Needless to say," he later wrote, "the Soviet position on this item stiffened, once recognition was in the bag, and no final agreement was ever arrived at."[57]

Trade was affected as well. On March 29, 1934 Amtorg approached Anderson, Clayton & Co. with an offer to buy 30,000 bales of cotton on 2 1/2 year terms. Will Clayton refused, telegraphing the Export-Import Bank that he did so partly because he feared he would be unable to "participate in arrangements you may work out for refinancing sales."[58] Bohlen, Kennan, Clayton, Henderson—these men would be around when FDR was gone and a new policy towards the Russians was being shaped, and they and their peers would all share the common memory of Litvinoff's deception.

It is impossible to say what affect this encounter had on the leaders of the Soviet Union and what common perception the members of the Soviet foreign office formed of America, but it is likely the results were as profound. The Soviets had acceded to all the American demands during the recognition negotiations and had courted Bullitt on his trip to Moscow as well, complying with whatever requests Bullitt made of them, but when the time came for the Americans to carry out their part of the bargain they reneged. At the end of World War II the Soviets would have the American bad faith to look back upon just as the Americans had the Russian bad faith to consider. Stalin was not the sort of man who did not learn from wasted kisses.

By early summer Bullitt began to assume that Litvinoff's failure to reach an agreement revealed a fundamentally hostile attitude towards the U.S. "I venture to express the opinion," he said to the State Department, "that so long as Litvinov adheres to his present attitude toward the United States we shall not be able to count on any genuinely friendly cooperation from him either at the forthcoming naval conference or elsewhere. . . ."[59] Far more important than personalities was the general conclusion that the State Department was working towards. Kelley had always argued that debts had to be settled before recognition, because if they were not settled friendly relations would be impossible. Now that it appeared that debts were not going to be settled, the idea that normal relations in other matters would be precluded gained credence. This assumption affected others besides Bullitt. In August Hull told Troyanovsky that "if it were not possible for the two Governments to reach a solution of the problem in hand, the first one to come to their attention and, in the Secretary's opinion, a relatively minor one, it could hardly be expected that they could collaborate with regard to larger world issues. . . . Certainly if the Secretary and Mr. Troyanovsky were not able to come to an agreement with regard to this minor matter, it would be quite futile to expect that when America representatives met Soviet representatives in London, Paris, Geneva, or elsewhere, any discussions between them would produce any fruitful results."[60]

To support the contention that deceitful behavior by the Soviets rendered international cooperation with them futile, the Eastern European Division was continuing to collect and disseminate examples of Soviet violations of the anti-propaganda pledge. Such Communist International proclamation as an early January 1934 statement that "in the United States there is a wave of mass strikes of workmen and indigent farmers against the bourgeois program of overcoming the crises" were diligently reported to Washington by the legation in Riga.[61] In early March, even before Bullitt's arrival in Moscow, Moore reported to Hull that "we are carefully watching for provable instances of the violation of Litvinov's promise to the President to prevent communist activities being projected from Russia and conducted in the United States with the encouragement or approval of the Soviet Government. Already there is pretty definite evidence of two or three such violations and as soon as more are discovered in the near future the facts will be brought to your attention to be dealt with by you in such manner as you may deem best."[62] By late May Hull was informing Bullitt that "from documents submitted to the Department it seems fairly certain that the propaganda pledge is being violated by activities stimulated and directed at Moscow."[63] By late June Moore was confronting the Russians with the issue. "I [Moore] said to Mr. Troynavosky that his own Government seems to have violated its pledge against propaganda by permitting the Third Internationale to send out from Moscow urgent suggestions that Communists everywhere should seek the overthrow of our Government and other governments by violent methods."[64] Although FDR disdained such rhetoric as nothing more than technical violations, by August Hull was accusing the Russians of bad faith in signing the anti-propaganda pledge.[65]

Helping Bullitt in Moscow interpret the debt, propaganda, and other issues in contention were the senior embassy staff. In intellectual attitude and gut feeling, they had the same outlook towards the Soviet Union as did Kelley, and from the beginning they helped shape Bullitt's evolving understanding of the nature of the Soviet Union. On April 13, in his first letter to FDR since his arrival in Moscow, Bullitt explained to the President why "the honeymoon atmosphere" had evaporated completely before his arrival. He wrote the President, "As Wiley says, 'the Japanese have let us down badly.' The Russians are convinced that Japan will not attack this spring or summer and, as they no longer feel that they need our immediate help, their underlying hostility to all capitalist countries now shows through the veneer of intimate friendship."[66] Kelley could not have put it any better. Henderson, however, not Wiley, was probably the most influential member of the staff. By default, Henderson ran the operation. He was "in effect, the administrator of the Embassy, since neither Bullitt nor Wiley was particularly gifted in that field."[67] As chief political officer of the embassy it was Henderson's function to interpret Soviet behavior for Bullitt, and Henderson brought to the job not only a preconceived perception of Soviet Russia but a strong and impressive personality. Kennan described Henderson during this period as "a man of so active an intelligence, such deep seriousness and impressive sincerity, and such unbending conscientiousness not only in the performance of his duties but in his entire effort to cope with the problems presented to us by Soviet communism, that he left his impression on everyone who was associated with him."[68] Bohlen described Henderson as "a man with a high sense of duty and honesty, he would go to any trouble to help a younger staff officer, of which I was one, to learn his trade. . . . During Stalin's great purges, when Henderson was chargé d'affaires for at least two years, he wrote some brilliant dispatches from Moscow."[69]

With the help of these men Bullitt came over the next year to accept the attitude of the State Department's Russian experts. The incident which finally drove Bullitt to believe that normal relations between the two countries were not possible occurred in the summer of 1935 when the Soviet Union hosted a meeting of the Communist International. This meeting of the Comintern was, in spite of the obligatory rhetoric, an abandonment of revolutionary action in an effort to strengthen European governments in their resistance to Nazi Germany. Bullitt, now

236

sharing the attitudes of the Russian experts, was outraged over what he considered to be a flagrant violation of the terms of the anti-propaganda pledge, and confident that communist theoretical writings automatically determined all communist behavior, he misinterpreted the meaning of the event. Bullitt viewed this as a complete breach of faith, and his initial optimism was now fully replaced by a furious bitterness. Kennan noted of these events that Bullitt became "the advocate of a hard line toward Moscow, a line which most of us in the embassy wholeheartedly supported."[70] From this point on, Bullitt remained "for the rest of his life a consistent and at times a violent opponent of the Soviet Union."[71]

On the day that Bullitt learned that the Comintern would be holding its first meeting on Russian soil he felt compelled to unleash a full blown exposition on his newly developed intimate understanding of the Soviet government's soul in a multi-page message to Washington. "Contrary to the comforting belief which the French now cherish, it is my conviction that there has been no decrease in the determination of the Soviet Government to produce world revolution. Diplomatic relations with friendly states are not regarded by the Soviet Government as normal friendly relations but 'armistice' relations and it is the conviction of the leaders of the Soviet Union that this 'armistice' can not possibly be ended by a definitive peace but only by a renewal of battle." Bullitt believed that "the Soviet Union genuinely desires peace on all fronts at the present time but this peace is looked upon merely as a happy respite in which future wars may be prepared." This conception was a matter of profound significance to Bullitt. "If this basic postulate of the Soviet Government is understood, there is little or nothing in Soviet domestic or foreign policy that is not clear."[72] By the time the Communist International adjourned, Bullitt had no doubt that it had constituted "a flagrant violation of Litvinov's pledge to the President."[73]

FDR refused to take the pretentious communist pronouncements regarding the impending revolution of the world proletariat as anything more serious than the natural detritus of the
Russian bureaucracy, and he specifically refused to categorize
such pronouncements as genuine violations of the anti-propaganda pledge. He referred to these as "technical" violations.
When Bullitt was attempting to prepare FDR for drastic action
shortly before the meeting of the Comintern, he approached the
subject with full knowledge of how little impressed FDR would
be with the idea. "I can hear you roar with laughter," he wrote
FDR, "over the idea of breaking relations on the basis of a mere
technical violation of Litvinov's pledge."[74] Understanding FDR's
resistance to this way of thinking, Bullitt insisted after the
meeting that he had now encountered "flagrant violations."

FDR did not consider these things to be matters of substance,
and he regarded them as slightly as he did so many of the pronouncements of his own bureaucracy. He thought this concentration upon rhetoric by the bureaucracies of both countries
to be a meaningless diversion, quite irrelevant to the realities of
international politics. In early 1935 FDR specifically advised Bullitt, who was recuperating in a hospital during a visit to the U.S.,
to avoid being caught up in that sort of foolishness, suggesting
that he "forget the whole crew of Bolshies and Career Men
(same idea)."[75] The fear of communism, however, had already
developed too great a hold on Bullitt.

Fear of the communist movement in America was always
crucial in producing the vehemence with which the Russian
experts held their views and by the time the meeting of the
Comintern was over Bullitt had the fear. "A cold appraisal of the
wisest course to pursue to defend the American people from the
efforts of the Soviet Government to produce bloody revolution
in the United States," led Bullitt to conclude that relations
should not be broken. A simple oral protest would certainly not
be adequate "to meet the menace set forth in the new 'united

front' tactics of the Soviet Government and its servant the Comintern," and Bullitt proposed to the State Department a detailed program for responding to the "menace."[76] Among the steps Bullitt recommended was the use of "this occasion to make clear to the American people the aims of the Soviet Government which lie behind the mask labeled 'united front against Fascism and war,'" and he suggested that a speech to that effect by the President "might have a powerful influence in stripping the mask from the united front movement."[77] Bullitt then sent a personal message to FDR telling him of the plan he had just sent to the State Department and advising him "to handle the matter from the domestic, not the foreign, political viewpoint." As enflamed as he was by the clarity of his anti-communist vision, Bullitt still realized how uncongenial FDR would find these words of admonition, but he nevertheless gave FDR his best piece of advice. "If by any chance you decide to follow the line I have recommended, do have Kelley in on all drafting. The technical complexities of Soviet organization are so great that his encyclopedic knowledge will be indispensible."[78] Bullitt had now come full circle.

In August 1936 FDR appointed Bullitt ambassador to France. Bullitt's legacy in Russia was lost opportunity, or rather, destroyed opportunity. As a summary of his handling of the debt negotiations, a comment by the British Ambassador to the United States, although made in a different context, is most fitting. "He may be regarded as thoroughly untrustworthy, and completely unscrupulous where there is a question of taking his objective." A comment by a member of the British Foreign Office best characterizes the essence of William Bullitt, the statesman. "I think Mr. Bullitt may do less harm in Moscow than in Washington, though he is the kind of man who does harm anywhere."[79]

The failure, however, was not only Bullitt's. Since 1917 most State Department professionals and policy makers, including

Under Secretaries and Secretaries of State, as well as Presidents had been impressed by the menace they thought inherent in Russian communism. It was the conventional habit of thought for the Americans who occupied these positions during this era, and Kelley's scholarly analyses of the potential danger seldom failed to arouse the passions of these men in addition to their intellects. Only a few did not become enflamed with the need to protect America, and of these few only FDR had the wisdom and the strength to ignore the issue entirely. Unlike his predecessors, FDR was determined to deal with the Soviet Union on the basis of practical international politics.

XIII

=====

Epilogue

IN 1920 SECRETARY OF STATE COLBY WAS CONCERNED ABOUT political intercourse with a country whose "spokesmen say that they sign agreements with no intention of keeping them."[1] In 1934, after the first official encounter with that country, the Russian promise of perfidy was fulfilled. As far as the State Department was concerned the Russians had come to this country with the idea of saying anything necessary to secure recognition, and afterwards they broke their word as quickly and as casually as they had always said they would. The State Department during this period put much emphasis on the sanctity of treaty obligations. In George Kennan's words, Americans wanted "their statesmanship impressive, unfunctional, with the emphasis on outward appearance rather than on inner reality."[2] To violate so blatantly a treaty agreement was seen by many diplomats as a fundamental moral failing, and for many it reestablished Russia as a country beyond the pale. The lesson for future dealings with that country was clear.

241

The violation of the treaty pledges eliminated something of a semantic problem for the Russian experts. If the Russians claimed that they broke their agreements and therefore what they said was unreliable, how could one know that they really would break their agreements. If an analytical structure for judging an opponent is based upon his own words, it is necessary to define some level of reliability at which his declarations can be accepted as a true expression of intent. The violation of the treaty pledges was interpreted by the Russian experts as meaning that the reliability level was further below the surface than anticipated, and below any level of visibility to outsiders. This was possible once the Russians actually broke their agreements because there was no longer any need to take the Russian word that they would break their word. Experience could be substituted for a tautology. With the semantic barrier removed the two level theory of Russian behavior took on a new significance for the Russian experts. The problem of defining and pointing out the hostile intent the Russian experts thought they saw behind all Soviet moves was made vastly easier. As Loy Henderson warned in late 1936, the "Soviet government in the conduct of international relations has shown a remarkable degree of flexibility," but it has thus far "displayed a fixed determination not to sacrifice any of the principles upon which it is based, and in my opinion it has no intention of doing so."[3] Whatever the Russian diplomatic gesture, the Russian experts, now having the benefit of firsthand experience, could be counted upon to interpolate the hostile intent lurking below the surface. Typical of this approach to Russian motivation, Kelley, Bullitt, and Henderson were all convinced that the real intent of the meeting of the Communist International in 1935 was to foment "bloody revolution."

Because FDR did not share their clear vision of the Russian communist soul the Russian experts were antagonistic towards his policy of recognition from the beginning. They saw in his decision to recognize a fundamental weakness in understanding. The Soviet Union's refusal to pay their debts only substantiated the Russian experts' belief that they had been right from the start and that FDR's involvement was naive, shallow, and politically motivated. Their belief that FDR was callowly and casually reacting to economic and political forces in deciding to recognize was a misunderstanding that became fundamental to their view. The reality was that FDR had created these forces to aide him in moving towards diplomatic contact. The real irony of these events is that it was FDR's almost total disdain for the economic issues and their political impact that had given the Russian experts the opportunity to take control of the debt repayment negotiations and which led directly to the breakdown in the discussions and the destruction of the goodwill already established and which became so important to the Russian experts in the reconfirmation of their bias regarding the expected behavior of the Soviet government.

Although Kelley was in a real sense dissembling while he was reworking the "gentleman's agreement," he and the other Russian experts convinced themselves and each other of the justification for and the fairness of their negotiating positions. They were not being consciously mutinous, but were so overwhelmed by their distrust and convinced of the validity of their suspicions that the exaggeratedly defensive nature of their positions subverted FDR's intent. As a result of their endeavors to prevent the Soviet Union from gaining any additional advantages in the struggle, they eliminated any possibility of building upon the recognition settlements.

As little as the Russian experts thought of FDR's Russian policy, they would have been appalled at the idea that they were deliberately manipulating a policy established by the President. The men in Kelley's division were career diplomats and looked upon themselves in this way. They defined themselves as professionals, and from this perspective the Russian division was regarded by its members as being among the most competent of the entire Department. Considering their professional approach to be both analytical and reserved, their judgment regarding Russia was, in fact, deeply flawed. In evaluating Soviet behavior, the Russian experts were incapable of seeing events from a Russian perspective. Their antipathy towards and fear of communism prevented them from accurately interpreting Russian behavior, and as in the case of the "gentleman's agreement" this led to many sincere but erroneous misreadings of events. This is not an uncommon mode of behavior for the leadership of states powerful enough to avoid realistically appraising international relationships, but not dominant enough to avoid feelings of insecurity. It certainly has been typical of 20th century American foreign policy. FDR's approach to foreign policy was different in a fundamental way because he had enormous faith in America and lacked the insecurity that drove so many others.

In recognizing the Soviet Union, FDR was not making a big political gamble by being far in front of public opinion but was simply implementing a change in policy that had become acceptable to the electorate, in spite of some very visible and vocal opposition. FDR's gift was in seeing what America was willing to accept before it was clearly apparent, not in leading or educating public opinion. His failure in the final agreements, however, and the way the Russians demonstrated bad faith, used up all his political credit for any future initiatives in this regard. Public support for or acquiescence in any deeper involvement almost totally evaporated. The whole business ended so badly, with Russia backtracking on its word—a belief that FDR also shared—that any further such undertakings could only be a political embarrassment. The identification of the Russian failure to pay its debts with the failure of many other European countries to pay their war debts compounded American feelings of mistrust and disgust for such dealings.

The increased Russian contact with U.S. businessmen that Kelley had worked so hard to control was effectively squelched. Trade development was limited, and Russia, in fact, went deeper into a period of autarky. With unofficial American contacts with Russia reduced to neglible proportions and increased diplomatic cooperation a political embarrassment, FDR's future initiatives in making Russian policy were much restricted. The failure meant that the U.S. would continue to be as far removed from Russia after recognition as it had been before and that a realistic appraisal and understanding of that country within America would not develop. Instead of building another step of international cooperation with Russia upon the successful first step of recognition, FDR was effectively precluded from doing any more. Both countries continued to operate largely in isolation as the forces for war were increasing in an unstable world. Bullitt went on to France, where for the rest of the decade he did his best from that post to prevent the Russians and the French from working together.

FDR also had preconceptions confirmed, particulary regarding the abilities of his foreign service officers. FDR came from the same strata of society from which so many of the senior members of the diplomatic corps were drawn. As a group he considered these men to have been cut off by their inherited wealth from gaining a true feeling for the broad texture of American life. In addition, years of overseas service and concentration upon international problems severely hampered this already deficient feeling for what America was about. In FDR's opinion, the foreign service officers' mode of existence rendered valueless their comprehension of the country's domestic life.

As FDR moved the country towards recognition the diplomats confirmed his preconceptions by their preoccupation with the importance of communist propaganda in America. Compounding this, the Russian experts' year long struggle to prevent recognition expressed itself in ways that further substantiated the President's view of his foreign service officers as narrow gauged and ineffective men. The diplomats had objected to including President Kalinin in his disarmament message to the heads of nations. They had long lists of problems regarding recognition that they thought could not be overcome. They had "fussed" over how to make the initial contact with the Soviet Union. They had gone into the negotiations with Litvinoff armed with stacks of analyses and memoranda and the discussions had almost immediately bogged down. From FDR's point of view they were superficial and legalistic men who operated by the book and who understood little of his policies. In FDR's overdrawn but potent stereotype, they were men who at the time of great events were worried about the spelling of "commissar." After recognition FDR routinely ignored the Russian experts and their point of view.

The United States government went into the last half of the 1930's with a policy towards the Soviet Union existing on two different levels, and with the people at each level disdainful of the policy of the other. At the top the President was attempting to work with Russia with whatever very limited means remained open to him. The fact that the Soviet Union was obsessively materialistic and boundlessly cynical did not mean that the country did not have national interests that could be expressed in their foreign policy, and which could indeed run parallel to those of other countries. This is the feeling that FDR imparted to Bullitt before Bullitt's appointment as ambassador, and that is why Bullitt kept writing back to Washington in early 1934 that he would try to maintain the best relations possible, even though the Russians lacked integrity. Although Bullitt had initially absorbed FDR's idea that the foreign policy of the two countries may at some time run parallel and that therefore the lines of communication should be kept open, he had come by the time he left the Soviet Union to accept the area specialists' view that that country was America's principal enemy.

246

At the area specialist level, American diplomats viewed the Soviet Union as a country which was immutably hostile to the U.S., and whose enmity was being faithlessly masked by whatever attitude its government thought would at the moment do it the most good on the international stage—just as the *lie* about paying the debts had been used to secure recognition. The monumental domestic barbarity of Russian communism during the mid-1930's reinvigorated the emotional revulsion of the older Russian experts and initiated these feeling in a new generation of Russian experts. It was a source of much frustration for these men, who believed that their firsthand experience with Russia validified their ideology, to have their advice regularly ignored by the President in his implementation of American policy.

Their lack of influence during FDR's tenure did not, however, alter the Russian experts' opinions. They remained as adamant and as convinced as ever of the clarity of their understanding of the true nature of the Soviet Union and the real meaning of its foreign policy. What they continued to lack as long as FDR was alive was a forum for expressing their views and superiors who would appreciate their credentials and grant them a serious hearing.

Notes

Abbreviations

FDR   Franklin D. Roosevelt
NA   National Archives
NA, DB   National Archives, Diplomatic Branch
FRUS   Foreign Relations of the United States
PSF   President's Secretary's File
PPF   President's Personal File
OF   Official File

Chapter I

1. FRUS, *The Soviet Union, 1933-1939* (Washington, 1952), p. 17. (711.61/287a).
2. James A. Farley, *Jim Farley's Story* (New York, 1948), p. 43. Sumner Welles, *The Time for Decision* (New York, 1944), p. 318.
3. *Ibid.,* p. 316. Joseph P. Lash (editor), *From the Diaries of Felix Frankfurter* (New York, 1975), p. 136.
4. FDR Library, Rexford Tugwell Papers, Box 19, Notes from a New Deal Diary, 1/29/1933, p. 86.
5. *Ibid.,* 1/25/1933, p. 83.
6. FDR Library, Henry Morganthau, Jr., FCA Diary, 5/2/1933, p. 7.
7. Lash (ed.), *Diaries of Frankfurter,* 3/20/1933, p. 136.
8. Rexford Tugwell, *In Search of Roosevelt* (Cambridge, 1972), pp. 192-194.
9. Edgar B. Nixon (editor), *Franklin D. Roosevelt and Foreign Affairs* (Cambridge, 1969), Vol. I, p. 55.

10. FRUS, *1920,* Vol. III, The Secretary of State to All Diplomatic and Consular Offices, 7/27/1920, p. 719. (661.119/541a).

11. FDR Library, Morganthau, Jr. Papers, Box 243 Russia, Memo dated 5/9/1933.

12. *Ibid.*

13. NA, Records of the Reconstruction Finance Corporation, Record Group No. 234, Administrative Subject File, Folder "Loans-Russia Part 3, 9/1/1933-9/30/1933," Letter, Smith W. Brookhart to John J. Blaine, 7/14/1933; Memo, Stanley Reed to Jesse Jones, 9/18/1933.

14. FDR Library, Morganthau, Jr., FCA Diary, 5/9/1933, p. 17.

15. *Ibid.,* 5/15/1933, p. 22.

16. Tugwell, *In Search of Roosevelt,* pp. 210, 211.

17. Yale University Library, Henry Stimson Personal Diary, 1/9/1933, p. 103.

18. Yale Library, Stimson Diary, 2/25/1933, pp. 96, 97.
Moley, *The First New Deal* (New York, 1966), p. 90.
FDR Library, Rexford Tugwell, Notes from a New Deal Diary, 2/26/1933, p. 104.
Documents on British Foreign Policy: 1919-1939 (London, 1956), Second Series, V. No. 527, 2/27/1933, pp. 774-775.

19. Yale Library, Stimson Diary, 2/26/1933, pp. 105, 106.

20. *Ibid.,* 3/3/1933, p. 130.

21. Harvard University, Houghton Library, J. P. Moffat Diary, 5/15/1933.

22. *Ibid.,* 5/16/1933.

23. *Complete Presidential Press Conferences of Franklin D. Roosevelt* (New York, 1972), Vol. 1-2, 1933, Press Conferences #25, 5/31/1933.

24. FDR Library, Morganthau, Jr., FCA Diary, 5/29/1933, p. 38.

25. *Ibid.,* p. 28.

26. Nixon (ed.), *FDR and Foreign Affairs,* Vol. I, June 1933-Feb. 1934, Letter, Henry A. Wallace to FDR, 5/27/1933, p. 186.

27. NA, Records of the RFC, Adm. Subj. File, Folder "Loans-Russia Part 1, 9/30/1932-7/25/1933"; Letter, A. J. Rosenshein to Henry Morganthau, 6/1/1933; Letter, Morganthau to Jesse Jones, 6/5/1933; Letter, Morganthau to Rosenshein, 6/5/1933.

28. *Ibid., Washington Herald,* 5/28/1933, copy of article.

29. *Ibid.,* Letter, S. Stern, Vice-President, The Chase National Bank to Jesse Jones, 6/13/1933.

30. *The New York Times,* 6/14/1933, p. 4.

31. Nixon (ed.), *FDR and Foreign Affairs*, Vol. I, pp. 27, 129, 165, 278, 279, 403.
32. NA, Records of the RFC, RFC Board Minutes, Vol. 17, Part 2, p. 1446.
33. NA, Records of the RFC, Adm. Subj. File, Folder "Loans-Russia Part 1, 9/30/1932-7/25/1933"; Letter, Anderson, Clayton & Co. to RFC, 1/6/1933; Letter, Anderson, Clayton & Co. to J. H. Jones, 1/10/1933.
34. FDR Library, Morganthau, Jr. Papers, Box 243, Russia, Letter, Jesse Jones to President, 6/24/1933.
35. *Ibid.*, Box 243, Russia, Letter, Jesse Jones to Henry Morganthau, 6/27/1933.
36. NA, Records of RFC, Adm. Subj. File, Folder "Loans-Russia Part 1, 9/30/1932-7/25/1933"; Press Release, 7/3/1933.

Chapter II

1. Robert E. Bowers, "American Diplomacy, the 1933 Wheat Conference, and Recognition of the Soviet Union," *Agricultural History*, XL, 1/1966, p. 49.
2. Cordell Hull, *The Memoirs of Cordell Hull* (New York, 1948), Vol. I, pp. 293, 294.
3. FDR Library, PSF, London Economic Conference, Box 156, Letter, Bullitt to FDR, 7/8/1933, p. 7.
4. James P. Warburg, *The Long Road Home* (Garden City, N.Y., 1964), p. 114.
5. Beatrice Farnsworth, *William C. Bullitt and the Soviet Union* (Bloomington and London, 1967), p. 4.
6. Orville Bullitt (editor), *For the President, Personal and Secret* (Boston, 1972), p. xliv.
Farnsworth, *Bullitt and Soviet Union*, p. 4.
7. Orville Bullitt (ed.), *For the President*, p. xliv.
8. *Ibid.*, p. xxxvii.
9. Farnsworth, *Bullitt and Soviet Union*, p. 5.
10. *Ibid.*, p. 7.
11. *Ibid.*, pp. 8-10.
12. *Ibid.*, pp. 33, 34.
13. Arthur Schlesinger, *The Coming of the New Deal* (Boston, 1959), p. 212.

14. Farnsworth, *Bullitt and Soviet Union*, p. 56.

15. Orville Bullitt (editor), *For the President*, p. xli.

16. Farnsworth, *Bullitt and Soviet Union*, p. 15.

17. Bullitt to House, 2/7/1918, House Papers as cited in Farnsworth, *Bullitt and Soviet Union*, p. 15.

18. Orville Bullitt (editor), *For the President*, p. 8.

19. Farnsworth, *Bullitt and Soviet Union*, p. 56.

20. *Ibid.*, pp. 58-63.

21. Lodge to White, 10/2/1919, Lodge Papers as cited in Farnsworth, *Bullitt and Soviet Union*, p. 65.

22. Farnsworth, *Bullitt and Soviet Union*, p. 88.

23. Letter, FDR to Herbert Bayard Swope, 9/30/1919, as cited in Frank Freidel, *Franklin D. Roosevelt, The Ordeal* (Boston, 1954), pp. 22, 23.

24. Raymond Moley, *After Seven Years* (New York, 1939), p. 136.

25. Herbert Feis, *1933: Characters in Crises* (Boston, 1966), p. 104.

26. James P. Warburg, *The Long Road Home* (Garden City, N.Y., 1964), p. 114.

27. Farnsworth, *Bullitt and Soviet Union*, p. 74.

28. Yale University Library, Edward House Collection, Letters, William Bullitt to Colonel House, 1/9/1932, 4/29/1932; Letter, Colonel House to William Bullitt, 5/11/1932.

29. Louis Wehle, *Hidden Threads of History* (New York, 1953), p. 112.

30. *Ibid.*, p. 112.
FDR Library, PPF, Box 693, Louis Wehle to FDR, 8/13/1932.

31. Yale University Library, Edward House Collection, Letter, Bullitt to House, 9/3/1932.

32. Wehle, *Hidden Threads*, pp. 114-115.

33. *Ibid.*, pp. 117, 118.

34. Farnsworth, *Bullitt and Soviet Union*, p. 82.

35. FDR Library, PPF, #693, Letter, Bullitt to Wehle, 12/3/1932, p. 5.

36. Wehle, *Hidden Threads*, p. 119.

37. Orville Bullitt (editor), *For the President*, pp. 24, 26-28.

38. *Ibid.*, p. 28.

39. Wehle, *Hidden Threads*, p. 121.

40. Moley, *After Seven Years*, pp. 136, 137.

41. Feis, *1933*, p. 180.

42. FDR Library, PSF, London Economic Conf., Box 156, Letter, Bullitt to FDR, 7/8/1933, p. 7.

43. Orville Bullitt (editor), *For the President*, p. xli.
44. *Ibid.*, p. xli.
45. *Ibid.*, p. 11.
46. *Ibid.*, p. xli.
47. Warburg, *The Long Road Home*, p. 129.
48. James Cox, *Journey Through My Years* (New York, 1946), p. 373.
49. Yale Library, Stimson Diary, 7/15/1933, p. 181.
50. Robert Bowers and Jeannette P. Nichols, "Roosevelt's Monetary Diplomacy in 1933," *The American Historical Review* (New York, 1951), Vol. LVI, 10/1950 to 7/1951, pp. 316, 317.
51. FDR Library, PSF, London Economic Conference, Box 156, Letter, Bullitt to FDR, 7/8/1933, pp. 4, 5.
52. *Ibid.*, pp. 5, 6, 3.
53. *Ibid.*, pp. 7, 8.
54. *Ibid.*, p. 8
FRUS, *The Soviet Union, 1933-1939*, Vol. III, Memorandum by the Secretary of State, 7/14/1933, p. 495. (893.50A/49).

Chapter III

1. Feis, *1933* p. 308.
2. NA, Diplomatic Branch, 800.00B/190, 2/20/1933; 800.00B/212, 10/18/1933; 150.069/213, 2/24/1933; 800.00B/193, 3/28/1933; 800.00B/192, 3/13/1933.
3. *Ibid.*, 861.51/2611, 10/9/1933; 800.00B-Communist International/134, 4/12/1933; 800.00B/211, 9/22/1933; 800.00B-Communist International/135, 5/26/1933; 661.1115/551, 7/26/1933; 800.00B-Communist International/139, 8/24/1933.
4. George F. Kennan, *The Decision to Intervene* (Princeton, N.J., 1958), p. 470.
5. Harvard Library, Phillips Journal, 12/22/1917, p. 305.
6. *Ibid.*, 1/3/1918, p. 317.
7. FRUS, *1920*, Vol. III, The Secretary of State to the Italian Ambassador (Avezzana), 8/10/1920, p. 468. (760c61/300b).
8. NA, Diplomatic Branch, 861.01/1415, Memo, Robert F. Kelley, April 12, 1929.
9. George F. Kennan, *Memoirs, 1925-1950* (Boston, 1967), p. 84.
10. *Ibid.*
11. *Ibid.*

12. Charles E. Bohlen, *Witness to History, 1929-1969* (New York, 1973), p. 39.
13. FRUS, *The Soviet Union 1933-1939*, 7/27/1933, p. 6-11. (711.61/ 287 3/4).
14. *Ibid.*, Secretary of State to Senator William E. Borah, 9/8/1932, pp. 1,2. (861.01/1786).
Harvard University, Houghton Library, Joseph C. Grew Diary, 10/21/ 1933, p. 742.
15. NA, DB, 661.1115/545, Letter, Dorsey Richardson to Cordell Hull, 5/13/1933.
16. *Ibid.*, 661.1115/545, Letter, Phillips to Lehman Brothers, 6/2/1933.

Chapter IV

1. NA, Records of the RFC, Adm. Subj. File, Folder "Loans-Russia Part 2, 7/26/1933-8/31/1933"; 3 letters, Lamar Fleming, Jr. to Jesse Jones, 7/28/1933.
2. *Ibid.*, Letter, Fleming to Jones, 8/19/1933.
3. FDR Library, Morganthau, Jr. Papers, Russia, Box 243, undated memorandum concerning $12,000,000 sale by The White Company. NA, Records of the RFC, Adm. Subj. File, Folder "Loans-Russia Part 3, 9/1/1933-9/30/1933"; Letter, Harris Creech to RFC, 7/31/1933; Letter, H. K. York to RFC, 8/3/1933; Letter, H. K. York to C. E. Merian, 8/8/1933; Letter, Claude M. Houchins to Stanley Reed, 8/18/ 1933; Letter, Frederic H. Tabor to H. K. York, 9/12/1933.
4. *Ibid.*, Letter, York to Merian, 8/8/1933.
5. *Ibid.*, Letter, Wilson McCarthy to J. C. Hoot, Alliance Machine Co., 8/29/1933.
6. FDR Library, Morganthau, Jr. Papers, Memorandum for Mr. Henry Morganthau, Jr. (Personal and Confidential), unsigned, 8/1/ 1933; Memorandum from Dorethea Greenbaum, 5/13/1933.
Ibid., Morganthau, Jr., FCA Diary, 5/9/1933, pp. 17, 18.
NA, Records of the RFC, Adm. Subj. File, Folder "Loans-Russia Part 1, 9/30/1932-7/25/1933"; Letter, Edward Greenbaum to Stanley Reed, 7/21/1933 and enclosure entitled "RE: Financing American Exports to Russia Through Cooperative Efforts"; Folder "Loans-Russia Part 3, 9/1/1933-9/30/1933"; "Memorandum to Mr. Jones" on Russia exports, from Stanley Reed, 9/18/1933.
Columbia University, Oral History Collection, Edward Samuel Greenbaum, pp. 150-155.

7. FDR Library, Morganthau, Jr. Papers, Russia, Box 243, Newspaper article dated 10/8/1933.

8. *Ibid.,* Letter, R. C. Horne, Jr. to Henry Morganthau, Jr., 10/9/1933.

9. *Ibid.,* "A Plan for Financing American Exports to Soviet Russia"; OF, 220A, Letter W. Irving Shuman to Marvin H. McIntyre, 8/12/1933.

10. *Ibid.,* Morganthau, Jr. papers, Russia Box 243, Letter R. C. Horne, Jr. to Henry Morganthau, Jr., 10/9/1933.

11. *Ibid.,* Letter, W. Irving Shuman to Marvin H. McIntyre, 8/12/1933, plus attached memo, Shuman to Walter Cummings, 8/12/1933.

12. *Ibid.,* Letter, Peter A. Bogdanov to Henry Morganthau, Jr., 8/18/1933, plus enclosures.

13. *Ibid.,* Letter, E. L. Packer to Mr. Carr, 8/25/1933, p. 1.

14. *Ibid.,* Bureau of Foreign and Domestic Commerce to Hersh & Morse, 7/13/1933.

15. *Ibid.,* Letter, E. L. Packer to Mr. Carr, 8/25/1933, p. 2.

16. *Ibid.,* Packer to Carr, "Subject: Plan Fostered by Mr. Max Rabinoff for the Facilitation of Trade with Russia," pp. 1, 4.

17. NA, Records of the RFC, Adm. Subj. File, Folder "Loans-Russia Part 4, 10/1/1933-11/30/1933"; Memorandum, J. A. Marcus to General William I. Westervelt, Director, A.A.A., 8/20/33.

Chapter V

1. Library of Congress, Manuscript Division, Cordell Hull Papers, Correspondence Reel #9, Memo, FDR to Secretary of State, 8/7/1933.

2. *Ibid.,* Hull to Norman Davis, 8/11/1933.

3. NA, DB, 837.00/3579 1/2, Letter, Sumner Welles to FDR, 7/17/1933; 837.00/3665, Telegram, Welles to Secretary of State, 8/15/1933, p. 4.

4. *Ibid.,* 837.00/3739, Telegram #186, Welles to Sec. of State, 8/30/1933.

5. *Ibid.,* 837.00/3666, Memo, Packer to Latin American Division, 8/9/1933.

6. *Ibid.,* 811.00B/1608, Memo on Problems Pertaining to Russian-American Relations, Question of "Communist Propaganda," No. 4, 10/20/1933, pp. 3, 4.

7. *Ibid.,* p. 40.

8. *Ibid.,* p. 59.

9. *Ibid.,* 837.00/3636 1/2, Memo of telephone call between Secre-

tary Hull and Mr. Caffery and Ambassador Welles from Habana, 8/15/
1933 at 10:30 a.m.

10. Bryce Wood, *The Making of the Good Neighbor Policy* (New York
and London, 1961), p. 71.

11. NA, DB, 837.00/3747, Telegram #191, Welles to Sec. of State,
9/5/1933.

12. *Ibid.*, 837.00/3753, Telegram #192, Welles to Sec. of State, 9/5/
1933.

13. *Ibid.*, 837.00/3757, Telegram #195, Welles to Sec. of State, 9/5/
1933.

14. *Ibid.*, 837.00/3755, Telegram #196, Welles to Sec. of State, 9/5/
1933.

15. *Ibid.*, 837.00/3759, Telegram #197, Welles to Sec. of State, 9/5/
1933.

16. *Ibid.*, 837.00/3756, Telegram #199, Welles to Sec. of State, 9/5/
1933.

17. *Ibid.*, 837.00/3761, Memo from the Commandant of the United
States Naval Station, Guantanamo Bay to Chief of Naval Operations,
9/5/1933.

18. *Ibid.*, 837.00/3773, Telegram from Corn Exchange Bank Trust
Co. to Dept. of State, 9/6/1933.

19. *Ibid.*, 837.00/3766, Telegram from The New York Trust Company to Dept. of State, 9/6/1933.

20. *Ibid.*, 837.00/3774, Telegram #361 from Dr. J. M. Puig Casaurano to Hull, 9/7/1933.

21. *Ibid.*, 837.00/3772, Telegram #178 from Daniels to Sec. of State,
9/6/1933.

22. *Ibid.*, 837.00.3774, Telegram #361 from Puig Casaurano to
Hull, 9/7/1933.

The concern of the American government regarding the importance
of the role of communism in the Cuban revolution was also reflected in
the Mexican government's description of three of the other members
of the Commission. "Mr. Guillermo Portela, who is Commissioner of
Foreign Relations in the new Government, is professor of criminal law,
a scientist of standing, with ample financial resources, of high social position, and who, as soon as the university problem arose, distinguished
himself as an opponent of President Machado. Dr. Ramón Grau San
Martin, Commissioner of Public Instruction and Health, was Dean of
the Medical Faculty, with non-Communistic ideas, [was] also distinguished in the university opposition to President Machado, and until

recently an exile in your country. Porfirio Franca, Commissioner of Finance, may be considered as one of the best prepared men in Cuba for that position, with the highest connections in the best banks, a man of means, of no communistic views or antecedents."

23. Hull, *Memoirs*, Vol. I, p. 316.

24. NA, DB, 837.00/4033, Letter, Daniels to Secretary Hull, 9/9/1933; 837.00/3940, Long Distance Telephone Conversation Between Secretary Hull at Washington and Ambassador Daniels at Mexico City, 1:00 p.m., 9/9/1933.

25. *Ibid.*, 837.00/3771, Telegram, Lawton in Guatemala to Sec. of State, 9/6/1933.

26. *Ibid.*, 837.00/3891, Letter, E. R. Leonard to Sec. of State, 9/7/1933; 837.00B/63, Letter, Frank C. Munson to Hull, 9/8/1933.

27. *Ibid.*, 837.00B/90, Memorandum of conversation between Dr. Marquez Sterling, and Asst. Sec. of State Jefferson Caffery, 9/8/1933. (originally 837.00/4218).

28. FDR Library, Official File 20, Letter from Phillips to FDR, 4/8/1933, p. 2.
NA, DB, 837.00/3940, Long distance telephone conversation between Sec. Hull at Washington and Ambassador Daniels at Mexico City, 1:00 o'clock p.m., 9/9/1933.

29. *Ibid.*, 837.00/3824, Long distance telephone conversation between Sec. Hull at Washington and Ambassador Welles at Habana, 10:30 a.m., 9/8/1933.

Chapter VI

1. *Ibid.*, 561.311 F 1 Advisory Comm./5, Letter, Mordecai Ezekial to Herbert Feis plus enclosure of cable to Ambassador Bingham, 9/14/1933.

2. *Ibid.*, 561.311 F 1 Advisory Comm./6, Memo, Herbert Feis, plus enclosure of cable to Ambassador Bingham, 9/14/1933.

3. NA, Records of the RFC, Adm, Subj. File, Folder "Loans-Russia Part 3, 9/1/1933-9/30/1933," Letter, Cordell Hull to Jesse Jones, 9/14/1933.

4. FDR Library, PPF, Felix Frankfurter #140, Letter, Frankfurter to FDR, 10/29/1933.

5. *Ibid.*

6. *The New York Times*, 9/16/1933, p. 1.

7. *Ibid.*, 9/17/1933, p. 15.

8. *Ibid.*

9. NA, Records of the RFC, Adm. Subj. File, Folder "Loans-Russia Part 3, 9/1/1933-9/30/1933," Letter, Mordecai Ezekial to Stanley Reed, 9/18/1933; Letter, Oscar Johnston to Jesse Jones, 9/22/1933. FDR Library, Morganthau, Jr., FCA Diary, 9/27/1933, p. 65.

10. *Ibid.*

11. NA, DB, 611.1115/558, Letter, Jesse Jones to Cordell Hull, 9/26/1933.

12. *Ibid.*, 837.00/3888, Telegram #259, Welles to Sec. of State, 9/15/1933.

13. Library of Congress, Raymond Clapper Papers, Diaries 1933, Container #8, 10/20/1933 plus report from JHB to RJB filed with 10/20 Diary pages.

14. NA, DB, 111.08/71, Memo, Secretary's Office, 9/18/1933 as cited in: Robert E. Bowers, *The Journal of American History*, "Hull, Russian Subversion in Cuba, and Recognition of the U.S.S.R.", Vol. 53, 12/1966, p. 550.

15. Harvard University Library, J. P. Moffat Diary, Monday, 9/18/1933.

16. Columbia University, Oral History Collection, Edward Samuel Greenbaum, p. 152.

17. FRUS, *The Soviet Union, 1933-1939*, Letter, Earl Packer to William Bullitt, 8/31/1933, p. 12. (711.61/287 3/4).

18. *Ibid.*, Letter, Cordell Hull to President Roosevelt, 9/21/1933, pp. 12, 13. (861.01/1968a).

19. NA, DB, Desp. from Carlson (Tallinn), Jan. 14, 1933, DSF 861.5017 Living Conditions/581 as cited in Donald Bishop, *The Roosevelt-Litvinov Agreements* (Syracuse, 1965), pp. 9, 253.

20. *Ibid.*, 800.51 W 89 USSR/11, Dispatch #497, Frank C. Lee to Sec. of State, 1/30/1933.

21. NA, DB, 661.1115/551, Dispatch No. 1505, Felix Cole to Sec. of State, 7/26/1933.

Packer at least initially disagreed with this assessment, believing that Germany was too tied up in credits to Russia "to do other than grant further facilities."

22. NA, DB, 861.51/2592, Dispatch No. 1550, Felix Cole to Sec. of State, 8/25/1933.

23. FRUS, *The Soviet Union, 1933-1939*, Letter, Cordell Hull to President Roosevelt, 9/21/1933, pp. 12, 13. (861.01/1968a).

24. Feis, *1933*, p. 312.

25. NA, DB, 837.00/3987, Telephone conversation, Hull and Welles, 3:00 p.m., 9/20/1933.

26. Arthur Krock, *Memoirs* (New York, 1968), p. 165.

27. Harvard Library, Moffat Diary, Monday, 8/21/1933.

28. Feis, *1933*, p. 309.

29. FDR Library, Morganthau, Jr., FCA Diary, 9/27/1933, p. 64.

30. Samuel N. Harper, *The Russia I Believe In* (Chicago, 1945), p. 202.

31. Harvard Library, Moffat Diary, Thursday, 11/9/1933.

32. Hull, *Memoirs*, Vol. I, p. 297.

33. Bernadotte E. Schmitt, *The American Historical Review*, "How Little Wisdom." Vol. LXVI, No. 2, 1/1961, p. 311.

34. Hull, *Memoirs*, Vol. I, p. 297.
Hull's discussion of the religious issue is anachronistic here. It was not a State Department concern in September and was introduced later by FDR.

35. FDR Library, Morganthau, Jr., FCA Diary, 5/9/1933, p. 17.

36. FDR Library, White House Usher's Diary, 9/21/1933.

37. NA, DB, 561.311 F 1 Advisory Comm./41, Memo, Feis to Hull, 9/22/1933.

38. *Ibid.*, 561.311 F 1 Advisory Comm./31, Memo, Robert F. Kelley to Feis, 9/23/1933, attached to back of telegram 256, 9/21/1933, Wallace to Ambassador Bingham.

39. Robert Paul Browder, *The Origins of Soviet-American Diplomacy* (Princeton, 1953), p. 116, citation of a personal interview with Robert Kelley.

40. William Phillips, *Ventures in Diplomacy* (Boston, 1952), p. 156. Browder, *Origins Soviet-American Diplomacy*, p. 115.

41. FRUS, *The Soviet Union, 1933-1939*, Letter, Robert F. Kelley to Phillips, 9/25/1933, p. 14. (711.61/287 7/8).

42. FDR Library, Robert W. Moore Papers, Box 18, Letter, Hull to Frank C. Walker, 10/28/1933.

43. *Ibid.*, Morganthau, Jr., FCA Diary, 9/26/1933, p. 61.

44. Henry Morganthau, Jr., "The Morganthau Diaries. Part III," *Colliers*, 10/11/1947, p. 21.

45. FDR Library, Morganthau, Jr., FCA Diary, 9/27/1933, pp. 63-65.

46. *Press Conferences of FDR*, Vol. 1-2, #55, 9/22/1933, pp. 290-292.

47. FDR Library, Morganthau, Jr., FCA Diary, 9/27/1933, pp. 63-65.

48. FRUS, *Soviet Union 1933-1939*, Letter, Hull to FDR, 9/21/1933, p. 13. (861.0l/1968a).
Ibid., Memo, Bullitt to Sec. of State 10/4/1933, p. 16. (711.61/289 2/3).
49. FDR Library, Morganthau, Jr., FCA Diary, 9/27/1933, p. 64.

Chapter VII

1. FRUS, *Soviet Union 1933-1939*, Letter, Hull to FDR, 10/5/1933, p. 15. (711.61/289 1/3).
2. FDR Library, Morganthau, Jr., FCA Diary, 10/18/1933, p. 72. Library of Congress, Manuscript Division, Cordell Hull Papers, Correspondence Reel #10, Letter, FDR to Cordell Hull.
Ibid., Memo, Hull to Mr. President, 10/9/1933.
3. FDR Library, Morganthau, Jr., FCA Diary, 10/1/1933, p. 66.
4. Orville Bullitt (ed.), *For the President*, Memo, FDR to Hull, 10/10/1933, p. 40.
5. FDR Library, Morganthau, Jr., FCA Diary, 10/18/1933, p. 72.
6. Orville Bullitt (ed.), *For the President*, Memo, William Bullitt to Hull, 10/11/1933, pp. 42, 43.
7. FRUS, *Soviet Union 1933-1939*, Letter, FDR to President Kalinin, 10/10/1933, pp. 17, 18. (711.61/287a).
8. Library of Congress, George Norris Papers, Russia 1931-1935, No. 18, Box 8, Tray 8, Letter, Smith Brookhart to George Norris, 9/27/1933.
9. FDR Library, Roosevelt Papers, Official File, #220 Russia, Letter, Father Walsh to President, 11/7/1933, attached behind letter, M. McIntyre to Father Walsh, 11/9/1933.
10. *Ibid.*, Memo, Walter G. Hooke, 10/15/1933.
11. *Ibid.*, Letter, Raymond Robbins to FDR, 10/14/1933, attached behind memo from FDR to Bullitt and Morganthau.
12. Browder, *Orgins Soviet-American Diplomacy*, citation of a personal interview with Robert Kelley, p. 114.
13. FDR Library, Official File, William Bullitt #799, Memo, FDR to Bullitt, 10/16/1933.
14. Robert I. Gannon, *The Cardinal Spellman Story* (Garden City, N.Y., 1962), Chapter XI, n. 2, p. 425.
15. Rev. Louis J. Gallagher, *Edmund A. Walsh, S. J., a Biography* (New York, 1962), p. 93.
16. Joseph F. Thorning, S. J., "What Russian Recognition Means," *America*, 12/2/1933, p. 200.

17. Excerpts from Cardinal Spellman's Diary, 11/7/1933 and 11/10/1933, cited in Gannon, *Spellman Story*, p. 98.
18. Eleanor Roosevelt, *This I Remember* (New York, 1949), p. 134. Grace Tully, *F.D.R. My Boss* (Chicago, 1949), pp. 66, 67.
19. *The New York Times*, 10/21/1933, p. 2.
20. FDR Library, Official File, #142 (A.F. of L.), Memo to FDR, 11/10/1933.
21. NA, DB, 811.00B/1478, Letter and attachment, William Green to Sec. of State, 11/10/1933.
22. FDR Library, Morganthau, Jr., FCA Diary, 9/26/1933, p. 61.
23. *The New York Times*, 11/18/1933, p. 5.
24. FDR Library, Morganthau, Jr., Russia Box 243, Memorandum, Bullitt to Morganthau, 10/17/1933 and attachments by Charles E. Stuart, The Russian Trade Organization and Methods, Handling of Trade Relations Were We to Recognize Russia, 10/16/1933.

Although there is no specific documentation that Stuart visited Bullitt on Monday, October 16, Stuart's documents are dated October 16, and they were sent from Bullitt to Morganthau on October 17.

25. *Ibid.*, attachment, The Russian Trade Organization and Methods, pp. 1, 3.
26. *Ibid.*, p. 5.
27. *Ibid.*
28. *Ibid.*, p. 8.
29. *Ibid.*, p. 5.
30. *Ibid.*, attachment, Handling of Trade Relations Were We to Recognize Russia, p. 5.
31. *Ibid.*, p. 2.
32. *Ibid.*, p. 1.
33. *Ibid.*, p. 3.
34. *Ibid.*
35. FDR Library, Morganthau, Jr., FCA Diary, 5/9/1933, p. 17.
36. Harper, *The Russia I Believe In*, p. 200.
37. NA, Industrial and Social Branch, Dept. of Commerce Files, Record Group 40, Letter Daniel C. Roper to Attorney General, 6/16/1933.
38. FDR Library, Morganthau Jr. Papers, Russia Box 243, Memo by Robert F. Kelley, 10/16/1933.
39. *Ibid.*
40. *Ibid.*, Robert W. Moore Collection, Container 18, Russia, 10/1933; Letter, Hull to Frank C. Walker, 10/28/1933.

41. Hull, *Memoirs*, Vol. I, p. 296.
42. NA, DB, 661.6215/104A, Hull (RFK) to Amconsul, Berlin, 10/12/1933; 661.6215/105, Consul J. H. Morgan, Report on "Unsatisfactory Results of Attempts of German Exporters to Build Up an Effective Central Organization for Carrying on Trade with Russia," completed 10/27/1933.

Chapter VIII

1. Orville Bullitt (ed.), *For the President*, Memo, William Bullitt to Hull, 10/19/1933, p. 44.
2. Harold Ickes, *The Secret Diary of Harold L. Ickes, The First Thousand Days 1933-1936* (New York, 1953), 10/20, 10/23/1933, pp. 111, 113.
3. FDR Library, Morganthau, Jr., FCA Diary, 10/18, 10/19/1933, pp. 71, 73-75.
4. *The New York Times*, 10/21/1933, p. 2.
5. *Ibid.*, p. 1.
6. Harper, *The Russia I Believe In*, pp. 200, 201.
Harper on page 200 wrote that he visited Kelley on October 23, but he has gotten his dates wrong. On page 201 he talks about a meeting with Skvirsky on Saturday, October 24. Saturday was October 21 and the previous day was Friday, October 20th, when he met Kelley.
7. Browder, *Origins Soviet-American Diplomacy*, p. 115.
8. Harper, *The Russia I Believe In*, p. 201.
9. NA, DB, 837.00B/83, Telegram #234, Welles to Hull, 9/30/1933; 837.00B/84, Telegram #143, Welles to Hull, 9/29/1933; 837.00B/85, Telegram #340, Welles to Hull, 10/4/1933; 837.00B/87, Telegram #153, Welles to Hull, 10/3/1933; 837.00B/88, Telegram #163, Welles to Hull 10/6/1933; 837.00B/89, Telegram #366, Welles to Hull, 10/16/1933; 837.00B/94,Telegram #387, Welles to Hull, 10/22/1933; 837.00B/96, Telegram #393, Welles to Hull, 10/24/1933; 837.00B/100, Telegram #410, Welles to Hull, 10/29/1933.
10. *Ibid.*, 837.00B/86, Telegram #38, Felix Cole to Hull, 10/9/1933.
11. FDR Library, Moore Papers, Box 18, Daily Report for Eastern Europe by Robert F. Kelley, 10/16/1933.
12. Library of Congress, Clapper Papers, Container #8, Diaries 1933, 10/20, page 1 and teletype insert from JHB to RJB.
In early 1934, Caffery, now Ambassador to Cuba, inquired "whether it would be practical" to confront the Soviet embassy in Washington with the telegram. The reply, drafted by Kelley, indicated the weakness of this evidence for any purpose other than offending State Depart-

ment sensibilities. "The information contained in the despatches referred to by Mr. Caffery is not such as would justify our discussing the matter with the Soviet Ambassador even in the most informal way." NA, DB, 83700/4719, Kelley to Wilson, 3/10/1934.

13. NA, DB, No. 1 800.51 W 89 U.S.S.R/13 3/4, 10/20/1933; No. 2, 861.51/2622 1/2, 10/20/1933; No. 3, 461.11/198 1/2, 10/20/1933; No. 4, 811.00B/1608, 10/20/1933; No. 5, 361.11/4089 1/2, 10/20/1933.

14. FDR Library, Moore Papers, Box 18, Russia Oct. '33, Dept. of State, Division of Current Information, Memorandum of the Press Conf., Saturday, 10/21/1933.

15. Harvard Library, Moffat Diary, MS Am 1407, Vol. 34, 10/23/1933.

16. Hull, *Memoirs,* Vol. I, p. 298.

17. FDR Library, Moore Papers, Box 18, Memo by Moore, 10/28/1933, p. 3.

Ibid., Memo, Moore to Hackworth, 10/24/1933.

18. *Ibid.,* Memo for the Secretary from Moore, 11/4/1933.

19. *Ibid.,* Memo by Moore, 10/28/1933, pp. 6, 1.

Ibid., Memo for the Secretary by Moore, 11/10/1933, pp. 1-5.

Ibid., Memo, Moore to Hackworth, 10/24/1933.

20. *Ibid.,* Memo, Moore to Hull, 10/30/1933.

21. *Ibid.*

22. *Ibid.,* Memo for the Secretary from Moore, 11/4/1933, p. 1.

23. *Ibid.*

24. *Ibid.,* Memo by Moore, 10/28/1933, p. 4.

25. *Ibid.,* Memo from Moore to Hull, 11/9/1933, 3 pages, p. 2. (one of three 11/9/1933 memos by Moore).

26. *Ibid.,* Notes of Conference held in office of Assistant Secretary Moore, 9:30 a.m. Monday, 10/30/1933, p. 4.

27. *Ibid.,* p. 3.

FRUS, *Soviet Union 1933-1939,* Memo by Kelley, 10/25/1933, pp. 23, 24. (861.01/1968a).

28. Library of Congress, Josephus Daniels Papers, Letter, Josephus Daniels to FDR, 10/21/1933.

29. FDR Library, Moore Papers, Box 18, Memo by Moore, 10/28/1933, p. 8.

30. *Ibid.,* p. 6.

31. FRUS, *Soviet Union 1933-1939,* Memo by Kelley, 10/25/1933, pp. 23, 24. (861.01/1968a).

32. NA, DB, 411.61-Assignments/1 1/4, No. 6, Russian Government Property in the United States, 10/26/1933.

33. Hull, *Memoirs*, Vol. I, p. 299.

34. NA, DB, 800.00B/227, Considerations and Recommendations with Respect to the Question of "Communist Propaganda" by Robert Kelley, 10/27/1933.

35. Hull, *Memoirs*, Vol, I, p. 299.

36. NA, DB, 800.00B/227, Considerations and Recommendations with Respect to the Question of "Communist Propaganda" by Robert Kelley, 10/27/1933.

37. *Ibid.*, 811.00B/1608, Question of "Communist Propaganda" No. 4, 10/20/1933, p. 79.

38. Harvard Library, William Phillips Papers, William Phillips Journal, 10/30/1933, p. 3.

39. *Ibid.*

40. *Ibid.*

FDR Library, Morganthau, Jr., FCA Diary, 10/27/1933, p. 84.

41. Harvard Library, Phillips Jour., 10/30/1933, pp. 3, 4.

42. FDR Library, Roosevelt Papers, PSF, Box 23, Memo by Hull, undated, as cited in: Donald G. Bishop, *The Roosevelt-Litvinov Agreements* (Syracuse, 1965), p. 18.

43. FDR Library, Moore Papers, Box 18, Meeting in Moore's Office, 10/30/1933, p. 5.

44. *Ibid.*, p. 6.

45. *Ibid.*, pp. 6, 7.

46. *Ibid.*, Memo by Moore, 10/28/1933, p. 8.

47. NA, DB, 800.51 W 89 U.S.S.R./21 3/4, Memo, Moore to Kelley, 1/16/1934 and attached memo by Kelley, Kelley memo, section 3.

48. Columbia University, Oral History Collection, James Warburg Diary, 10/11/1933, pp. 1561, 1564, 1571-1573.

49. FDR Library, Morganthau, Jr., FCA Diary, 10/23/1933, pp. 76, 77.

50. *Ibid.*, Morganthau, Jr. Papers, Box 243, Russia, Letter, Frank C. Walker to The Governor of the Farm Credit Administration, 10/25/1933.

51. *Ibid.*, Morganthau, Jr., FCA Diary, 11/1/1933, p. 93.

52. *Ibid.*, 10/16-11/13/1933, pp. 69-101.

53. FDR Library, Moore Papers, Box 18, Memo, Moore to Mr. Kelley and Mr. Hackworth, 10/30/1933.

54. NA, DB, 661.61/11, No. 7, Estimate of Maximum Value of Possible Annual Imports Into the United States of Merchandise of Russian Origin.

264

55. *Ibid.,* 861.44/Litvinov, M.M./15, No. 8, Statements by Litvinov on Matters of Foreign Policy that are of Interest to the United States, 11/3/1933, p. 6.
56. *Ibid.,* p. 69.
57. Hull, *Memoirs,* Vol. I, p. 300.
58. FDR Library, Morganthau, Jr., FCA Diary, 10/25/1933, p. 81.

Chapter IX

1. *The New York Times,* 10/29/1933, p. 1.
Ibid., 11/8/1933, p. 24.
Although the State Department spelled the Russian negotiator's name as "Litvinov," this book uses the spelling "Litvinoff" because that is the way he signed his name to the recognition agreements.
2. FDR Library, Moore Papers, Box 18, Memorandum As To The Russian Conversations, by Moore, 11/10/1933, p. 1.
3. Harvard Library, Phillips Jour., 10/8/1933, p. 21.
4. FDR Library, Morganthau, Jr., FCA Diary, 11/6/1933, pp. 98, 99.
5. Ickes, *Secret Diary,* 11/8/1933, p. 117.
6. FDR Library, Morganthau, Jr., FCA Diary, 11/6/1933, p. 99.
Ibid., Moore Papers, Box 18, Memo, For Mr. Hull from Moore, 11/9/1933, 2 pages, (one of three 11/9/1933 memos by Moore).
7. FDR Library, Moore Papers, Box 18, Moore to Sec. of State, 11/9/1933, 3 pages (one of three 11/9/1933 memos by Moore), p. 1.
8. *Ibid.,* Box 18, Memo, For Mr. Hull from Moore, 11/9/1933, 2 pages, (one of three 11/9/1933 memos by Moore).
9. Harvard Library, Phillips Jour., 11/9/1933, p. 23.
10. FDR Library, Moore Papers, Box 18, 11/10/1933, pp. 3, 4.
11. *Ibid.,* Box 18, Memo For The Secretary from Moore, 11/9/1933, 3 pages, (one of three 11/9/1933 memos by Moore).
12. Harvard Library, Phillips Jour., 11/9/1933, p. 24.
13. *Ibid.,* 11/10/1933, pp. 26, 27.
14. *Ibid.,* p. 27.
15. Ickes, *Secret Diary,* 11/10/1933, p. 118.
16. James A. Farley, *Jim Farley's Story* (New York, 1948), p. 44.
The date for this often told story by FDR is not certain. Farley states that FDR told him of it during a White House dinner while the negotiations were in progress. If Farley's memory is accurate, the White House logs fix this date as Friday, November 10.

17. *The New York Times*, 11/11/1933, p. 9.

18. *Press Conferences of FDR*, Vol. 1-2, #67, 11/8/1933.

19. Orville Bullitt (ed.), *For the President*, handwritten undated memo from FDR to Bullitt, pp. 47, 48.
In less specific terms, FDR told Farley that he "made it clear that everything must be cleared up first." Farley, *Farley's Story*, p. 44.

20. FRUS, Soviet Union 1933-1939, Telegram #478, Bullitt to Secretary of State, 11/9/1935, p. 265. (711.61/573).

21. Harvard Library, Phillips Jour., 11/11/1933, p. 28.

22. *Press Conferences of FDR*, Vol. 1-2, #68, 11/10/1933.

23. *The New York Times*, 11/11/1933, p. 1.

24. Harvard Library, Phillips Jour., 11/11/1933, pp. 28, 29.

25. *The New York Times*, 11/12/1933, p. 1.

26. *Ibid.*, p. 3.

27. *Ibid.*, 11/13/1933, pp. 1, 2.
FDR Library, White House Usher's Diary, 11/11, 11/12/1933.

28. Harvard Library, Phillips Jour., 11/13/1933, p. 30.

29. *The New York Times*, 11/13/1933, p. 1.

30. Harvard Library, Phillips Jour., 11/13/1933, p. 31; 11/14/1933, p. 34.
FDR Library, White House Usher's Diary and FDR Appointment Calendar, 11/13, 11/14/1933.

31. Harvard Library, Moffat Diary, MS Am 1407, Vol. 34, 11/18, 11/19/1933, p. 2.

32. William Bullitt, *Life Magazine*, 8/30/1948, p. 84.

33. Browder, *Origins Soviet-American Diplomacy*, p. 133, note 21.

34. Harvard Library, Phillips Jour., 11/13/1933, pp. 31, 32.

35. *Ibid.*, 11/13, 11/14/1933, pp. 3l, 32, 34.
FDR Library, White House Usher's Diary, 11/15/1933.

36. *Press Conferences of FDR*, Vol. 1-2, #69, 11/15/1933.

37. FRUS, *Soviet Union 1933-1939*, Memo, Bullitt to President, 11/15/1933, p. 25. (711.61/353a).

38. Gannon, *Spellman Story*, p. 157.

39. FRUS, *Soviet Union 1933-1939*, Memo, Bullitt to President, 11/15/1933, p. 26. (711.61/353a).

40. FDR Library, Roosevelt Papers, Official File #229, Memo, M. H. M. (McIntyre) to the President, 11/15/1933.

41. FRUS, *Soviet Union 1933-1939*, Memo, Bullitt to President, 11/15/1933, p. 26. (711.61/333).

42. *Ibid.*
43. *Ibid.*
44. NA, DB, 711.61/406, Address by Honorable R. Walton Moore, 11/22/1933, p. 4.
45. FRUS, *Soviet Union 1933-1939*, Memo, Bullitt to Sec. of State, 10/4/1933, p. 16. (711.61/289 2/3).
46. *Ibid.*, Memo, Bullitt to President, 11/15/1933, p. 26. (711.61/353a).
47. FRUS, *Soviet Union 1933-1939*, Memo by President Roosevelt and the Soviet Commissar for Foreign Affairs (Litvinov), 11/15/1933, p. 27. (711.61/353 1/2).
48. Harvard Library, Phillips Jour., 11/16/1933, pp. 37, 38.
49. *The New York Times*, 11/17/1933, p. 1.
FDR Library, Morganthau, Jr., FCA Diary, 11/16/1933, p. 102.
Library of Congress, Wilbur J. Carr Papers, Box 4, Diary 11/16, 11/17/1933.
50. Harvard Library, Phillips Jour., 11/16/1933, pp. 39, 40.
51. Tugwell, *In Search of Roosevelt*, p. 309.
52. Harvard Library, Phillips Jour., 11/16/1933, p. 39.
53. Harvard Library, Moffat Diary, MS Am 1407, Vol. 34, 11/17/1933.
54. *The New York Times*, 11/18/1933, p. 5.
55. Farley, *Story*, p. 44.
56. Ickes, *Secret Diary*, 11/17/1933, p. 124.
57. Harvard Library, Phillips Jour., 11/18/1933, pp. 41, 42.
58. *The New York Times*, 11/18/1933, p. 2.
59. *Press Conferences of FDR*, Vol, 1-2, #70, 11/17/1933.
60. *The New York Times*, 11/18/1933, p. 2.
61. *Press Conferences of FDR*, Vol. 1-2, #70, 11/17/1933.
62. *Ibid.*
63. *Ibid.*
FDR Library, White House Usher's Diary, White House Appointment Calendar, 11/17/1933.
64. *The New York Times*, 11/18/1933, p. 1.
65. *Ibid.*, p. 2.
66. *The Wall Street Journal*, 11/20/1933, p. 8.
67. *The Washington Post*, 11/18/1933, p. 1.
68. George Q. Flynn, *American Catholics & the Roosevelt Presidency 1932-1936* (Lexington, Ky., 1968), p. 148.

69. *Ibid.*, p. 147

70. Joseph F. Thorning, S. J., "What Russian Recognition Means," *America*, 12/2/1933, p. 200.

71. FDR Library, Roosevelt Papers, Official File #229, Letter, Key Pittman to President, 11/23/1933, p. 3.

72. *The New York Times*, 11/19/1933, p. 28.

73. FDR Library, Roosevelt Papers, PPF #88 (Bernard Baruch), Memo, L. H. (Louis Howe) to President, 11/23/1933, and attached letter from Bernard Baruch to Lou Howe, 11/18/1933. Library of Congress, Frankfurter Papers, Foreign Affairs, Russia #97, Letter, Frankfurter to President, 11/23/1933.

74. FDR Library, Roosevelt Papers, PPF #86 (Josephus Daniels), Letter, Daniels to Franklin D. Roosevelt, 11/18/1933.

75. FDR Library, Roosevelt Papers, PPF 1006 (Frank L. Polk), Letter, FDR to Frank Polk, 12/5/1933 and attached letter, Frank Polk to Pres., 11/24/1933.

76. NA, DB, 711.61/406, Address by Honorable R. Walton Moore, 11/22/1933, p. 7.

77. Harvard Library, Moffat Diary, MS Am 1407, Vol. 34, 11/17/1933, pp. 1, 2.

78. Harvard Library, Phillips Jour., 11/18/1933, p. 44.

79. Columbia University Oral Histories, William Phillips, Micro Fiche page 2 of 2, p. 105.

80. Kennan, *Memoirs*, p. 56.

81. Browder, *Origins Soviet-American Diplomacy*, p. 148.

82. Frances Perkins, *The Roosevelt I Knew* (New York, 1946), p. 143.

83. Harper, *The Russia I Believe In*, p. 203.

84. FDR Library, Morganthau, Jr., FCA Diary, 11/6/1933, p. 99.

85. Gannon, *Spellman Story*, p. 157.

86. FDR Library, Roosevelt Papers, PSF Box 67, Memo, Moore to the President, 11/11/1933, incorrectly attached to and filed behind memo by Green Hackworth.

87. Harvard Library, Phillips Jour., 11/13/1933, p. 30.

88. FDR Library, Moore Papers, Box 24 File "H", Letter, Moore to Hull, 11/13/1933.

89. *The Public Papers and Addresses of Franklin D. Roosevelt* (New York, 1938), Vol. 2, The Year of Crises 1933, Address delivered at Savanah, Georgia, "The American March of Progress," 11/18/1933, p. 492.

90. FRUS, *Soviet Union 1933-1939*, Pres. Roosevelt to the Soviet Commissar for Foreign Affairs, 11/16/1933, p. 29. (711.61/343 2/8).

91. *Press Conferences of FDR*, Vol. 1-2, #70, 11/17/1933.

92. NA, DB, 361.11/4089 1/2, No. 5, Treaty Rights Essential to the Welfare and Protection of American Nationals in Russia, 10/20/1933, pp. 12, 13.

93. *Ibid.*, p. 11.

94. *Ibid.*, p. 12.

95. George F. Kennan, *Memoirs, 1925-1950* (Boston, 1967), pp. 47-54.

96. FRUS, *Soviet Union 1933-1939*, The Soviet Commissar for For. Affrs. (Litvinov) to President Roosevelt, 11/16/1933, pp. 35, 36. (711.61/343 6/8).

97. NA, DB, 411.61 Assignments/6, Letter, Secretary Hull to Attorney General Cummings, 9/21/1934.

98. NA, DB, 411.61 Assignments/1 1/4, Russian Government Property in the United States, No. 6, 10/26/1933.
FDR Library, Morganthau, Jr. Diary, 5/11/1937, p. 244.
FDR Library, Roosevelt Papers, Official File, #220 Russia, Conditions on which Recognition of the Union of Soviet Socialist Republics may be granted by the United States, Explanation of the Alternative Drafts of Section X.
NA, DB, 311.6153/4, Letter, Ughet to Kelley, 5/16/1930.

99. FDR Library, Morganthau, Jr. Diary, 5/11/1937, p. 242.

100. *Ibid.*, p. 245.

101. FRUS, *Soviet Union 1933-1939*, The Soviet Commissar for For. Affrs. (Litvinov) to President Roosevelt, 11/16/1933, p. 36. (711.61/343 7/8).

102. Alexander Baykov, *Soviet Foreign Trade* (Princeton, 1946), p. 60.

103. NA, DB, 711.61/406, Address by Walton Moore, 11/22/1933, p. 3.

104. FDR Library, Roosevelt Papers, Official File, Box 799, Memo for Sec. of State, 3/3/1934, as cited in: Donald Bishop, *The Roosevelt-Litvinov Agreements*, p. 254, n. 61.

105. FDR Library, Morganthau, Jr. Papers, Box 243, Russia, Memo, Oliphant to Morganthau, 11/13/1933 and Memo, Oliphant to Morganthau, 11/29/1933.

106. Harvard Library, Moffatt Diary, MS Am 1407, Vol. 34, 11/18, 11/19/1933, p. 2.

107. Orville Bullitt (ed.) *For the President*, Letter, Bullitt to LeHand, 1/22/1933, p. 26.

108. FDR Library, John Wiley Papers, Box 1-3, Letter, Wiley to Bullitt, 12/14/1933.

109. Orville Bullitt (ed.), *For the President*, p. xliii.

110. *Ibid.*, p. 33

Chapter X

1. NA, DB, 861.51/2618, Conversation, Boris Skvirsky and Robert Kelley, 11/21/1933.

2. *The New York Times*, 11/18/1933, p. 5.
Harvard Library, Phillips Jour., 11/18/1933, p. 43.

3. *Ibid.*, 1/18/1933, pp. 43, 44.

4. Columbia University, Oral History Collection, James Warburg Diary, 11/18/1933, pp. 1764, 1765.

5. *The New York Times*, 11/19/1933, p. 1.
Ibid., 11/21/1933, p. 8.

6. *Ibid.*

7. Harvard Library, Phillips Jour., 11/20/1933, p. 46.

8. *The New York Times*, 11/22/1933, p. 9.
Harvard Library, Phillips Jour., 11/22/1933, p. 51.
FDR Library, Roosevelt Papers, Official File, #220 Russia, Letter, Litvinoff to President, 11/22/1933.

9. *The New York Times*, 11/23/1933. p. 9.

10. Harvard Library, Phillips Jour., 11/22/1933, p. 51.

11. *The Washington Post*, 11/18/1933, p. 6; 11/19/1933, p. 6.

12. Harvard Library, Phillips Jour., 11/27/1933, p. 61.

13. *The New York Times*, 12/11/1933, p. 3.
FDR Library, Roosevelt Papers, PSF, Russia, Box 67, Letter, Bullitt to President, 1/1/1934, p. 3.

14. *Ibid.*

15. *Ibid.*, pp. 6, 7.

16. *Ibid.*, p. 8.

17. *Ibid.*, p. 4.

18. *Ibid.*, p. 7.

19. *Ibid.*, p. 17.

20. *Ibid.*, p. 5.

21. *The New York Times*, 12/14/1933, p. 14.

22. FDR Library, Roosevelt Papers, PSF, Russia, Box 67, Letter, Bullitt to President, 1/1/1934, pp. 5, 6.

23. *Ibid.,* p. 6
24. *Ibid.,* p. 8.
25. *Ibid.,* p. 9.
26. *Ibid.,* p. 11.
27. *Ibid.,* pp. 11-17.
28. *Ibid.,* pp. 18-20.
29. *Ibid.,* p. 22.
30. *Ibid.,* p. 5.
31. *Ibid.,* p. 8.
32. *Ibid.,* p. 10.
33. *Ibid.,* p. 16.
34. *Ibid.,* p. 11.
35. *Ibid.,* p. 6.
36. *Ibid.,* p. 17.
37. *Ibid.,* p. 14.
38. *Ibid.,* pp. 25, 22; Telegram, Bullitt to Hull, 12/24/1933, p. 4.

Chapter XI

1. NA, DB, 800.51 W 89 U.S.S.R./16, Memo, Moore to Phillips, 12/7/1933.
2. *Ibid.,* 800.51 W. 89 U.S.S.R./14, Memo, John C. Wiley, 12/5/1933; 800.51 W 89 U.S.S.R./15, Memo, Moore to Phillips, 12/5/1933.
3. FDR Library, John Wiley Papers, Box 1-3, Letter, Wiley to Bullitt, 12/14/1933, p. 2.
NA, DB, 800.51 W 89 U.S.S.R./14, Memo by Wiley, 12/5/1933, pp. 4. 5.
4. FDR Library, Wiley Papers, Box 1-3, Letter, Wiley to Bullitt, 12/14/1933, p. 2.
NA, DB, 800.51 W 89 U.S.S.R./14, Memo by Wiley, 12/5/1933, p. 4.
5. FDR Library, Wiley Papers, Box 1-3, Letter, Wiley to Bullitt, 12/14/1933, p. 2.
Columbia University, Oral History Collection, James Warburg Diary, 10/11/1933, pp. 1572, 1573.
6. FDR Library, Wiley Papers, Box 1-3, Letter, Wiley to Bullitt, 12/14/1933, pp. 2, 3.
7. FRUS, *Soviet Union 1933-1939,* The Acting Sec. of State to the Ambassador of Germany (Dodd), 12/8/1933, pp. 47-48. (800.51 W 89 U.S.S.R./16: Telegram).
8. NA, DB, 800.51 W 89 U.S.S.R./21 3/4, Memo, Moore to Kelley, 1/16/1934 and attached memo by Kelley, Kelley memo section 3.
9. FRUS, *The Soviet Union 1933-1939,* The Acting Sec. of State to

the Ambassador in Germany (Dodd), 12/8/1933, pp. 47-48. (800.51 W 89 U.S.S.R./16: Telegram).

10. *Ibid.*

11. FDR Library, Roosevelt Papers, Official File, #198 Germany, Memo by Phillips, 12/9/1933.

12. FRUS, *Soviet Union 1933-1939*, The Acting Sec. of State to the Ambassador in Germany (Dodd), 12/21/1933, p. 52. (800.51 W 89 U.S.S.R./16: Telegram).

13. *Ibid.*, The Ambassador in Germany (Dodd) to the Acting Sec. of State, 12/23/1933, p. 52. (800.51 W 89 U.S.S.R./18: Telegram).

14. FDR Library, Wiley Papers, Box 1-3, Letter, Wiley to Bullitt, 12/14/1933.

15. *Ibid.*
Harvard Library, Phillips Jour., 11/29/1933, p. 65.

16. Feis, *The Diplomacy of the Dollar* (Hamden, Connecticut, 1965), p. 19.

17. *Ibid.*, p. 46.

18. *The New York Times*, 1/8/1934, pp. 1, 3.

19. *Ibid.*, 1/9/1934, p. 3.

20. NA, DB, 800.51 W 89 U.S.S.R./19, Telegram #578, Marriner to Sec. of State, 12/27/33.

21. FDR Library, Roosevelt Papers, PSF, Russia Box 67, Letter, Bullitt to President, 1/1/1934, p. 21.

22. *The New York Times*, 12/28/1933, p. 8.

23. *Ibid.*, 1/9/1934, p. 15.

24. *Ibid.*

25. Orville Bullitt (ed.), *For the President*, Letter, FDR to Bullitt, 1/7/1934, pp. 75-77.

26. NA, DB, 800.51 W 89 U.S.S.R./21 3/4, Memo, Moore to Kelley, 1/16/1934 and attached memo by Kelley, Kelley memo, section 3.

27. *Ibid.*

28. *Ibid.*, Moore memo, p. 1.

29. *Ibid.*, Kelley memo, section 4.

30. William C. Bullitt, The Establishment of Normal Relations Between the United States and the Union of Soviet Socialist Republics, Address before the Chamber of Commerce of Philadelphia, 1/19/1934, The Department of State Eastern European Series, No. 3, U.S. Government Printing Office (Washington, 1934), Publication No. 553.

31. *The New York Times*, 1/20/1934, p. 8.

32. William C. Bullitt, *Life Magazine*, "How We Won the War and Lost the Peace," 8/30/1948, p. 83.

NA, DB, 800.51 Johnson Act/2A, Letter, Moore to Senator Joe Robinson, 1/27/1934.

33. FDR Library, White House Usher's Diary, 2/7/1934.

34. FDR Library, White House Usher's Diary, White House Appointment Calendar, 1/8/1934-2/13/1934.

35. NA, DB, 800.51 W 89 U.S.S.R./21 3/4, Memo, Moore to Kelley, 1/16/1934 and attached memo by Kelley, Memo by Kelley, section 4.

36. *Ibid.*, Kelly memo, section 6.

37. *Ibid.*

38. FDR Library, Moore Papers, Box 6, Export-Import Bank, Memo, Moore to Sec., 2/23/1934 with attached memo by Kelley, p. 2.

39. NA, DB, 800.51 W 89 U.S.S.R./21 3/4, Memo, Moore to Kelley, 1/16/1934 with attached memo by Kelley, Kelley Memo, section 10.

40. *Ibid.*, Kelly memo, section 6.

41. Harvard Library, Phillips Jour., 11/29/1933, p. 66.

42. *Ibid.*

43. *Ibid.*, 12/14/1933, p. 91.

44. FDR Library, Moore Papers, Box 18, Russia, 12/1933, Memo, Kelley to Phillips, 12/18/1933, p. 3.

45. FDR Library, Roosevelt Papers, White House Calendar, 12/19/ 1933.

FRUS *Soviet Union 1933-1939*, Memorandum, The Dept. of State to the Soviet Embassy, 12/20/1933, p. 51. (701.6111/744).

46. FDR Library, Wiley Papers, Box 1-3, Letter, Wiley to Bullitt, 12/14/1933.

47. NA, DB, 611.1115/580, Memo, Kelley to Phillips, 1/9/1934 attached behind letter, Rodney E. Marshall to Phillips, 12/16/1933.

48. Columbia University, Oral History Collection, Edward Samuel Greenbaum, pp. 150, 151.

49. Minutes of the Export-Import Bank of Washington, Export-Import Bank of Washington, p. 6(A) and 6(C-1).

50. Ibid., pp. 15, 16, 28.

51. *Ibid.*, pp. 15-20.

University of Missouri Library, Western Historical Manuscripts Collection, George Peek Papers, Folder No. 2335, interview, 2/27/34, p. 2.

52. Harvard Library, Phillips Jour., 2/27/1934, pp. 86, 87.

53. Harvard Library, Phillips Jour., 1/22/1934, p. 43

54. NA, DB, 800.51 W 89 U.S.S.R./22 1/2, Memo, Bullitt for Sec. 2/10/1934..

55. *Ibid.*

56. Yale Library, Stimson Diary, 11/28/1932, p. 136.

57. NA, DB, 800.51 W 89 U.S.S.R./21A, Telegram, Sec. Hull to Bullitt, 3/2/1934.

58. NA, DB, 800.15 W 89 U.S.S.R./22 1/2, Memo, Bullitt to Sec., 2/10/1934.

59. *Ibid.*

60. NA, DB, 800.51 W 89 U.S.S.R./27A, Telegram, Hull to American Embassy Moscow, 4/7/1934.

61. FDR Library, Roosevelt Papers, White House Calendar, Usher's Diary, 2/9-2/13/1934.

62. Bohlen, *Witness to History 1929-1969*, p. 16.

63. FDR Library, Morganthau, Jr., FCA Diary, 9/27/1933, p. 64.

64. The Department of State, *Foreign Service List* (Washington, 1934), 4/l/1934, p. 27.

65. Bohlen, *Witness 1929-1969*, p. 17.
FDR Library, Wiley Papers, Box 1-3, Letters between Wiley and Kelley, 1931, 1932.

66. Bohlen, *Witness 1929-1969*, p. 17

67. Dept. of State, *Foreign Service List*, 4/1/1934, p. 27.

68. NA, DB, 800.51 W 89 U.S.S.R./27A, Telegram, Hull to Amer. Embassy Moscow, 4/7/1934.

69. *Documents on British Foreign Policy: 1919-1939* (London, 1956), Second Series, V, No. 521, 1/30/1933, p. 749; No. 524, 2/21/1933, p. 770.
Moley, *After Seven Years*, p. 202.
Harvard Library, Phillips Jour., 11/13/1933, p. 31.

70. NA, DB, 861.51/2613, Letter, Dean Acheson to Sec. Hull, 11/2/1933.

71. NA, DB, 800.51 W 89 U.S.S.R./27A, Telegram, Hull to Amembassy Moscow, 4/7/1934.

72. NA, DB, 800.51 W 89 U.S.S.R./62, Telegram, Bullitt to Sec. of State, 5/24/1934.

73. NA, DB, 800.51 W 89 U.S.S.R./27A, Telegram, Hull to Amembassy Moscow, 4/7/1934.

74. NA, DB, 800.51 W 89 U.S.S.R./21A, Telegram, Hull to Bullitt in Warsaw, 3/2/1934.
NA, DB 800.51 W 89 U.S.S.R./21 1/2, Memo by Kelley, 2/21/1934.

Chapter XII

1. Bohlen, *Witness 1929-1969*, p. 14.

2. NA, DB, 800.51 W 89 U.S.S.R./22, Telegram #13, Bullitt to Sec. of State, 3/15/1934.

3. *Ibid.*

4. *Ibid.*

5. Export-Import Bank of Washington, Minutes, 3/16/1934, p. 39.

6. *Ibid.*

7. *Ibid.,* p. 40.

8. *Ibid.*

9. NA, DB, 800.51 W 89 U.S.S.R./22, Telegram, Hull to Bullitt in Moscow, 3/17/1934.

10. NA, DB, 800.51 W 89 U.S.S.R./23, Telegram #20, Bullitt to Sec. of State, 3/18/1934.

11. NA, DB, 800.51 W 89 U.S.S.R./34, Memo by Kelley, 4/9/1934.

12. NA, DB, 800.51 W 89 U.S.S.R./24, Telegram #24, Bullitt to Sec. of State, 3/21/1934.

13. NA, DB, 800.51 W 89 U.S.S.R./26, Memo by Hull, 3/26/1934.

14. *Ibid.*

15. NA, DB, 800.51 W 89 U.S.S.R./25, Telegram #27, Bullitt to Sec. of State, 3/23/1934.

16. NA, DB, 800.51 W 89 U.S.S.R./27, Telegram #33, Bullitt to Sec. of State, 4/2/1934.

17. *Ibid.*

18. *Ibid.,* Telegram, Hull to Bullitt at Amembassy Moscow, 4/5/1934, attached to back of telegram, Bullitt to Sec. of State, 4/2/1934.

19. NA, DB, 800.51 W 89 U.S.S.R/46B, Telegram, Hull to Bullitt at Amembassy Moscow, 5/7/1934.

20. NA, DB, 800.51 W 89 U.S.S.R./49, Telegram, Hull to Bullitt at Amembassy Moscow, 5/15/1934.

21. NA, DB, 800.51 W 89 U.S.S.R./47, Press release by Dept. of State of letter by Attorney General Homer Cummings, 5/5/1934, p. 9.

22. NA, DB, 800.51 W 89 U.S.S.R./51, Department of State, For the Press, 5/7/1934.

23. NA, DB, 800.51 W 89 U.S.S.R./27, Telegram, Hull to Bullitt at Amembassy Moscow, 4/5/1934, attached behind telegram, Bullitt to Hull, 4/2/1934.

24. NA, DB, 800.51 W 89 U.S.S.R/28, Telegram #43, Bullitt to Hull, 4/8/1934, p. 1.

25. NA, DB, 800.51 W 89 U.S.S.R./21 3/4, Memo by Kelley attached behind memo from Moore to Kelley, 1/16/1934, section 6.
FDR Library, Moore Papers, Box 6, Export-Import Bank, Memo by Kelley, 2/23/1934.

275

26. NA, DB, 800.51 W 89 U.S.S.R./28, Telegram #43, Bullitt to Sec of State, 4/8/1934.

27. NA, DB, 800.51 W 89 U.S.S.R./45, Enclosure No. 1 attached to Dispatch No. 29, Bullitt to Sec. of State, 4/20/1934.

28. NA, DB, 800.51 W 89 U.S.S.R./28, Telegram #43, Bullitt to Sec. of State, 4/8/1934.

29. NA, DB, 800.51 W 89 U.S.S.R./36, Telegram, Hull to Bullitt at Amembassy Moscow, 4/18/1934.

30. *Ibid.*

31. NA, DB, 800.51 W 89 U.S.S.R./39A, Telegram from Moore signed by Phillips to Bullitt at Amembassy Moscow, 4/23/1934. FDR Library, Moore Papers, Box 3, Letter, Moore to Bullitt, 4/24/1934.

32. Orville Bullitt (ed.), *For the President*, Letter, Moore to Bullitt, 5/8/1934, p. 86.

33. NA, DB, 800.51 W 89 U.S.S.R./43A, Telegram Hull to Bullitt at Amembassy Moscow, 5/1/1934.

34. NA, DB, 800.51 W 89 U.S.S.R./44, Telegram #71, Bullitt to Sec. of State, 5/2/1934; Telegram, Hull to Bullitt, 5/3/1934.

35. NA, DB, 800.51 W 89 U.S.S.R./48, Telegram #79, Bullitt to Sec. of State, 5/9/1934,

36. *Ibid.*, Telegram, Hull to Bullitt at Amembassy Moscow, 5/11/1934.

37. NA, DB, 800.51 W 89 U.S.S.R./49, Telegram #81, Bullitt to Sec. of State, 5/13/1934.

38. Export-Import Bank of Washington, Minutes, 5/15/1934, p. 64.

39. *Ibid.*, 5/15/1934, p. 65.

40. *Ibid.*, 5/15/1934, p. 66.

41. NA, DB, 800.51 W 89 U.S.S.R./49, Telegram, Hull to Bullitt at Amembassy Moscow, 5/15/1934.

42. NA, DB, 800.51 W 89 U.S.S.R./57, Telegram #85, Bullitt to Sec. of State, 5/16/1934.

43. NA, DB, 800.51 W 89 U.S.S.R./60, Telegram #90, Bullitt to Sec. of State, 5/21/1934.

44. U. of Missouri Library, W. Historical Manuscripts Col., Peek Papers, 1911-1947, Col. No. 2270, Folder No. 467, memo with attachments from Charles E. Stuart to George Peek, 7/28/1934, pp. 2, 3, 10.

45. NA, DB, 800.51 W 89 U.S.S.R./60, Telegram #90, Bullitt to Sec. of State, 5/21/1934.

46. NA, DB, 800.51 W 89 U.S.S.R./69, Telegram #140, Bullitt to Sec. of State, 6/14/1934.

47. Bohlen, *Witness 1929-1969*, pp. 32, 33.

48. NA, DB, 800.51 W 89 U.S.S.R./72, Telegram #145, Bullitt to Sec. of State, 6/16/1934.

49. *Ibid.,* Telegram #146, Bullitt to Secretary of State, 6/16/1934.

50. William Bullitt, *Life Magazine*, "How We Won the War and Lost the Peace," 8/30/1948, p. 84.

51. Bohlen, *Witness 1929-1969*, p. 34.

52. Orville Bullitt (ed.), *For the President*, Letter, Moore to Bullitt, 4/10/1934, p. 81.

53. Harvard Library, Phillips Jour., 4/7/1934, p. 162.

54. Hull, *Memoirs*, Vol. I, p. 307.

55. Bohlen, *Witness 1929-1969*, p. 14, 33, 35.

56. Bohlen, *The Transformation of American Foreign Policy* (New York, 1969), p. 56.

57. George Kennan, *Russia and the West under Lenin and Stalin* (Boston, 1960, 1961), p. 298.

58. Harry S. Truman Library, Papers of William L. Clayton, Telegram, W. L. Clayton to George Peek, 4/2/1934.

59. NA, DB, 800.51 W 89 U.S.S.R./76, Telegram #167, Bullitt to Sec. of State, 6/30/1934.

60. NA, DB, 800.51 W 89 U.S.S.R./103, Memorandum of Conversation by Kelley, 8/10/1934.

61. NA, DB, 800.00B/217, Telegram from Cole to Secretary of State, 1/5/1934.

62. Orville Bullitt (ed.), *For the President*, Memo, Moore to Sec. of State, 3/5/1934, pp. 76, 77.

63. NA, DB, 800.51 W 89 U.S.S.R./57, Telegram, Hull to Bullitt at Amembassy Moscow, 5/23/1934.

64. NA, DB, 800.51 W 89 U.S.S.R./74, Memorandum of Conversation between the Russian Ambassador and Assistant Sec. of State Moore, 6/20/1934.

65. NA, DB, 800.51 W 89 U.S.S.R./103, Memorandum of Conversation, Troyanovsky, Hull, Moore, Kelley, 8/10/1934.

66. Orville Bullitt (ed.), *For the President*, Letter, Bullitt to President, 4/13/1934, p. 83.

67. Bohlen, *Witness 1929-1969*, p. 17.

68. Kennan, *Memoirs,* p. 61.

69. Bohlen, *Witness 1929-1969*, p. 17.

70. Kennan, *Memoirs*, p. 80.

71. Bohlen, *Transformation*, p. 57.

72. FRUS, *Soviet Union 1933-1939*, The Ambassador in the Soviet Union (Bullitt) to the Secretary of State, No. 730, 7/19/1935, p. 224. (761.00/260).

73. *Ibid.*, Ambassador in the Soviet Union (Bullitt) to the Sec. of State, 8/21/1935, p. 244. (861.00 Congress, Communist International, VII/56-82: Telegram).

74. Orville Bullitt (ed.), *For the President*, Letter, Bullitt to President, 7/15/1935, p. 130.

75. *Ibid.*, Letter, FDR to Bullitt, 2/6/1935, p. 102.

76. FRUS, *Soviet Union 1933-1939*, The Ambassador in the Soviet Union (Bullitt) to the Sec. of State, 8/21/1935, p. 246. (861.00 Congress, Communist International, VII/56-62: Telegram).

77. *Ibid.*, Ambassador in the Soviet Union (Bullitt) to the Sec. of State, 8/21/1935, pp. 246, 248. (861.00 Congress, Communist International, VII/56-62: Telegram).

78. *Ibid.*, Ambassador in the Soviet Union (Bullitt) to the Sec. of State, 8/21/1935, p. 246. (861.00 Communist International, VI/56-62: Telegram).

79. British Foreign Office, FO 371/16599, A1 668 4954 372, 3/4/1933; FO N8689, FO 311/17255, 4954 254, 12/6/1933, as cited in Orville Bullitt (ed.), *For the President*, p. 58.

ChapterXIII

1. FRUS, *1920*, Vol. III, The Secretary of State to the Italian Ambassador (Arezzana), 8/10/1920, p. 468. (760c61/300b).

2. George F. Kennan, *Realities of American Foreign Policy* (London, 1954), p. 15.

3. FRUS, *The Soviet Union, 1933-1939*, Vol. III, The Chargé in the Soviet Union (Henderson) to the Secretary of State, 11/16/1936, p. 308. (711.61/611).

Bibliography

Columbia Oral History Collection, Columbia University, New York, New York.
  Edward Samuel Greenbaum
  William Phillips
  James P. Warburg

Export-Import Bank of Washington, Washington, D.C.

Harvard University, Cambridge, Massachusetts
  Joseph C. Grew papers
  Jay Pierrepont Moffat papers
  William Phillips papers

Library of Congress, Washington, D.C.
  Wilbur J. Carr papers
  Raymond Clapper papers
  Josephus Daniels papers
  Felix Frankfurter papers
  Cordell Hull papers
  George W. Norris papers

National Archives, Washington, D.C.
  General Records of The Department of State, Record Group 59
  Records of the R.F.C., Record Group 234
  Records of The Department of Commerce, Record Group 40

Franklin D. Roosevelt Library, Hyde Park, New York
    Robert Walton Moore papers
    Henry M. Morganthau, Jr., papers
    Franklin D. Roosevelt: Official File
    Franklin D. Roosevelt: President's Personal File
    Franklin D. Roosevelt: President's Secretary's File
    Rexford G. Tugwell papers
    John C. Wiley papers

Harry S. Truman Library, Independence, Missouri
    William L. Clayton papers

University of Missouri, Columbia, Missouri
    George N. Peek papers

Yale University, New Haven, Connecticut
    Edward M. House papers
    Henry L. Stimson papers

Bishop, Donald G. *The Roosevelt-Litvinov Agreements.* Syracuse, 1965.

Bohlen, Charles E. *The Transformation of American Foreign Policy.* New York, 1969.

———— *Witness to History, 1929-1969.* New York, 1973.

Bowers, Robert E. "American Diplomacy, the 1933 Wheat Conference and Recognition of the Soviet Union." *Agricultural History.* vol. XL. 1/1966.

———— "Hull, Russian Subversion in Cuba, and Recognition of the U.S.S.R." *The Journal of American History.* vol. 53, 12/1966.

Bowers, Robert E. and Nichols, Jeannette P. "Roosevelt's Monetary Diplomacy in 1933." *The American Historical Review.* vol. LVI. 10/1950 to 7/1951.

Browder, Robert Paul. *The Origins of Soviet-American Diplomacy.* Princeton, N.J. 1953.

Bullitt, Orville H., ed. *For the President: Personal and Secret: Correspondence Between Franklin D. Roosevelt and William C. Bullitt.* Boston, 1972.

Bullitt, William C. "How We Won the War and Lost the Peace." *Life.* 8/30/1948.

Complete Presidential Press Conferences of Franklin D. Roosevelt. vols. 1-2. New York, 1972.

Cox, James. *Journey Through My Years.* New York, 1946.

Documents on British Foreign Policy: 1919-1939. Second Series. vol. V. London, 1956.

Farley, James A. *Jim Farley's Story.* New York, 1948.

Farnsworth, Beatrice. *William C. Bullitt and the Soviet Union.* Bloomington, Indiana, 1967.

Feis, Herbert. *1933: Characters in Crises.* Boston, 1966.

——— *The Diplomacy of the Dollar.* Hamden, Connecticut, 1965.

Flynn, George Q. *American Catholics & the Roosevelt Presidency 1932-1936.* Lexington, Ky., 1968.

Freidel, Frank. *Franklin D. Roosevelt, The Ordeal.* Boston, 1954.

Gallagher, Louis J. *Edmund A. Walsh, S.J., A Biography.* New York, 1962.

Gannon, Robert I. *The Cardinal Spellman Story.* Garden City, N.Y., 1962.

Harper, Samuel N. *The Russia I Believe In.* Chicago, 1945.

Hull, Cordell. *The Memoirs of Cordell Hull.* vol. 1. New York, 1948.

Ickes, Harold L. *The Secret Diary of Harold L. Ickes, The First Thousand Days 1933-1936.* New York, 1953.

Kennan, George F. *The Decision to Intervene.* Princeton, 1958.

——— *Memoirs 1925-1950.* Boston, 1967.

——— *Realities of American Foreign Policy.* London, 1954.

——— *Russia and the West Under Lenin and Stalin.* Boston, 1960, 1961.

Krock, Arthur. *Memoirs.* New York, 1968.

Lash, Joseph P., ed. *From the Diaries of Felix Frankfurter.* New York, 1975.

Moley, Raymond. *After Seven Years.* New York, 1939.

——— *The First New Deal.* New York, 1966.

Morganthau, Henry, Jr. "The Morganthau Diaries. Part III." *Colliers.* 10/11/1947.

Nixon, Edgar B., ed. *Franklin D. Roosevelt and Foreign Affairs.* vol. 1. Cambridge, Mass., 1969.

Perkins, Frances. *The Roosevelt I Knew.* New York, 1946.

Phillips, William. *Ventures in Diplomacy.* Boston, 1952.

The Public Papers and Addresses of Franklin D. Roosevelt. vol. 2. New York, 1938.

Roosevelt, Eleanor. *This I Remember.* New York, 1949.

Schlesinger, Arthur. *The Coming of the New Deal.* Boston, 1959.

Schmitt, Bernadotte E. "How Little Wisdom." *The American Historical Review.* vol. LXVI, No. 2. 1/1961.

Thorning, Joseph F. "What Russian Recognition Means." *America.* 12/2/1933.

Tugwell, Rexford. *In Search of Roosevelt.* Cambridge, Mass., 1972.

Tully, Grace. *F.D.R. My Boss.* Chicago, 1949.

United States Department of State. *Foreign Relations of the United States* (cited as FRUS). Washington, D.C.

Warburg, James P. *The Long Road Home.* Garden City, N.Y., 1964.

Wehle, Louis B. *Hidden Threads of History.* New York, 1953.

Welles, Sumner. *The Time for Decision.* New York, 1944.

Wood, Bryce. *The Making of the Good Neighbor Policy.* New York, 1961.

Index

283